YOUR MOST COMPREHENSIVE AND REVEALING INDIVIDUAL FORECAST

SUPER HOROSCOPE

TAURUS

19 99

April 21 - May 20

B

BERKLEY BOOKS, NEW YORK

The publishers regret that they cannot answer
individual letters requesting personal horoscope information.

1999 SUPER HOROSCOPE TAURUS

PRINTING HISTORY
Berkley Trade Edition / August 1998

The Penguin Putnam Inc. World Wide Web site address is
http://www.penguinputnam.com

ISBN: 0-425-16325-3

BERKLEY®
Berkley Books are published by The Berkley Publishing Group,
a member of Penguin Putnam Inc.,
200 Madison Avenue, New York, New York 10016.
"BERKLEY" and the "B" logo
are trademarks belonging to Berkley Publishing Corporation.

PRINTED IN THE UNITED STATES OF AMERICA

10 9 8 7 6 5 4 3 2 1

CONTENTS

THE CUSP-BORN TAURUS

Are you *really* a Taurus? If your birthday falls during the fourth week of April, at the beginning of Taurus, will you still retain the traits of Aries, the sign of the Zodiac before Taurus? And what if you were born late in May—are you more Gemini than Taurus? Many people born at the edge, or cusp, of a sign have difficulty determining exactly what sign they are. If you are one of these people, here's how you can figure it out, once and for all.

Consult the cusp table on the facing page, then locate the year of your birth. The table will tell you the precise days on which the Sun entered and left your sign for the year of your birth. In that way you can determine if you are a true Taurus—or whether you are an Aries or a Gemini—according to the variations in cusp dates from year to year (see also page 17).

If you were born at the beginning or end of Taurus, yours is a lifetime reflecting a process of subtle transformation. Your life on Earth will symbolize a significant change in consciousness, for you are either about to enter a whole new way of living or are leaving one behind.

If you were born toward the end of April, you may want to read the horoscope book for Aries as well as for Taurus. The investment might be strangely revealing, for Aries contains the secret to many of your complexities and unexpressed assets and liabilities.

But this is the very irony of an Aries-Taurus cusp. The more fixed you become, the less able you are to seek out adventure, take chances, gamble—and win. Your natural tendency is to acquire, build, and collect. The more you possess, the more permanent your status in life; thus, the less able you are to simply pick up and go back to zero. Fulfillment comes through loyalty, constancy, and success in the material world.

If you were born during the third week of May, you may want to see the Gemini horoscope book as well as Taurus, for without Gemini your assets are often too stable, too fixed. Gemini provides you with fluidity and gets you moving.

You are a blend of stability and mobility—rich, raw material—with a dexterity of mind and body. Even around a fixed and con-

4

stant center, change is always taking place. No matter how you hang on, there will be a series of changes, experiences, new people, new faces, places, facts, and events.

You are conservative with the very definite hint of an open mind, the blend of hardheaded realism and freewheeling experimentalism, earthy, tactile sensuality, and bold participation in life's joys.

THE CUSPS OF TAURUS

DATES SUN ENTERS TAURUS (LEAVES ARIES)

April 20 every year from 1900 to 2000, except for the following:

April 19			April 21
1948	1972	1988	1903
52	76	89	07
56	80	92	11
60	81	93	19
64	84	96	
68	85	97	

DATES SUN LEAVES TAURUS (ENTERS GEMINI)

May 21 every year from 1900 to 2000, except for the following:

May 20			May 22
1948	1972	1988	1903
52	76	89	07
56	80	92	11
60	81	93	19
64	84	96	
68	85	97	

THE ASCENDANT: TAURUS RISING

Could you be a "double" Taurus? That is, could you have Taurus as your Rising sign as well as your Sun sign? The tables on pages 8–9 will tell you Taurus what your Rising sign happens to be. Just find the hour of your birth, then find the day of your birth, and you will see which sign of the Zodiac is your Ascendant, as the Rising sign is called. The Ascendant is called that because it is the sign rising on the eastern horizon at the time of your birth. For a more detailed discussion of the Rising sign and the twelve houses of the Zodiac, see pages 17–20.

The Ascendant, or Rising sign, is placed on the 1st house in a horoscope, of which there are twelve houses. The 1st house represents your response to the environment—your unique response. Call it identity, personality, ego, self-image, facade, come-on, body-mind-spirit—whatever term best conveys to you the meaning of the you that acts and reacts in the world. It is a you that is always changing, discovering a new you. Your identity started with birth and early environment, over which you had little conscious control, and continues to experience, to adjust, to express itself. The 1st house also represents how others see you. Has anyone ever guessed your sign to be your Rising sign? People may respond to that personality, that facade, that body type governed by your Rising sign.

Your Ascendant, or Rising sign, modifies your basic Sun sign personality, and it affects the way you act out the daily predictions for your Sun sign. If your Rising sign is indeed Taurus, what follows is a description of its effects on your horoscope. If your Rising sign is not Taurus, but some other sign of the Zodiac, you may wish to read the horoscope book for that sign as well.

With Taurus on the Ascendant, that is, in your 1st house, the planet rising in the 1st house is Venus, ruler of Taurus. Venus confers an intuitive, creative mind, and a liking for ease and luxury. Venus here gives you a sociable nature—loyal, lovable, and loving. But there are contradictions! Like the Bull, the zodiacal symbol of Taurus, you strike contrasting poses. In repose, you can be seen sweetly, peaceably smelling the flowers. Enraged, you trample the very turf that supports you. A passionate, selfish, demanding streak overcomes the mild, gentle, docile mood.

You have a well-developed need for people. Personal relationships are important to you, often centering around your love life. Bestowed with ample good looks and sensual appeal, you do not lack for admirers. In fact, you are sought after, often chased. Though generally loyal and steadfast, and capable of success in marriage, you may, however, have an irresistible urge for secret affairs, which arouse other people's jealousy and antagonism. There is also the danger that you can be caught between a fierce possessiveness and a thoughtless desire to acquire popularity in an indiscriminating way.

You have an even greater need for money. For you with Taurus Rising, money symbolizes the successful self. You intend to earn money in a steady, practical way, especially one that is time-honored and contains few risks. But you tend to spend money lavishly, when your comfort and edification demand it. You like sparkle and glitter, ornamentation, and nourishment. Food, clothes, "things" can become extravagances you cannot afford. Only when threats to your personal security loom do you jealously guard your money. You may also confuse money and love, using the one to get the other and vice versa.

You have a strong creative drive, tending toward the arts and crafts. Your self-expression is best achieved by creating sensations that are pleasing to the eye and to the body in general. You are, however, capable of sustained efforts of the mind, for you are both patient and intuitive. For you, the creator, one problem lies in being too fixed in your vision, too proud to ask for help, and too self-centered to think you need it. If you get bogged down, you abandon your undertakings for a lazy, self-indulgent spell. You also keep a too tenacious hold on your creations.

Because you are basically cautious, what you create or build is usually very sound. Success through stability is your motto. Your efforts, focused in a relationship or in a product, have a tempering, personalizing influence. Sometimes you shy away from group efforts if they stress generalities or nonpersonal goals. In a setting where intimacy is discouraged, your drive is inhibited. On the other hand, you have deep compassion and an unselfish need to serve others. When an activity or cause sponsors both personal satisfaction and kindly justice, you will work for it laboriously. Otherwise, you prefer the pursuit of heady living, sometimes alone, sometimes with a partner.

For Taurus Rising, two key words are sense and sensibility. Weave them together into a rich, thick tapestry, rather than raveling them in bits and pieces of pleasure.

RISING SIGNS FOR TAURUS

Hour of Birth*	Day of Birth		
	April 20–25	**April 26–29**	**April 30–May 4**
Midnight	Capricorn	Capricorn	Capricorn
1 AM	Capricorn	Aquarius	Aquarius
2 AM	Aquarius	Aquarius	Aquarius; Pisces 5/4
3 AM	Pisces	Pisces	Pisces
4 AM	Pisces; Aries 4/22	Aries	Aties
5 AM	Aries	Taurus	Taurus
6 AM	Taurus	Taurus	Taurus; Gemini 5/4
7 AM	Gemini	Gemini	Gemini
8 AM	Gemini	Gemini	Gemini; Cancer 5/2
9 AM	Cancer	Cancer	Cancer
10 AM	Cancer	Cancer	Cancer
11 AM	Cancer; Leo 4/22	Leo	Leo
Noon	Leo	Leo	Leo
1 PM	Leo	Leo	Virgo
2 PM	Virgo	Virgo	Virgo
3 PM	Virgo	Virgo	Virgo
4 PM	Virgo; Libra 4/23	Libra	Libra
5 PM	Libra	Libra	Libra
6 PM	Libra	Libra; Scorpio 4/29	Scorpio
7 PM	Scorpio	Scorpio	Scorpio
8 PM	Scorpio	Scorpio	Scorpio
9 PM	Scorpio; Sagittarius 4/23	Sagittarius	Sagittarius
10 PM	Sagittarius	Sagittarius	Sagittarius
11 PM	Sagittarius	Sagittarius; Capricorn 4/27	Capricorn

*See note on facing page.

Hour of Birth*	Day of Birth		
	May 5–10	May 11–15	May 16–21
Midnight	Capricorn	Aquarius	Aquarius
1 AM	Aquarius	Aquarius	Aquarius; Pisces 5/18
2 AM	Pisces	Pisces	Pisces
3 AM	Pisces; Aries 5/6	Aries	Aries
4 AM	Aries	Taurus	Taurus
5 AM	Taurus	Taurus	Taurus; Gemini 5/19
6 AM	Gemini	Gemini	Gemini
7 AM	Gemini	Gemini	Gemini; Cancer 5/18
8 AM	Cancer	Cancer	Cancer
9 AM	Cancer	Cancer	Cancer
10 AM	Cancer; Leo 5/8	Leo	Leo
11 AM	Leo	Leo	Leo
Noon	Leo	Leo	Virgo
1 PM	Virgo	Virgo	Virgo
2 PM	Virgo	Virgo	Virgo
3 PM	Virgo; Libra 5/8	Libra	Libra
4 PM	Libra	Libra	Libra
5 PM	Libra	Scorpio	Scorpio
6 PM	Scorpio	Scorpio	Scorpio
7 PM	Scorpio	Scorpio	Scorpio
8 PM	Scorpio; Sagittarius 5/8	Sagittarius	Sagittarius
9 PM	Sagittarius	Sagittarius	Sagittarius
10 PM	Sagittarius	Sagittarius; Capricorn 5/12	Capricorn
11 PM	Capricorn	Capricorn	Capricorn

*Hour of birth given here is for Standard Time in any time zone. If your hour of birth was recorded in Daylight Saving Time, subtract one hour from it and consult that hour in the table above. For example, if you were born at 6 AM D.S.T., see 5 AM above.

THE PLACE OF ASTROLOGY IN TODAY'S WORLD

Does astrology have a place in the fast-moving, ultra-scientific world we live in today? Can it be justified in a sophisticated society whose outriders are already preparing to step off the moon into the deep space of the planets themselves? Or is it just a hangover of ancient superstition, a psychological dummy for neurotics and dreamers of every historical age?

These are the kind of questions that any inquiring person can be expected to ask when they approach a subject like astrology which goes beyond, but never excludes, the materialistic side of life.

The simple, single answer is that astrology works. It works for many millions of people in the western world alone. In the United States there are 10 million followers and in Europe, an estimated 25 million. America has more than 4000 practicing astrologers, Europe nearly three times as many. Even down-under Australia has its hundreds of thousands of adherents. In the eastern countries, astrology has enormous followings, again, because it has been proved to work. In India, for example, brides and grooms for centuries have been chosen on the basis of their astrological compatibility.

Astrology today is more vital than ever before, more practicable because all over the world the media devotes much space and time to it, more valid because science itself is confirming the precepts of astrological knowledge with every new exciting step. The ordinary person who daily applies astrology intelligently does not have to wonder whether it is true nor believe in it blindly. He can see it working for himself. And, if he can use it—and this book is designed to help the reader to do just that—he can make living a far richer experience, and become a more developed personality and a better person.

Astrology and Relationships

Astrology is the science of relationships. It is not just a study of planetary influences on man and his environment. It is the study of man himself.

We are at the center of our personal universe, of all our relationships. And our happiness or sadness depends on how we act, how we relate to the people and things that surround us. The emotions that we generate have a distinct effect—for better or worse—on the world around us. Our friends and our enemies will confirm this. Just look in the mirror the next time you are angry. In other words, each of us is a kind of sun or planet or star radiating our feelings on the environment around us. Our influence on our personal universe, whether loving, helpful, or destructive, varies with our changing moods, expressed through our individual character.

Our personal "radiations" are potent in the way they affect our moods and our ability to control them. But we usually are able to throw off our emotion in some sort of action—we have a good cry, walk it off, or tell someone our troubles—before it can build up too far and make us physically ill. Astrology helps us to understand the universal forces working on us, and through this understanding, we can become more properly adjusted to our surroundings so that we find ourselves coping where others may flounder.

The Challenge of Love

The challenge of love lies in recognizing the difference between infatuation, emotion, sex, and, sometimes, the intentional deceit of the other person. Mankind, with its record of broken marriages, despair, and disillusionment, is obviously not very good at making these distinctions.

Can astrology help?

Yes. In the same way that advance knowledge can usually help in any human situation. And there is probably no situation as human, as poignant, as pathetic and universal, as the failure of man's love.

Love, of course, is not just between man and woman. It involves love of children, parents, home, and friends. But the big problems usually involve the choice of partner.

Astrology has established degrees of compatibility that exist between people born under the various signs of the Zodiac. Because people are individuals, there are numerous variations and modifications. So the astrologer, when approached on mate and marriage matters, makes allowances for them. But the fact remains that some groups of people are suited for each other and some are not, and astrology has expressed this in terms of characteristics we all can study and use as a personal guide.

No matter how much enjoyment and pleasure we find in the different aspects of each other's character, if it is not an overall compatibility, the chances of our finding fulfillment or enduring happiness in each other are pretty hopeless. And astrology can help us to find someone compatible.

Astrology and Science

Closely related to our emotions is the "other side" of our personal universe, our physical welfare. Our body, of course, is largely influenced by things around us over which we have very little control. The phone rings, we hear it. The train runs late. We snag our stocking or cut our face shaving. Our body is under a constant bombardment of events that influence our daily lives to varying degrees.

The question that arises from all this is, what makes each of us act so that we have to involve other people and keep the ball of activity and evolution rolling? This is the question that both science and astrology are involved with. The scientists have attacked it from different angles: anthropology, the study of human evolution as body, mind and response to environment; anatomy, the study of bodily structure; psychology, the science of the human mind; and so on. These studies have produced very impressive classifications and valuable information, but because the approach to the problem is fragmented, so is the result. They remain "branches" of science. Science generally studies effects. It keeps turning up wonderful answers but no lasting solutions. Astrology, on the other hand, approaches the question from the broader viewpoint. Astrology began its inquiry with the totality of human experience and saw it as an effect. It then looked to find the cause, or at least the prime movers, and during thousands of years of observation of man and his *universal* environment came up with the extraordinary principle of planetary influence—or astrology, which, from the Greek, means the science of the stars.

Modern science, as we shall see, has confirmed much of astrology's foundations—most of it unintentionally, some of it reluctantly, but still, indisputably.

It is not difficult to imagine that there must be a connection between outer space and Earth. Even today, scientists are not too sure how our Earth was created, but it is generally agreed that it is only a tiny part of the universe. And as a part of the universe, people on Earth see and feel the influence of heavenly bodies in almost every aspect of our existence. There is no doubt that the Sun has the greatest influence on life on this planet. Without it there would be no life, for without it there would be no warmth, no division into day and night, no cycles of time or season at all. This is clear and easy to see. The influence of the Moon, on the other hand, is more subtle, though no less definite.

There are many ways in which the influence of the Moon manifests itself here on Earth, both on human and animal life. It is a well-known fact, for instance, that the large movements of water on our planet—that is the ebb and flow of the tides—are caused by the Moon's gravitational pull. Since this is so, it follows that these water movements do not occur only in the oceans, but that all bodies of water are affected, even down to the tiniest puddle.

The human body, too, which consists of about 70 percent water, falls within the scope of this lunar influence. For example the menstrual cycle of most women corresponds to the 28-day lunar month; the period of pregnancy in humans is 273 days, or equal to nine lunar months. Similarly, many illnesses reach a crisis at the change of the Moon, and statistics in many countries have shown that the crime rate is highest at the time of the Full Moon. Even human sexual desire has been associated with the phases of the Moon. But it is in the movement of the tides that we get the clearest demonstration of planetary influence, which leads to the irresistible correspondence between the so-called metaphysical and the physical.

Tide tables are prepared years in advance by calculating the future positions of the Moon. Science has known for a long time that the Moon is the main cause of tidal action. But only in the last few years has it begun to realize the possible extent of this influence on mankind. To begin with, the ocean tides do not rise and fall as we might imagine from our personal observations of them. The Moon as it orbits around Earth sets up a circular wave of attraction which pulls the oceans of the world after it, broadly in an east to west direction. This influence is like a phantom wave crest, a loop of power stretching from pole to pole which passes over and around the Earth like an invisible shadow. It travels with equal effect across the land masses and, as scientists were recently amazed to observe, caused oysters placed in the dark in the middle of the United States where there is no sea to open their shells to receive the nonexistent tide. If the land-locked oysters react to this invisible signal, what effect does it have on us who not so long ago in evolutionary time came out of the sea and still have its salt in our blood and sweat?

Less well known is the fact that the Moon is also the primary force behind the circulation of blood in human beings and animals, and the movement of sap in trees and plants. Agriculturists have established that the Moon has a distinct influence on crops, which explains why for centuries people have planted according to Moon cycles. The habits of many animals, too, are directed by the movement of the Moon. Migratory birds, for instance, depart only at or near the time of the Full Moon. And certain sea creatures, eels in particular, move only in accordance with certain phases of the Moon.

Know Thyself—Why?

In today's fast-changing world, everyone still longs to know what the future holds. It is the one thing that everyone has in common: rich and poor, famous and infamous, all are deeply concerned about tomorrow.

But the key to the future, as every historian knows, lies in the past. This is as true of individual people as it is of nations. You cannot understand your future without first understanding your past, which is simply another way of saying that you must first of all know yourself.

The motto "know thyself" seems obvious enough nowadays, but it was originally put forward as the foundation of wisdom by the ancient Greek philosophers. It was then adopted by the "mystery religions" of the ancient Middle East, Greece, Rome, and is still used in all genuine schools of mind training or mystical discipline, both in those of the East, based on yoga, and those of the West. So it is universally accepted now, and has been through the ages.

But how do you go about discovering what sort of person you are? The first step is usually classification into some sort of system of types. Astrology did this long before the birth of Christ. Psychology has also done it. So has modern medicine, in its way.

One system classifies people according to the source of the impulses they respond to most readily: the muscles, leading to direct bodily action; the digestive organs, resulting in emotion; or the brain and nerves, giving rise to thinking. Another such system says that character is determined by the endocrine glands, and gives us such labels as "pituitary," "thyroid," and "hyperthyroid" types. These different systems are neither contradictory nor mutually exclusive. In fact, they are very often different ways of saying the same thing.

Very popular, useful classifications were devised by Carl Jung, the eminent disciple of Freud. Jung observed among the different faculties of the mind, four which have a predominant influence on character. These four faculties exist in all of us without exception, but not in perfect balance. So when we say, for instance, that someone is a "thinking type," it means that in any situation he or she tries to be rational. Emotion, which may be the opposite of thinking, will be his or her weakest function. This thinking type can be sensible and reasonable, or calculating and unsympathetic. The emotional type, on the other hand, can often be recognized by exaggerated language—everything is either marvelous or terrible—and in extreme cases they even invent dramas and quarrels out of nothing just to make life more interesting.

The other two faculties are intuition and physical sensation. The sensation type does not only care for food and drink, nice clothes and furniture; he or she is also interested in all forms of physical experience. Many scientists are sensation types as are athletes and nature-lovers. Like sensation, intuition is a form of perception and we all possess it. But it works through that part of the mind which is not under conscious control—consequently it sees meanings and connections which are not obvious to thought or emotion. Inventors and original thinkers are always intuitive, but so, too, are superstitious people who see meanings where none exist.

Thus, sensation tells us what is going on in the world, feeling (that is, emotion) tells us how important it is to ourselves, thinking enables us to interpret it and work out what we should do about it, and intuition tells us what it means to ourselves and others. All four faculties are essential, and all are present in every one of us. But some people are guided chiefly by one, others by another. In addition, Jung also observed a division of the human personality into the extrovert and the introvert, which cuts across these four types.

A disadvantage of all these systems of classification is that one cannot tell very easily where to place oneself. Some people are reluctant to admit that they act to please their emotions. So they deceive themselves for years by trying to belong to whichever type they think is the "best." Of course, there is no best; each has its faults and each has its good points.

The advantage of the signs of the Zodiac is that they simplify classification. Not only that, but your date of birth is personal—it is unarguably yours. What better way to know yourself than by going back as far as possible to the very moment of your birth? And this is precisely what your horoscope is all about, as we shall see in the next section.

WHAT IS A HOROSCOPE?

If you had been able to take a picture of the skies at the moment of your birth, that photograph would be your horoscope. Lacking such a snapshot, it is still possible to recreate the picture—and this is at the basis of the astrologer's art. In other words, your horoscope is a representation of the skies with the planets in the exact positions they occupied at the time you were born.

The year of birth tells an astrologer the positions of the distant, slow-moving planets Jupiter, Saturn, Uranus, Neptune, and Pluto. The month of birth indicates the Sun sign, or birth sign as it is commonly called, as well as indicating the positions of the rapidly moving planets Venus, Mercury, and Mars. The day and time of birth will locate the position of our Moon. And the moment—the exact hour and minute—of birth determines the houses through what is called the Ascendant, or Rising sign.

With this information the astrologer consults various tables to calculate the specific positions of the Sun, Moon, and other planets relative to your birthplace at the moment you were born. Then he or she locates them by means of the Zodiac.

The Zodiac

The Zodiac is a band of stars (constellations) in the skies, centered on the Sun's apparent path around the Earth, and is divided into twelve equal segments, or signs. What we are actually dividing up is the Earth's path around the Sun. But from our point of view here on Earth, it seems as if the Sun is making a great circle around our planet in the sky, so we say it is the Sun's apparent path. This twelvefold division, the Zodiac, is a reference system for the astrologer. At any given moment the planets—and in astrology both the Sun and Moon are considered to be planets—can all be located at a specific point along this path.

Now where in all this are you, the subject of the horoscope? Your character is largely determined by the sign the Sun is in. So that is where the astrologer looks first in your horoscope, at your Sun sign.

The Sun Sign and the Cusp

There are twelve signs in the Zodiac, and the Sun spends approximately one month in each sign. But because of the motion of the Earth around the Sun—the Sun's apparent motion—the dates when the Sun enters and leaves each sign may change from year to year. Some people born near the cusp, or edge, of a sign have difficulty determining which is their Sun sign. But in this book a Table of Cusps is provided for the years 1900 to 2000 (page 5) so you can find out what your true Sun sign is.

Here are the twelve signs of the Zodiac, their ancient zodiacal symbol, and the dates when the Sun enters and leaves each sign for the year 1999. Remember, these dates may change from year to year.

ARIES	Ram	March 20–April 20
TAURUS	Bull	April 20–May 21
GEMINI	Twins	May 21–June 21
CANCER	Crab	June 21–July 23
LEO	Lion	July 23–August 23
VIRGO	Virgin	August 23–September 23
LIBRA	Scales	September 23–October 23
SCORPIO	Scorpion	October 23–November 22
SAGITTARIUS	Archer	November 22–December 22
CAPRICORN	Sea Goat	December 22–January 20
AQUARIUS	Water Bearer	January 20–February 18
PISCES	Fish	February 18–March 20

It is possible to draw significant conclusions and make meaningful predictions based simply on the Sun sign of a person. There are many people who have been amazed at the accuracy of the description of their own character based only on the Sun sign. But an astrologer needs more information than just your Sun sign to interpret the photograph that is your horoscope.

The Rising Sign and the Zodiacal Houses

An astrologer needs the exact time and place of your birth in order to construct and interpret your horoscope. The illustration on the next page shows the flat chart, or natural wheel, an astrologer uses. Note the inner circle of the wheel labeled 1 through 12. These 12 divisions are known as the houses of the Zodiac.

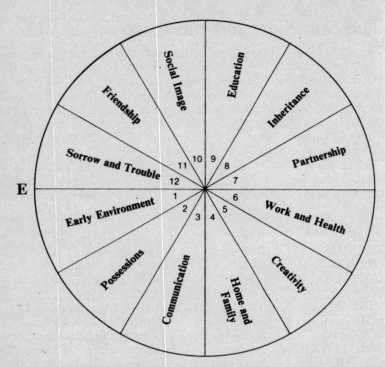

The 1st house always starts from the position marked E, which corresponds to the eastern horizon. The rest of the houses 2 through 12 follow around in a "counterclockwise" direction. The point where each house starts is known as a cusp, or edge.

The cusp, or edge, of the 1st house (point E) is where an astrologer would place your Rising sign, the Ascendant. And, as already noted, the exact time of your birth determines your Rising sign. Let's see how this works.

As the Earth rotates on its axis once every 24 hours, each one of the twelve signs of the Zodiac appears to be "rising" on the horizon, with a new one appearing about every 2 hours. Actually it is the turning of the Earth that exposes each sign to view, but in our astrological work we are discussing apparent motion. This Rising sign marks the Ascendant, and it colors the whole orientation of a horoscope. It indicates the sign governing the 1st house of the chart, and will thus determine which signs will govern all the other houses.

To visualize this idea, imagine two color wheels with twelve divisions superimposed upon each other. For just as the Zodiac is divided into twelve constellations that we identify as the signs, another twelvefold division is used to denote the houses. Now imagine one wheel (the signs) moving slowly while the other wheel (the houses) remains still. This analogy may help you see how the signs keep shifting the "color" of the houses as the Rising sign continues to change every two hours. To simplify things, a Table of Rising Signs has been provided (pages 8–9) for your specific Sun sign.

Once your Rising sign has been placed on the cusp of the 1st house, the signs that govern the rest of the 11 houses can be placed on the chart. In any individual's horoscope the signs do not necessarily correspond with the houses. For example, it could be that a sign covers part of two adjacent houses. It is the interpretation of such variations in an individual's horoscope that marks the professional astrologer.

But to gain a workable understanding of astrology, it is not necessary to go into great detail. In fact, we just need a description of the houses and their meanings, as is shown in the illustration above and in the table below.

THE 12 HOUSES OF THE ZODIAC

1st	Individuality, body appearance, general outlook on life	Personality house
2nd	Finance, possessions, ethical principles, gain or loss	Money house
3rd	Relatives, communication, short journeys, writing, education	Relatives house
4th	Family and home, parental ties, land and property, security	Home house
5th	Pleasure, children, creativity, entertainment, risk	Pleasure house
6th	Health, harvest, hygiene, work and service, employees	Health house
7th	Marriage and divorce, the law, partnerships and alliances	Marriage house
8th	Inheritance, secret deals, sex, death, regeneration	Inheritance house
9th	Travel, sports, study, philosophy and religion	Travel house
10th	Career, social standing, success and honor	Business house
11th	Friendship, social life, hopes and wishes	Friends house
12th	Troubles, illness, secret enemies, hidden agendas	Trouble house

The Planets in the Houses

An astrologer, knowing the exact time and place of your birth, will use tables of planetary motion in order to locate the planets in your horoscope chart. He or she will determine which planet or planets are in which sign and in which house. It is not uncommon, in an individual's horoscope, for there to be two or more planets in the same sign and in the same house.

The characteristics of the planets modify the influence of the Sun according to their natures and strengths.

Sun: Source of life. Basic temperament according to the Sun sign. The conscious will. Human potential.

Moon: Emotions. Moods. Customs. Habits. Changeable. Adaptive. Nurturing.

Mercury: Communication. Intellect. Reasoning power. Curiosity. Short travels.

Venus: Love. Delight. Charm. Harmony. Balance. Art. Beautiful possessions.

Mars: Energy. Initiative. War. Anger. Adventure. Courage. Daring. Impulse.

Jupiter: Luck. Optimism. Generous. Expansive. Opportunities. Protection.

Saturn: Pessimism. Privation. Obstacles. Delay. Hard work. Research. Lasting rewards after long struggle.

Uranus: Fashion. Electricity. Revolution. Independence. Freedom. Sudden changes. Modern science.

Neptune: Sensationalism. Theater. Dreams. Inspiration. Illusion. Deception.

Pluto: Creation and destruction. Total transformation. Lust for power. Strong obsessions.

Superimpose the characteristics of the planets on the functions of the house in which they appear. Express the result through the character of the Sun sign, and you will get the basic idea.

Of course, many other considerations have been taken into account in producing the carefully worked out predictions in this book: the aspects of the planets to each other; their strength according to position and sign; whether they are in a house of exaltation or decline; whether they are natural enemies or not; whether a planet occupies its own sign; the position of a planet in relation to its own house or sign; whether the sign is male or female; whether the sign is a fire, earth, water, or air sign. These are only a few of the colors on the astrologer's pallet which he or she must mix with the inspiration of the artist and the accuracy of the mathematician.

How To Use These Predictions

A person reading the predictions in this book should understand that they are produced from the daily position of the planets for a group of people and are not, of course, individually specialized. To get the full benefit of them our readers should relate the predictions to their own character and circumstances, coordinate them, and draw their own conclusions from them.

If you are a serious observer of your own life, you should find a definite pattern emerging that will be a helpful and reliable guide.

The point is that we always retain our free will. The stars indicate certain directional tendencies but we are not compelled to follow. We can do or not do, and wisdom must make the choice.

We all have our good and bad days. Sometimes they extend into cycles of weeks. It is therefore advisable to study daily predictions in a span ranging from the day before to several days ahead.

Daily predictions should be taken very generally. The word "difficult" does not necessarily indicate a whole day of obstruction or inconvenience. It is a warning to you to be cautious. Your caution will often see you around the difficulty before you are involved. This is the correct use of astrology.

In another section (pages 78–84), detailed information is given about the influence of the Moon as it passes through each of the twelve signs of the Zodiac. There are instructions on how to use the Moon Tables (pages 85–92), which provide Moon Sign Dates throughout the year as well as the Moon's role in health and daily affairs. This information should be used in conjunction with the daily forecasts to give a fuller picture of the astrological trends.

HISTORY OF ASTROLOGY

The origins of astrology have been lost far back in history, but we do know that reference is made to it as far back as the first written records of the human race. It is not hard to see why. Even in primitive times, people must have looked for an explanation for the various happenings in their lives. They must have wanted to know why people were different from one another. And in their search they turned to the regular movements of the Sun, Moon, and stars to see if they could provide an answer.

It is interesting to note that as soon as man learned to use his tools in any type of design, or his mind in any kind of calculation, he turned his attention to the heavens. Ancient cave dwellings reveal dim crescents and circles representative of the Sun and Moon, rulers of day and night. Mesopotamia and the civilization of Chaldea, in itself the foundation of those of Babylonia and Assyria, show a complete picture of astronomical observation and well-developed astrological interpretation.

Humanity has a natural instinct for order. The study of anthropology reveals that primitive people—even as far back as prehistoric times—were striving to achieve a certain order in their lives. They tried to organize the apparent chaos of the universe. They had the desire to attach meaning to things. This demand for order has persisted throughout the history of man. So that observing the regularity of the heavenly bodies made it logical that primitive peoples should turn heavenward in their search for an understanding of the world in which they found themselves so random and alone.

And they did find a significance in the movements of the stars. Shepherds tending their flocks, for instance, observed that when the cluster of stars now known as the constellation Aries was in sight, it was the time of fertility and they associated it with the Ram. And they noticed that the growth of plants and plant life corresponded with different phases of the Moon, so that certain times were favorable for the planting of crops, and other times were not. In this way, there grew up a tradition of seasons and causes connected with the passage of the Sun through the twelve signs of the Zodiac.

Astrology was valued so highly that the king was kept informed of the daily and monthly changes in the heavenly bodies, and the results of astrological studies regarding events of the future. Head astrologers were clearly men of great rank and position, and the office was said to be a hereditary one.

Omens were taken, not only from eclipses and conjunctions of the Moon or Sun with one of the planets, but also from storms and earthquakes. In the eastern civilizations, particularly, the reverence inspired by astrology appears to have remained unbroken since the very earliest days. In ancient China, astrology, astronomy, and religion went hand in hand. The astrologer, who was also an astronomer, was part of the official government service and had his own corner in the Imperial Palace. The duties of the Imperial astrologer, whose office was one of the most important in the land, were clearly defined, as this extract from early records shows:

> This exalted gentleman must concern himself with the stars in the heavens, keeping a record of the changes and movements of the Planets, the Sun and the Moon, in order to examine the movements of the terrestrial world with the object of prognosticating good and bad fortune. He divides the territories of the nine regions of the empire in accordance with their dependence on particular celestial bodies. All the fiefs and principalities are connected with the stars and from this their prosperity or misfortune should be ascertained. He makes prognostications according to the twelve years of the Jupiter cycle of good and evil of the terrestrial world. From the colors of the five kinds of clouds, he determines the coming of floods or droughts, abundance or famine. From the twelve winds, he draws conclusions about the state of harmony of heaven and earth, and takes note of good and bad signs that result from their accord or disaccord. In general, he concerns himself with five kinds of phenomena so as to warn the Emperor to come to the aid of the government and to allow for variations in the ceremonies according to their circumstances.

The Chinese were also keen observers of the fixed stars, giving them such unusual names as Ghost Vehicle, Sun of Imperial Concubine, Imperial Prince, Pivot of Heaven, Twinkling Brilliance, Weaving Girl. But, great astrologers though they may have been, the Chinese lacked one aspect of mathematics that the Greeks applied to astrology—deductive geometry. Deductive geometry was the basis of much classical astrology in and after the time of the Greeks, and this explains the different methods of prognostication used in the East and West.

Down through the ages the astrologer's art has depended, not so much on the uncovering of new facts, though this is important, as on the interpretation of the facts already known. This is the essence of the astrologer's skill.

But why should the signs of the Zodiac have any effect at all on the formation of human character? It is easy to see why people thought they did, and even now we constantly use astrological expressions in our everyday speech. The thoughts of "lucky star," "ill-fated," "star-crossed," "mooning around," are interwoven into the very structure of our language.

Wherever the concept of the Zodiac is understood and used, it could well appear to have an influence on the human character. Does this mean, then, that the human race, in whose civilization the idea of the twelve signs of the Zodiac has long been embedded, is divided into only twelve types? Can we honestly believe that it is really as simple as that? If so, there must be pretty wide ranges of variation within each type. And if, to explain the variation, we call in heredity and environment, experiences in early childhood, the thyroid and other glands, and also the four functions of the mind together with extroversion and introversion, then one begins to wonder if the original classification was worth making at all. No sensible person believes that his favorite system explains everything. But even so, he will not find the system much use at all if it does not even save him the trouble of bothering with the others.

In the same way, if we were to put every person under only one sign of the Zodiac, the system becomes too rigid and unlike life. Besides, it was never intended to be used like that. It may be convenient to have only twelve types, but we know that in practice there is every possible gradation between aggressiveness and timidity, or between conscientiousness and laziness. How, then, do we account for this?

A person born under any given Sun sign can be mainly influenced by one or two of the other signs that appear in their individual horoscope. For instance, famous persons born under the sign of Gemini include Henry VIII, whom nothing and no one could have induced to abdicate, and Edward VIII, who did just that. Obviously, then, the sign Gemini does not fully explain the complete character of either of them.

Again, under the opposite sign, Sagittarius, were both Stalin, who was totally consumed with the notion of power, and Charles V, who freely gave up an empire because he preferred to go into a monastery. And we find under Scorpio many uncompromising characters such as Luther, de Gaulle, Indira Gandhi, and Montgomery, but also Petain, a successful commander whose name later became synonymous with collaboration.

A single sign is therefore obviously inadequate to explain the differences between people; it can only explain resemblances, such as the combativeness of the Scorpio group, or the far-reaching devotion of Charles V and Stalin to their respective ideals—the Christian heaven and the Communist utopia.

But very few people have only one sign in their horoscope chart. In addition to the month of birth, the day and, even more, the hour to the nearest minute if possible, ought to be considered. Without this, it is impossible to have an actual horoscope, for the word horoscope literally means "a consideration of the hour."

The month of birth tells you only which sign of the Zodiac was occupied by the Sun. The day and hour tell you what sign was occupied by the Moon. And the minute tells you which sign was rising on the eastern horizon. This is called the Ascendant, and, as some astrologers believe, it is supposed to be the most important thing in the whole horoscope.

The Sun is said to signify one's heart, that is to say, one's deepest desires and inmost nature. This is quite different from the Moon, which signifies one's superficial way of behaving. When the ancient Romans referred to the Emperor Augustus as a Capricorn, they meant that he had the Moon in Capricorn. Or, to take another example, a modern astrologer would call Disraeli a Scorpion because he had Scorpio Rising, but most people would call him Sagittarius because he had the Sun there. The Romans would have called him Leo because his Moon was in Leo.

So if one does not seem to fit one's birth month, it is always worthwhile reading the other signs, for one may have been born at a time when any of them were rising or occupied by the Moon. It also seems to be the case that the influence of the Sun develops as life goes on, so that the month of birth is easier to guess in people over the age of forty. The young are supposed to be influenced mainly by their Ascendant, the Rising sign, which characterizes the body and physical personality as a whole.

It is nonsense to assume that all people born at a certain time will exhibit the same characteristics, or that they will even behave in the same manner. It is quite obvious that, from the very moment of its birth, a child is subject to the effects of its environment, and that this in turn will influence its character and heritage to a decisive extent. Also to be taken into account are education and economic conditions, which play a very important part in the formation of one's character as well.

People have, in general, certain character traits and qualities which, according to their environment, develop in either a positive or a negative manner. Therefore, selfishness (inherent selfishness, that is) might emerge as unselfishness; kindness and consideration as cruelty and lack of consideration toward others. In the same way, a naturally constructive person may, through frustration, become destructive, and so on. The latent characteristics with which people are born can, therefore, through environment and good or bad training, become something that would appear to be its opposite, and so give the lie to the astrologer's description of their character. But this is not the case. The true character is still there, but it is buried deep beneath these external superficialities.

Careful study of the character traits of various signs of the Zodiac are of immeasurable help, and can render beneficial service to the intelligent person. Undoubtedly, the reader will already have discovered that, while he is able to get on very well with some people, he just "cannot stand" others. The causes sometimes seem inexplicable. At times there is intense dislike, at other times immediate sympathy. And there is, too, the phenomenon of love at first sight, which is also apparently inexplicable. People appear to be either sympathetic or unsympathetic toward each other for no apparent reason.

Now if we look at this in the light of the Zodiac, we find that people born under different signs are either compatible or incompatible with each other. In other words, there are good and bad interrelating factors among the various signs. This does not, of course, mean that humanity can be divided into groups of hostile camps. It would be quite wrong to be hostile or indifferent toward people who happen to be born under an incompatible sign. There is no reason why everybody should not, or cannot, learn to control and adjust their feelings and actions, especially after they are aware of the positive qualities of other people by studying their character analyses, among other things.

Every person born under a certain sign has both positive and negative qualities, which are developed more or less according to our free will. Nobody is entirely good or entirely bad, and it is up to each of us to learn to control ourselves on the one hand and at the same time to endeavor to learn about ourselves and others.

It cannot be emphasized often enough that it is free will that determines whether we will make really good use of our talents and abilities. Using our free will, we can either overcome our failings or allow them to rule us. Our free will enables us to exert sufficient willpower to control our failings so that they do not harm ourselves or others.

Astrology can reveal our inclinations and tendencies. Astrology can tell us about ourselves so that we are able to use our free will to overcome our shortcomings. In this way astrology helps us do our best to become needed and valuable members of society as well as helpmates to our family and our friends. Astrology also can save us a great deal of unhappiness and remorse.

Yet it may seem absurd that an ancient philosophy could be a prop to modern men and women. But below the materialistic surface of modern life, there are hidden streams of feeling and thought. Symbology is reappearing as a study worthy of the scholar; the psychosomatic factor in illness has passed from the writings of the crank to those of the specialist; spiritual healing in all its forms is no longer a pious hope but an accepted phenomenon. And it is into this context that we consider astrology, in the sense that it is an analysis of human types.

Astrology and medicine had a long journey together, and only parted company a couple of centuries ago. There still remain in medical language such astrological terms as "saturnine," "choleric," and "mercurial," used in the diagnosis of physical tendencies. The herbalist, for long the handyman of the medical profession, has been dominated by astrology since the days of the Greeks. Certain herbs traditionally respond to certain planetary influences, and diseases must therefore be treated to ensure harmony between the medicine and the disease.

But the stars are expected to foretell and not only to diagnose.

Astrological forecasting has been remarkably accurate, but often it is wide of the mark. The brave person who cares to predict world events takes dangerous chances. Individual forecasting is less clear cut; it can be a help or a disillusionment. Then we come to the nagging question: if it is possible to foreknow, is it right to foretell? This is a point of ethics on which it is hard to pronounce judgment. The doctor faces the same dilemma if he finds that symptoms of a mortal disease are present in his patient and that he can only prognosticate a steady decline. How much to tell an individual in a crisis is a problem that has perplexed many distinguished scholars. Honest and conscientious astrologers in this modern world, where so many people are seeking guidance, face the same problem.

Five hundred years ago it was customary to call in a learned man who was an astrologer who was probably also a doctor and a philosopher. By his knowledge of astrology, his study of planetary influences, he felt himself qualified to guide those in distress. The world has moved forward at a fantastic rate since then, and yet people are still uncertain of themselves. At first sight it seems fantastic in the light of modern thinking that they turn to the most ancient of all studies, and get someone to calculate a horoscope for them. But is it *really* so fantastic if you take a second look? For astrology is concerned with tomorrow, with survival. And in a world such as ours, tomorrow and survival are the keywords for the twenty-first century.

ASTROLOGICAL BRIDGE TO THE 21st CENTURY

As the last decade of the twentieth century comes to a close, planetary aspects for its final years connect you with the future. Major changes completed in 1995 and 1996 give rise to new planetary cycles that form the bridge to the twenty-first century and new horizons. The years 1996 through 1999 and into the year 2000 reveal hidden paths and personal hints for achieving your potential, for making the most of your message from the planets.

All the major planets begin new cycles in the late 1990s. Jupiter, planet of good fortune, transits four zodiacal signs from 1996 through 1999 and goes through a complete cycle in each of the elements earth, air, fire, and water. Jupiter is in Capricorn, then in Aquarius, next in Pisces, and finally in Aries as the century turns. With the dawning of the twenty-first century, each new yearly Jupiter cycle follows the natural progression of the Zodiac, from Aries in 2000, then Taurus in 2001, next Gemini in 2002, and so on through Pisces in 2011. The beneficent planet Jupiter promotes your professional and educational goals while urging informed choice and deliberation. Jupiter sharpens your focus and hones your skills. And while safeguarding good luck, Jupiter can turn unusual risks into achievable aims.

Saturn, planet of reason and responsibility, has begun a new cycle in the spring of 1996 when it entered fiery Aries. Saturn in Aries through March 1999 heightens a longing for independence. Your movements are freed from everyday restrictions, allowing you to travel, to explore, to act on a variety of choices. With Saturn in Aries you get set to blaze a new trail. Saturn enters earthy Taurus in March 1999 for a three-year stay over the turn of the century into the year 2002. Saturn in Taurus inspires industry and affection. Practicality, perseverance, and planning can reverse setbacks and minimize risk. Saturn in Taurus lends beauty, order, and structure to your life. In order to take advantage of opportunity through responsibility, to persevere against adversity, look to beautiful planet Saturn.

Uranus, planet of innovation and surprise, started an important new cycle in January of 1996. At that time Uranus entered its natural home in airy Aquarius. Uranus in Aquarius into the year 2003 has a profound effect on your personality and the lens through which you see the world. A basic change in the way you project yourself is just one impact of Uranus in Aquarius. More significantly, a whole new consciousness is evolving. Winds of change blowing your way emphasize movement and freedom. Uranus in Aquarius poses involvement in the larger community beyond self, family, friends, lovers, associates. Radical ideas and progressive thought signal a journey of liberation. As the century turns, follow Uranus on the path of humanitarianism. While you carve a prestigious niche in public life, while you preach social reform and justice, you will be striving to make the world a better place for all people.

Neptune, planet of vision and mystery, is in earthy Capricorn until late 1998. Neptune in Capricorn excites creativity while restraining fanciful thinking. Wise use of resources helps you build persona and prestige. Then Neptune enters airy Aquarius during November 1998 and is there into the year 2011. Neptune in Aquarius, the sign of the Water Bearer, represents two sides of the coin of wisdom: inspiration and reason. Here Neptune stirs powerful currents bearing a rich and varied harvest, the fertile breeding ground for idealistic aims and practical considerations. Neptune's fine intuition tunes in to your dreams, your imagination, your spirituality. You can never turn your back on the mysteries of life. Uranus and Neptune, the planets of enlightenment and renewed idealism both in the sign of Aquarius, give you glimpses into the future, letting you peek through secret doorways into the twenty-first century.

Pluto, planet of beginnings and endings, has completed one cycle of growth November 1995 in the sign of Scorpio. Pluto in Scorpio marked a long period of experimentation and rejuvenation. Then Pluto entered the fiery sign of Sagittarius on November 10, 1995 and is there into the year 2007. Pluto in Sagittarius during its long stay of twelve years can create significant change. The great power of Pluto in Sagittarius may already be starting its transformation of your character and lifestyle. Pluto in Sagittarius takes you on a new journey of exploration and learning. The awakening you experience on intellectual and artistic levels heralds a new cycle of growth. Uncompromising Pluto, seeker of truth, challenges your identity, persona, and self-expression. Uncovering the real you, Pluto holds the key to understanding and meaningful communication. Pluto in Sagittarius can be the guiding light illuminating the first decade of the twenty-first century. Good luck is riding on the waves of change.

THE SIGNS OF THE ZODIAC

Dominant Characteristics

Aries: March 21–April 20

The Positive Side of Aries

The Aries has many positive points to his character. People born under this first sign of the Zodiac are often quite strong and enthusiastic. On the whole, they are forward-looking people who are not easily discouraged by temporary setbacks. They know what they want out of life and they go out after it. Their personalities are strong. Others are usually quite impressed by the Ram's way of doing things. Quite often they are sources of inspiration for others traveling the same route. Aries men and women have a special zest for life that can be contagious; for others, they are a fine example of how life should be lived.

The Aries person usually has a quick and active mind. He is imaginative and inventive. He enjoys keeping busy and active. He generally gets along well with all kinds of people. He is interested in mankind, as a whole. He likes to be challenged. Some would say he thrives on opposition, for it is when he is set against that he often does his best. Getting over or around obstacles is a challenge he generally enjoys. All in all, Aries is quite positive and young-thinking. He likes to keep abreast of new things that are happening in the world. Aries are often fond of speed. They like things to be done quickly, and this sometimes aggravates their slower colleagues and associates.

The Aries man or woman always seems to remain young. Their whole approach to life is youthful and optimistic. They never say die, no matter what the odds. They may have an occasional setback, but it is not long before they are back on their feet again.

The Negative Side of Aries

Everybody has his less positive qualities—and Aries is no exception. Sometimes the Aries man or woman is not very tactful in communicating with others; in his hurry to get things done he is apt to be a little callous or inconsiderate. Sensitive people are likely to find him somewhat sharp-tongued in some situations. Often in his eagerness to get the show on the road, he misses the mark altogether and cannot achieve his aims.

At times Aries can be too impulsive. He can occasionally be stubborn and refuse to listen to reason. If things do not move quickly enough to suit the Aries man or woman, he or she is apt to become rather nervous or irritable. The uncultivated Aries is not unfamiliar with moments of doubt and fear. He is capable of being destructive if he does not get his way. He can overcome some of his emotional problems by steadily trying to express himself as he really is, but this requires effort.

Taurus: April 21–May 20

The Positive Side of Taurus

The Taurus person is known for his ability to concentrate and for his tenacity. These are perhaps his strongest qualities. The Taurus man or woman generally has very little trouble in getting along with others; it's his nature to be helpful toward people in need. He can always be depended on by his friends, especially those in trouble.

Taurus generally achieves what he wants through his ability to persevere. He never leaves anything unfinished but works on something until it has been completed. People can usually take him at his word; he is honest and forthright in most of his dealings. The Taurus person has a good chance to make a success of his life because of his many positive qualities. The Taurus who aims high seldom falls short of his mark. He learns well by experience. He is thorough and does not believe in shortcuts of any kind. The Bull's thoroughness pays off in the end, for through his deliberateness he learns how to rely on himself and what he has learned. The Taurus person tries to get along with others, as a rule. He is not overly critical and likes people to be themselves. He is a tolerant person and enjoys peace and harmony—especially in his home life.

Taurus is usually cautious in all that he does. He is not a person who believes in taking unnecessary risks. Before adopting any one line of action, he will weigh all of the pros and cons. The Taurus person is steadfast. Once his mind is made up it seldom changes. The person born under this sign usually is a good family person—reliable and loving.

The Negative Side of Taurus

Sometimes the Taurus man or woman is a bit too stubborn. He won't listen to other points of view if his mind is set on something. To others, this can be quite annoying. Taurus also does not like to be told what to do. He becomes rather angry if others think him not too bright. He does not like to be told he is wrong, even when he is. He dislikes being contradicted.

Some people who are born under this sign are very suspicious of others—even of those persons close to them. They find it difficult to trust people fully. They are often afraid of being deceived or taken advantage of. The Bull often finds it difficult to forget or forgive. His love of material things sometimes makes him rather avaricious and petty.

Gemini: May 21–June 20

The Positive Side of Gemini

The person born under this sign of the Heavenly Twins is usually quite bright and quick-witted. Some of them are capable of doing many different things. The Gemini person very often has many different interests. He keeps an open mind and is always anxious to learn new things.

Gemini is often an analytical person. He is a person who enjoys making use of his intellect. He is governed more by his mind than by his emotions. He is a person who is not confined to one view; he can often understand both sides to a problem or question. He knows how to reason, how to make rapid decisions if need be.

He is an adaptable person and can make himself at home almost anywhere. There are all kinds of situations he can adapt to. He is a person who seldom doubts himself; he is sure of his talents and his ability to think and reason. Gemini is generally most satisfied

when he is in a situation where he can make use of his intellect. Never short of imagination, he often has strong talents for invention. He is rather a modern person when it comes to life; Gemini almost always moves along with the times—perhaps that is why he remains so youthful throughout most of his life.

Literature and art appeal to the person born under this sign. Creativity in almost any form will interest and intrigue the Gemini man or woman.

The Gemini is often quite charming. A good talker, he often is the center of attraction at any gathering. People find it easy to like a person born under this sign because he can appear easygoing and usually has a good sense of humor.

The Negative Side of Gemini

Sometimes the Gemini person tries to do too many things at one time—and as a result, winds up finishing nothing. Some Twins are easily distracted and find it rather difficult to concentrate on one thing for too long a time. Sometimes they give in to trifling fancies and find it rather boring to become too serious about any one thing. Some of them are never dependable, no matter what they promise.

Although the Gemini man or woman often appears to be well-versed on many subjects, this is sometimes just a veneer. His knowledge may be only superficial, but because he speaks so well he gives people the impression of erudition. Some Geminis are sharp-tongued and inconsiderate; they think only of themselves and their own pleasure.

Cancer: June 21–July 20

The Positive Side of Cancer

The Moon Child's most positive point is his understanding nature. On the whole, he is a loving and sympathetic person. He would never go out of his way to hurt anyone. The Cancer man or woman is often very kind and tender; they give what they can to others. They hate to see others suffering and will do what they can to help someone in less fortunate circumstances than themselves. They are often very concerned about the world. Their interest in people generally goes beyond that of just their own families and close friends; they have a deep sense of community and respect humanitarian values. The Moon Child means what he says, as a rule; he is honest about his feelings.

The Cancer man or woman is a person who knows the art of patience. When something seems difficult, he is willing to wait until the situation becomes manageable again. He is a person who knows how to bide his time. Cancer knows how to concentrate on one thing at a time. When he has made his mind up he generally sticks with what he does, seeing it through to the end.

Cancer is a person who loves his home. He enjoys being surrounded by familiar things and the people he loves. Of all the signs, Cancer is the most maternal. Even the men born under this sign often have a motherly or protective quality about them. They like to take care of people in their family—to see that they are well loved and well provided for. They are usually loyal and faithful. Family ties mean a lot to the Cancer man or woman. Parents and in-laws are respected and loved. Young Cancer responds very well to adults who show faith in him. The Moon Child has a strong sense of tradition. He is very sensitive to the moods of others.

The Negative Side of Cancer

Sometimes Cancer finds it rather hard to face life. It becomes too much for him. He can be a little timid and retiring, when things don't go too well. When unfortunate things happen, he is apt to just shrug and say, "Whatever will be will be." He can be fatalistic to a fault. The uncultivated Cancer is a bit lazy. He doesn't have very much ambition. Anything that seems a bit difficult he'll gladly leave to others. He may be lacking in initiative. Too sensitive, when he feels he's been injured, he'll crawl back into his shell and nurse his imaginary wounds. The immature Moon Child often is given to crying when the smallest thing goes wrong.

Some Cancers find it difficult to enjoy themselves in environments outside their homes. They make heavy demands on others, and need to be constantly reassured that they are loved. Lacking such reassurance, they may resort to sulking in silence.

Leo: July 21–August 21

The Positive Side of Leo

Often Leos make good leaders. They seem to be good organizers and administrators. Usually they are quite popular with others. Whatever group it is that they belong to, the Leo man or woman is almost sure to be or become the leader. Loyalty, one of the Lion's noblest traits, enables him or her to maintain this leadership position.

Leo is generous most of the time. It is his best characteristic. He or she likes to give gifts and presents. In making others happy, the Leo person becomes happy himself. He likes to splurge when spending money on others. In some instances it may seem that the Lion's generosity knows no boundaries. A hospitable person, the Leo man or woman is very fond of welcoming people to his house and entertaining them. He is never short of company.

Leo has plenty of energy and drive. He enjoys working toward some specific goal. When he applies himself correctly, he gets what he wants most often. The Leo person is almost never unsure of himself. He has plenty of confidence and aplomb. He is a person who is direct in almost everything he does. He has a quick mind and can make a decision in a very short time.

He usually sets a good example for others because of his ambitious manner and positive ways. He knows how to stick to something once he's started. Although Leo may be good at making a joke, he is not superficial or glib. He is a loving person, kind and thoughtful.

There is generally nothing small or petty about the Leo man or woman. He does what he can for those who are deserving. He is a person others can rely upon at all times. He means what he says. An honest person, generally speaking, he is a friend who is valued and sought out.

The Negative Side of Leo

Leo, however, does have his faults. At times, he can be just a bit too arrogant. He thinks that no one deserves a leadership position except him. Only he is capable of doing things well. His opinion of himself is often much too high. Because of his conceit, he is

sometimes rather unpopular with a good many people. Some Leos are too materialistic; they can only think in terms of money and profit.

Some Leos enjoy lording it over others—at home or at their place of business. What is more, they feel they have the right to. Egocentric to an impossible degree, this sort of Leo cares little about how others think or feel. He can be rude and cutting.

Virgo: August 22–September 22

The Positive Side of Virgo

The person born under the sign of Virgo is generally a busy person. He knows how to arrange and organize things. He is a good planner. Above all, he is practical and is not afraid of hard work.

Often called the sign of the Harvester, Virgo knows how to attain what he desires. He sticks with something until it is finished. He never shirks his duties, and can always be depended upon. The Virgo person can be thoroughly trusted at all times.

The man or woman born under this sign tries to do everything to perfection. He doesn't believe in doing anything halfway. He always aims for the top. He is the sort of a person who is always learning and constantly striving to better himself—not because he wants more money or glory, but because it gives him a feeling of accomplishment.

The Virgo man or woman is a very observant person. He is sensitive to how others feel, and can see things below the surface of a situation. He usually puts this talent to constructive use.

It is not difficult for the Virgo to be open and earnest. He believes in putting his cards on the table. He is never secretive or underhanded. He's as good as his word. The Virgo person is generally plainspoken and down to earth. He has no trouble in expressing himself.

The Virgo person likes to keep up to date on new developments in his particular field. Well-informed, generally, he sometimes has a keen interest in the arts or literature. What he knows, he knows well. His ability to use his critical faculties is well-developed and sometimes startles others because of its accuracy.

Virgos adhere to a moderate way of life; they avoid excesses. Virgo is a responsible person and enjoys being of service.

The Negative Side of Virgo

Sometimes a Virgo person is too critical. He thinks that only he can do something the way it should be done. Whatever anyone else does is inferior. He can be rather annoying in the way he quibbles over insignificant details. In telling others how things should be done, he can be rather tactless and mean.

Some Virgos seem rather emotionless and cool. They feel emotional involvement is beneath them. They are sometimes too tidy, too neat. With money they can be rather miserly. Some Virgos try to force their opinions and ideas on others.

Libra: September 23–October 22

The Positive Side of Libra

Libras love harmony. It is one of their most outstanding character traits. They are interested in achieving balance; they admire beauty and grace in things as well as in people. Generally speaking, they are kind and considerate people. Libras are usually very sympathetic. They go out of their way not to hurt another person's feelings. They are outgoing and do what they can to help those in need.

People born under the sign of Libra almost always make good friends. They are loyal and amiable. They enjoy the company of others. Many of them are rather moderate in their views; they believe in keeping an open mind, however, and weighing both sides of an issue fairly before making a decision.

Alert and intelligent, Libra, often known as the Lawgiver, is always fair-minded and tries to put himself in the position of the other person. They are against injustice; quite often they take up for the underdog. In most of their social dealings, they try to be tactful and kind. They dislike discord and bickering, and most Libras strive for peace and harmony in all their relationships.

The Libra man or woman has a keen sense of beauty. They appreciate handsome furnishings and clothes. Many of them are artistically inclined. Their taste is usually impeccable. They know how to use color. Their homes are almost always attractively arranged and inviting. They enjoy entertaining people and see to it that their guests always feel at home and welcome.

Libra gets along with almost everyone. He is well-liked and socially much in demand.

The Negative Side of Libra

Some people born under this sign tend to be rather insincere. So eager are they to achieve harmony in all relationships that they will even go so far as to lie. Many of them are escapists. They find facing the truth an ordeal and prefer living in a world of make-believe.

In a serious argument, some Libras give in rather easily even when they know they are right. Arguing, even about something they believe in, is too unsettling for some of them.

Libras sometimes care too much for material things. They enjoy possessions and luxuries. Some are vain and tend to be jealous.

Scorpio: October 23–November 22

The Positive Side of Scorpio

The Scorpio man or woman generally knows what he or she wants out of life. He is a determined person. He sees something through to the end. Scorpio is quite sincere, and seldom says anything he doesn't mean. When he sets a goal for himself he tries to go about achieving it in a very direct way.

The Scorpion is brave and courageous. They are not afraid of hard work. Obstacles do not frighten them. They forge ahead until they achieve what they set out for. The Scorpio man or woman has a strong will.

Although Scorpio may seem rather fixed and determined, inside he is often quite tender and loving. He can care very much for others. He believes in sincerity in all relationships. His feelings about someone tend to last; they are profound and not superficial.

The Scorpio person is someone who adheres to his principles no matter what happens. He will not be deterred from a path he believes to be right.

Because of his many positive strengths, the Scorpion can often achieve happiness for himself and for those that he loves.

He is a constructive person by nature. He often has a deep understanding of people and of life, in general. He is perceptive and unafraid. Obstacles often seem to spur him on. He is a positive person who enjoys winning. He has many strengths and resources; challenge of any sort often brings out the best in him.

The Negative Side of Scorpio

The Scorpio person is sometimes hypersensitive. Often he imagines injury when there is none. He feels that others do not bother to recognize him for his true worth. Sometimes he is given to excessive boasting in order to compensate for what he feels is neglect.

Scorpio can be proud, arrogant, and competitive. They can be sly when they put their minds to it and they enjoy outwitting persons or institutions noted for their cleverness.

Their tactics for getting what they want are sometimes devious and ruthless. They don't care too much about what others may think. If they feel others have done them an injustice, they will do their best to seek revenge. The Scorpion often has a sudden, violent temper; and this person's interest in sex is sometimes quite unbalanced or excessive.

Sagittarius: November 23–December 20

The Positive Side of Sagittarius

People born under this sign are honest and forthright. Their approach to life is earnest and open. Sagittarius is often quite adult in his way of seeing things. They are broad-minded and tolerant people. When dealing with others the person born under the sign of the Archer is almost always open and forthright. He doesn't believe in deceit or pretension. His standards are high. People who associate with Sagittarius generally admire and respect his tolerant viewpoint.

The Archer trusts others easily and expects them to trust him. He is never suspicious or envious and almost always thinks well of others. People always enjoy his company because he is so friendly and easygoing. The Sagittarius man or woman is often good-humored. He can always be depended upon by his friends, family, and co-workers.

The person born under this sign of the Zodiac likes a good joke every now and then. Sagittarius is eager for fun and laughs, which makes him very popular with others.

A lively person, he enjoys sports and outdoor life. The Archer is fond of animals. Intelligent and interesting, he can begin an

animated conversation with ease. He likes exchanging ideas and discussing various views.

He is not selfish or proud. If someone proposes an idea or plan that is better than his, he will immediately adopt it. Imaginative yet practical, he knows how to put ideas into practice.

The Archer enjoys sport and games, and it doesn't matter if he wins or loses. He is a forgiving person, and never sulks over something that has not worked out in his favor.

He is seldom critical, and is almost always generous.

The Negative Side of Sagittarius

Some Sagittarius are restless. They take foolish risks and seldom learn from the mistakes they make. They don't have heads for money and are often mismanaging their finances. Some of them devote much of their time to gambling.

Some are too outspoken and tactless, always putting their feet in their mouths. They hurt others carelessly by being honest at the wrong time. Sometimes they make promises which they don't keep. They don't stick close enough to their plans and go from one failure to another. They are undisciplined and waste a lot of energy.

Capricorn: December 21–January 19

The Positive Side of Capricorn

The person born under the sign of Capricorn, known variously as the Mountain Goat or Sea Goat, is usually very stable and patient. He sticks to whatever tasks he has and sees them through. He can always be relied upon and he is not averse to work.

An honest person, Capricorn is generally serious about whatever he does. He does not take his duties lightly. He is a practical person and believes in keeping his feet on the ground.

Quite often the person born under this sign is ambitious and knows how to get what he wants out of life. The Goat forges ahead and never gives up his goal. When he is determined about something, he almost always wins. He is a good worker—a hard worker. Although things may not come easy to him, he will not complain, but continue working until his chores are finished.

He is usually good at business matters and knows the value of money. He is not a spendthrift and knows how to put something away for a rainy day; he dislikes waste and unnecessary loss.

Capricorn knows how to make use of his self-control. He can apply himself to almost anything once he puts his mind to it. His ability to concentrate sometimes astounds others. He is diligent and does well when involved in detail work.

The Capricorn man or woman is charitable, generally speaking, and will do what is possible to help others less fortunate. As a friend, he is loyal and trustworthy. He never shirks his duties or responsibilities. He is self-reliant and never expects too much of the other fellow. He does what he can on his own. If someone does him a good turn, then he will do his best to return the favor.

The Negative Side of Capricorn

Like everyone, Capricorn, too, has faults. At times, the Goat can be overcritical of others. He expects others to live up to his own high standards. He thinks highly of himself and tends to look down on others.

His interest in material things may be exaggerated. The Capricorn man or woman thinks too much about getting on in the world and having something to show for it. He may even be a little greedy.

He sometimes thinks he knows what's best for everyone. He is too bossy. He is always trying to organize and correct others. He may be a little narrow in his thinking.

Aquarius: January 20–February 18

The Positive Side of Aquarius

The Aquarius man or woman is usually very honest and forthright. These are his two greatest qualities. His standards for himself are generally very high. He can always be relied upon by others. His word is his bond.

Aquarius is perhaps the most tolerant of all the Zodiac personalities. He respects other people's beliefs and feels that everyone is entitled to his own approach to life.

He would never do anything to injure another's feelings. He is never unkind or cruel. Always considerate of others, the Water

Bearer is always willing to help a person in need. He feels a very strong tie between himself and all the other members of mankind.

The person born under this sign, called the Water Bearer, is almost always an individualist. He does not believe in teaming up with the masses, but prefers going his own way. His ideas about life and mankind are often quite advanced. There is a saying to the effect that the average Aquarius is fifty years ahead of his time.

Aquarius is community-minded. The problems of the world concern him greatly. He is interested in helping others no matter what part of the globe they live in. He is truly a humanitarian sort. He likes to be of service to others.

Giving, considerate, and without prejudice, Aquarius have no trouble getting along with others.

The Negative Side of Aquarius

Aquarius may be too much of a dreamer. He makes plans but seldom carries them out. He is rather unrealistic. His imagination has a tendency to run away with him. Because many of his plans are impractical, he is always in some sort of a dither.

Others may not approve of him at all times because of his unconventional behavior. He may be a bit eccentric. Sometimes he is so busy with his own thoughts that he loses touch with the realities of existence.

Some Aquarius feel they are more clever and intelligent than others. They seldom admit to their own faults, even when they are quite apparent. Some become rather fanatic in their views. Their criticism of others is sometimes destructive and negative.

Pisces: February 19–March 20

The Positive Side of Pisces

Known as the sign of the Fishes, Pisces has a sympathetic nature. Kindly, he is often dedicated in the way he goes about helping others. The sick and the troubled often turn to him for advice and assistance. Possessing keen intuition, Pisces can easily understand people's deepest problems.

He is very broad-minded and does not criticize others for their faults. He knows how to accept people for what they are. On the whole, he is a trustworthy and earnest person. He is loyal to his friends and will do what he can to help them in time of need. Generous and good-natured, he is a lover of peace; he is often willing to help others solve their differences. People who have taken a wrong turn in life often interest him and he will do what he can to persuade them to rehabilitate themselves.

He has a strong intuitive sense and most of the time he knows how to make it work for him. Pisces is unusually perceptive and often knows what is bothering someone before that person, himself, is aware of it. The Pisces man or woman is an idealistic person, basically, and is interested in making the world a better place in which to live. Pisces believes that everyone should help each other. He is willing to do more than his share in order to achieve cooperation with others.

The person born under this sign often is talented in music or art. He is a receptive person; he is able to take the ups and downs of life with philosophic calm.

The Negative Side of Pisces

Some Pisces are often depressed; their outlook on life is rather glum. They may feel that they have been given a bad deal in life and that others are always taking unfair advantage of them. Pisces sometimes feel that the world is a cold and cruel place. The Fishes can be easily discouraged. The Pisces man or woman may even withdraw from the harshness of reality into a secret shell of his own where he dreams and idles away a good deal of his time.

Pisces can be lazy. He lets things happen without giving the least bit of resistance. He drifts along, whether on the high road or on the low. He can be lacking in willpower.

Some Pisces people seek escape through drugs or alcohol. When temptation comes along they find it hard to resist. In matters of sex, they can be rather permissive.

Sun Sign Personalities

ARIES: Hans Christian Andersen, Pearl Bailey, Marlon Brando, Wernher Von Braun, Charlie Chaplin, Joan Crawford, Da Vinci, Bette Davis, Doris Day, W. C. Fields, Alec Guinness, Adolf Hitler, William Holden, Thomas Jefferson, Nikita Khrushchev, Elton John, Arturo Toscanini, J. P. Morgan, Paul Robeson, Gloria Steinem, Sarah Vaughn, Vincent van Gogh, Tennessee Williams

TAURUS: Fred Astaire, Charlotte Brontë, Carol Burnett, Irving Berlin, Bing Crosby, Salvador Dali, Tchaikovsky, Queen Elizabeth II, Duke Ellington, Ella Fitzgerald, Henry Fonda, Sigmund Freud, Orson Welles, Joe Louis, Lenin, Karl Marx, Golda Meir, Eva Peron, Bertrand Russell, Shakespeare, Kate Smith, Benjamin Spock, Barbra Streisand, Shirley Temple, Harry Truman

GEMINI: Ruth Benedict, Josephine Baker, Rachel Carson, Carlos Chavez, Walt Whitman, Bob Dylan, Ralph Waldo Emerson, Judy Garland, Paul Gauguin, Allen Ginsberg, Benny Goodman, Bob Hope, Burl Ives, John F. Kennedy, Peggy Lee, Marilyn Monroe, Joe Namath, Cole Porter, Laurence Olivier, Harriet Beecher Stowe, Queen Victoria, John Wayne, Frank Lloyd Wright

CANCER: "Dear Abby," Lizzie Borden, David Brinkley, Yul Brynner, Pearl Buck, Marc Chagall, Princess Diana, Babe Didrikson, Mary Baker Eddy, Henry VIII, John Glenn, Ernest Hemingway, Lena Horne, Oscar Hammerstein, Helen Keller, Ann Landers, George Orwell, Nancy Reagan, Rembrandt, Richard Rodgers, Ginger Rogers, Rubens, Jean-Paul Sartre, O. J. Simpson

LEO: Neil Armstrong, James Baldwin, Lucille Ball, Emily Brontë, Wilt Chamberlain, Julia Child, William J. Clinton, Cecil B. De Mille, Ogden Nash, Amelia Earhart, Edna Ferber, Arthur Goldberg, Alfred Hitchcock, Mick Jagger, George Meany, Annie Oakley, George Bernard Shaw, Napoleon, Jacqueline Onassis, Henry Ford, Francis Scott Key, Andy Warhol, Mae West, Orville Wright

VIRGO: Ingrid Bergman, Warren Burger, Maurice Chevalier, Agatha Christie, Sean Connery, Lafayette, Peter Falk, Greta Garbo, Althea Gibson, Arthur Godfrey, Goethe, Buddy Hackett, Michael Jackson, Lyndon Johnson, D. H. Lawrence, Sophia Loren, Grandma Moses, Arnold Palmer, Queen Elizabeth I, Walter Reuther, Peter Sellers, Lily Tomlin, George Wallace

LIBRA: Brigitte Bardot, Art Buchwald, Truman Capote, Dwight D. Eisenhower, William Faulkner, F. Scott Fitzgerald, Gandhi, George Gershwin, Micky Mantle, Helen Hayes, Vladimir Horowitz, Doris Lessing, Martina Navratalova, Eugene O'Neill, Luciano Pavarotti, Emily Post, Eleanor Roosevelt, Bruce Springsteen, Margaret Thatcher, Gore Vidal, Barbara Walters, Oscar Wilde

SCORPIO: Vivien Leigh, Richard Burton, Art Carney, Johnny Carson, Billy Graham, Grace Kelly, Walter Cronkite, Marie Curie, Charles de Gaulle, Linda Evans, Indira Gandhi, Theodore Roosevelt, Rock Hudson, Katherine Hepburn, Robert F. Kennedy, Billie Jean King, Martin Luther, Georgia O'Keeffe, Pablo Picasso, Jonas Salk, Alan Shepard, Robert Louis Stevenson

SAGITTARIUS: Jane Austen, Louisa May Alcott, Woody Allen, Beethoven, Willy Brandt, Mary Martin, William F. Buckley, Maria Callas, Winston Churchill, Noel Coward, Emily Dickinson, Walt Disney, Benjamin Disraeli, James Doolittle, Kirk Douglas, Chet Huntley, Jane Fonda, Chris Evert Lloyd, Margaret Mead, Charles Schulz, John Milton, Frank Sinatra, Steven Spielberg

CAPRICORN: Muhammad Ali, Isaac Asimov, Pablo Casals, Dizzy Dean, Marlene Dietrich, James Farmer, Ava Gardner, Barry Goldwater, Cary Grant, J. Edgar Hoover, Howard Hughes, Joan of Arc, Gypsy Rose Lee, Martin Luther King, Jr., Rudyard Kipling, Mao Tse-tung, Richard Nixon, Gamal Nasser, Louis Pasteur, Albert Schweitzer, Stalin, Benjamin Franklin, Elvis Presley

AQUARIUS: Marian Anderson, Susan B. Anthony, Jack Benny, John Barrymore, Mikhail Baryshnikov, Charles Darwin, Charles Dickens, Thomas Edison, Clark Gable, Jascha Heifetz, Abraham Lincoln, Yehudi Menuhin, Mozart, Jack Nicklaus, Ronald Reagan, Jackie Robinson, Norman Rockwell, Franklin D. Roosevelt, Gertrude Stein, Charles Lindbergh, Margaret Truman

PISCES: Edward Albee, Harry Belafonte, Alexander Graham Bell, Chopin, Adelle Davis, Albert Einstein, Golda Meir, Jackie Gleason, Winslow Homer, Edward M. Kennedy, Victor Hugo, Mike Mansfield, Michelangelo, Edna St. Vincent Millay, Liza Minelli, John Steinbeck, Linus Pauling, Ravel, Renoir, Diana Ross, William Shirer, Elizabeth Taylor, George Washington

The Signs and Their Key Words

		POSITIVE	NEGATIVE
ARIES	self	courage, initiative, pioneer instinct	brash rudeness, selfish impetuosity
TAURUS	money	endurance, loyalty, wealth	obstinacy, gluttony
GEMINI	mind	versatility	capriciousness, unreliability
CANCER	family	sympathy, homing instinct	clannishness, childishness
LEO	children	love, authority, integrity	egotism, force
VIRGO	work	purity, industry, analysis	faultfinding, cynicism
LIBRA	marriage	harmony, justice	vacillation, superficiality
SCORPIO	sex	survival, regeneration	vengeance, discord
SAGITTARIUS	travel	optimism, higher learning	lawlessness
CAPRICORN	career	depth	narrowness, gloom
AQUARIUS	friends	human fellowship, genius	perverse unpredictability
PISCES	confine-ment	spiritual love, universality	diffusion, escapism

The Elements and Qualities of The Signs

Every sign has both an *element* and a *quality* associated with it. The element indicates the basic makeup of the sign, and the quality describes the kind of activity associated with each.

Element	Sign	Quality	Sign
FIRE	ARIES	CARDINAL	ARIES
	LEO		LIBRA
	SAGITTARIUS		CANCER
			CAPRICORN
EARTH	TAURUS		
	VIRGO		
	CAPRICORN	FIXED	TAURUS
			LEO
			SCORPIO
AIR.........	GEMINI		AQUARIUS
	LIBRA		
	AQUARIUS		
		MUTABLE	GEMINI
WATER....	CANCER		VIRGO
	SCORPIO		SAGITTARIUS
	PISCES		PISCES

Signs can be grouped together according to their element and quality. Signs of the same element share many basic traits in common. They tend to form stable configurations and ultimately harmonious relationships. Signs of the same quality are often less harmonious, but they share many dynamic potentials for growth as well as profound fulfillment.

Further discussion of each of these sign groupings is provided on the following pages.

The Fire Signs

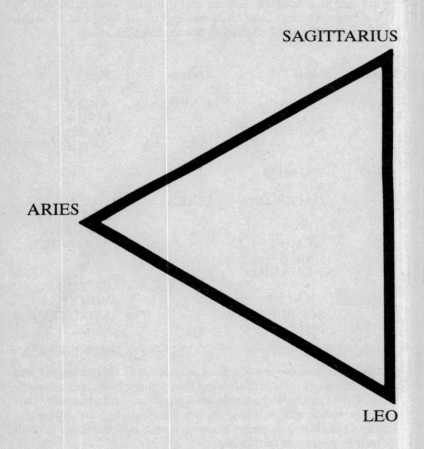

This is the fire group. On the whole these are emotional, volatile types, quick to anger, quick to forgive. They are adventurous, powerful people and act as a source of inspiration for everyone. They spark into action with immediate exuberant impulses. They are intelligent, self-involved, creative, and idealistic. They all share a certain vibrancy and glow that outwardly reflects an inner flame and passion for living.

The Earth Signs

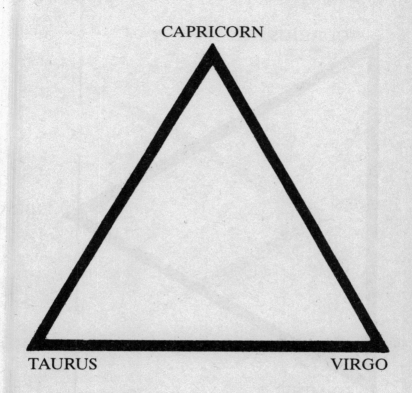

CAPRICORN

TAURUS

VIRGO

This is the earth group. They are in constant touch with the material world and tend to be conservative. Although they are all capable of spartan self-discipline, they are earthy, sensual people who are stimulated by the tangible, elegant, and luxurious. The thread of their lives is always practical, but they do fantasize and are often attracted to dark, mysterious, emotional people. They are like great cliffs overhanging the sea, forever married to the ocean but always resisting erosion from the dark, emotional forces that thunder at their feet.

The Air Signs

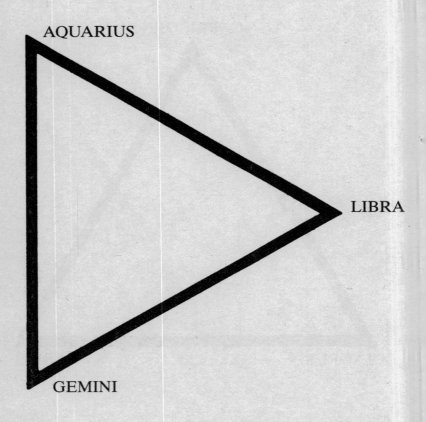

AQUARIUS

LIBRA

GEMINI

This is the air group. They are light, mental creatures desirous of contact, communication, and relationship. They are involved with people and the forming of ties on many levels. Original thinkers, they are the bearers of human news. Their language is their sense of word, color, style, and beauty. They provide an atmosphere suitable and pleasant for living. They add change and versatility to the scene, and it is through them that we can explore new territory of human intelligence and experience.

The Water Signs

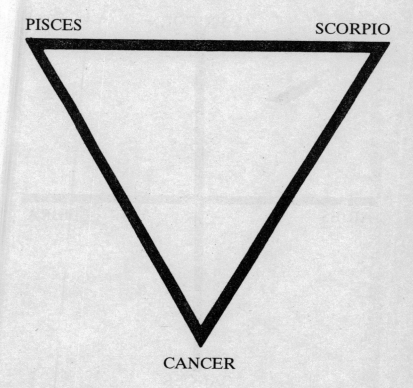

PISCES

SCORPIO

CANCER

This is the water group. Through the water people, we are all joined together on emotional, nonverbal levels. They are silent, mysterious types whose magic hypnotizes even the most determined realist. They have uncanny perceptions about people and are as rich as the oceans when it comes to feeling, emotion, or imagination. They are sensitive, mystical creatures with memories that go back beyond time. Through water, life is sustained. These people have the potential for the depths of darkness or the heights of mysticism and art.

The Cardinal Signs

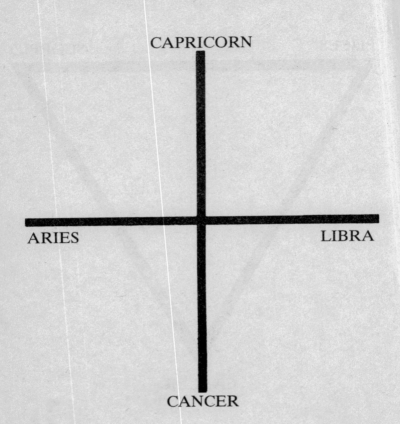

CAPRICORN

ARIES

LIBRA

CANCER

Put together, this is a clear-cut picture of dynamism, activity, tremendous stress, and remarkable achievement. These people know the meaning of great change since their lives are often characterized by significant crises and major successes. This combination is like a simultaneous storm of summer, fall, winter, and spring. The danger is chaotic diffusion of energy; the potential is irrepressible growth and victory.

The Fixed Signs

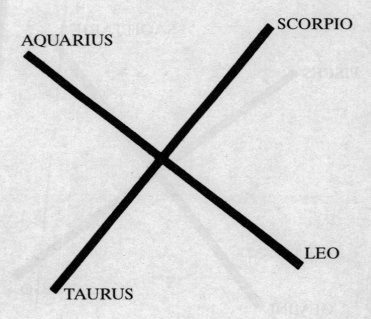

AQUARIUS

SCORPIO

LEO

TAURUS

Fixed signs are always establishing themselves in a given place or area of experience. Like explorers who arrive and plant a flag, these people claim a position from which they do not enjoy being deposed. They are staunch, stalwart, upright, trusty, honorable people, although their obstinacy is well-known. Their contribution is fixity, and they are the angels who support our visible world.

The Mutable Signs

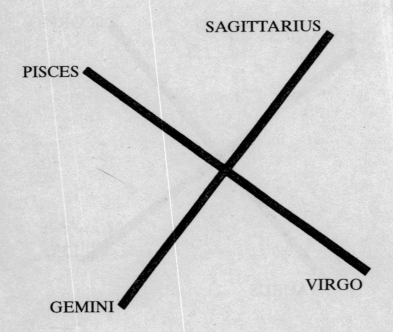

Mutable people are versatile, sensitive, intelligent, nervous, and deeply curious about life. They are the translators of all energy. They often carry out or complete tasks initiated by others. Combinations of these signs have highly developed minds; they are imaginative and jumpy and think and talk a lot. At worst their lives are a Tower of Babel. At best they are adaptable and ready creatures who can assimilate one kind of experience and enjoy it while anticipating coming changes.

THE PLANETS OF THE SOLAR SYSTEM

This section describes the planets of the solar system. In astrology, both the Sun and the Moon are considered to be planets. Because of the Moon's influence in our day-to-day lives, the Moon is described in a separate section following this one.

The Planets and the Signs They Rule

The signs of the Zodiac are linked to the planets in the following way. Each sign is governed or ruled by one or more planets. No matter where the planets are located in the sky at any given moment, they still rule their respective signs, and when they travel through the signs they rule, they have special dignity and their effects are stronger.

Following is a list of the planets and the signs they rule. After looking at the list, read the definitions of the planets and see if you can determine how the planet ruling *your* Sun sign has affected your life.

SIGNS	RULING PLANETS
Aries	Mars, Pluto
Taurus	Venus
Gemini	Mercury
Cancer	Moon
Leo	Sun
Virgo	Mercury
Libra	Venus
Scorpio	Mars, Pluto
Sagittarius	Jupiter
Capricorn	Saturn
Aquarius	Saturn, Uranus
Pisces	Jupiter, Neptune

Characteristics of the Planets

The following pages give the meaning and characteristics of the planets of the solar system. They all travel around the Sun at different speeds and different distances. Taken with the Sun, they all distribute individual intelligence and ability throughout the entire chart.

The planets modify the influence of the Sun in a chart according to their own particular natures, strengths, and positions. Their positions must be calculated for each year and day, and their function and expression in a horoscope will change as they move from one area of the Zodiac to another.

We start with a description of the sun.

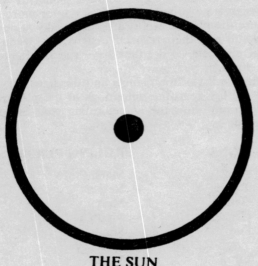

THE SUN

SUN

This is the center of existence. Around this flaming sphere all the planets revolve in endless orbits. Our star is constantly sending out its beams of light and energy without which no life on Earth would be possible. In astrology it symbolizes everything we are trying to become, the center around which all of our activity in life will always revolve. It is the symbol of our basic nature and describes the natural and constant thread that runs through everything that we do from birth to death on this planet.

To early astrologers, the Sun seemed to be another planet because it crossed the heavens every day, just like the rest of the bodies in the sky.

It is the only star near enough to be seen well—it is, in fact, a dwarf star. Approximately 860,000 miles in diameter, it is about ten times as wide as the giant planet Jupiter. The next nearest star is nearly 300,000 times as far away, and if the Sun were located as far away as most of the bright stars, it would be too faint to be seen without a telescope.

Everything in the horoscope ultimately revolves around this singular body. Although other forces may be prominent in the charts of some individuals, still the Sun is the total nucleus of being and symbolizes the complete potential of every human being alive. It is vitality and the life force. Your whole essence comes from the position of the Sun.

You are always trying to express the Sun according to its position by house and sign. Possibility for all development is found in the Sun, and it marks the fundamental character of your personal radiations all around you.

It is the symbol of strength, vigor, wisdom, dignity, ardor, and generosity, and the ability for a person to function as a mature individual. It is also a creative force in society. It is consciousness of the gift of life.

The underdeveloped solar nature is arrogant, pushy, undependable, and proud, and is constantly using force.

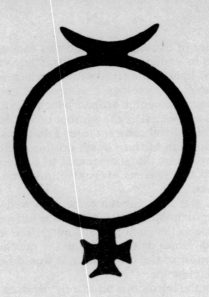

MERCURY

Mercury is the planet closest to the Sun. It races around our star, gathering information and translating it to the rest of the system. Mercury represents your capacity to understand the desires of your own will and to translate those desires into action.

In other words it is the planet of mind and the power of communication. Through Mercury we develop an ability to think, write, speak, and observe—to become aware of the world around us. It colors our attitudes and vision of the world, as well as our capacity to communicate our inner responses to the outside world. Some people who have serious disabilities in their power of verbal communication have often wrongly been described as people lacking intelligence.

Although this planet (and its position in the horoscope) indicates your power to communicate your thoughts and perceptions to the world, intelligence is something deeper. Intelligence is distributed throughout all the planets. It is the relationship of the planets to each other that truly describes what we call intelligence. Mercury rules speaking, language, mathematics, draft and design, students, messengers, young people, offices, teachers, and any pursuits where the mind of man has wings.

VENUS

Venus is beauty. It symbolizes the harmony and radiance of a rare and elusive quality: beauty itself. It is refinement and delicacy, softness and charm. In astrology it indicates grace, balance, and the aesthetic sense. Where Venus is we see beauty, a gentle drawing in of energy and the need for satisfaction and completion. It is a special touch that finishes off rough edges. It is sensitivity, and affection, and it is always the place for that other elusive phenomenon: love. Venus describes our sense of what is beautiful and loving. Poorly developed, it is vulgar, tasteless, and self-indulgent. But its ideal is the flame of spiritual love—Aphrodite, goddess of love, and the sweetness and power of personal beauty.

MARS

Mars is raw, crude energy. The planet next to Earth but outward from the Sun is a fiery red sphere that charges through the horoscope with force and fury. It represents the way you reach out for new adventure and new experience. It is energy and drive, initiative, courage, and daring. It is the power to start something and see it through. It can be thoughtless, cruel and wild, angry and hostile, causing cuts, burns, scalds, and wounds. It can stab its way through a chart, or it can be the symbol of healthy spirited adventure, well-channeled constructive power to begin and keep up the drive. If you have trouble starting things, if you lack the get-up-and-go to start the ball rolling, if you lack aggressiveness and self-confidence, chances are there's another planet influencing your Mars. Mars rules soldiers, butchers, surgeons, salesmen—any field that requires daring, bold skill, operational technique, or self-promotion.

JUPITER

This is the largest planet of the solar system. Scientists have recently learned that Jupiter reflects more light than it receives from the Sun. In a sense it is like a star itself. In astrology it rules good luck and good cheer, health, wealth, optimism, happiness, success, and joy. It is the symbol of opportunity and always opens the way for new possibilities in your life. It rules exuberance, enthusiasm, wisdom, knowledge, generosity, and all forms of expansion in general. It rules actors, statesmen, clerics, professional people, religion, publishing, and the distribution of many people over large areas.

Sometimes Jupiter makes you think you deserve everything, and you become sloppy, wasteful, careless and rude, prodigal and lawless, in the illusion that nothing can ever go wrong. Then there is the danger of overconfidence, exaggeration, undependability, and overindulgence.

Jupiter is the minimization of limitation and the emphasis on spirituality and potential. It is the thirst for knowledge and higher learning.

SATURN

Saturn circles our system in dark splendor with its mysterious rings, forcing us to be awakened to whatever we have neglected in the past. It will present real puzzles and problems to be solved, causing delays, obstacles, and hindrances. By doing so, Saturn stirs our own sensitivity to those areas where we are laziest.

Here we must patiently develop *method*, and only through painstaking effort can our ends be achieved. It brings order to a horoscope and imposes reason just where we are feeling least reasonable. By creating limitations and boundary, Saturn shows the consequences of being human and demands that we accept the changing cycles inevitable in human life. Saturn rules time, old age, and sobriety. It can bring depression, gloom, jealousy, and greed, or serious acceptance of responsibilities out of which success will develop. With Saturn there is nothing to do but face facts. It rules laborers, stones, granite, rocks, and crystals of all kinds.

THE OUTER PLANETS:
URANUS, NEPTUNE, PLUTO

Uranus, Neptune, Pluto are the outer planets. They liberate human beings from cultural conditioning, and in that sense are the lawbreakers. In early times it was thought that Saturn was the last planet of the system—the outer limit beyond which we could never go. The discovery of the next three planets ushered in new phases of human history, revolution, and technology.

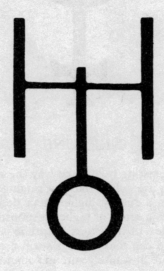

URANUS

Uranus rules unexpected change, upheaval, revolution. It is the symbol of total independence and asserts the freedom of an individual from all restriction and restraint. It is a breakthrough planet and indicates talent, originality, and genius in a horoscope. It usually causes last-minute reversals and changes of plan, unwanted separations, accidents, catastrophes, and eccentric behavior. It can add irrational rebelliousness and perverse bohemianism to a personality or a streak of unaffected brilliance in science and art. It rules technology, aviation, and all forms of electrical and electronic advancement. It governs great leaps forward and topsy-turvy situations, and *always* turns things around at the last minute. Its effects are difficult to predict, since it rules sudden last-minute decisions and events that come like lightning out of the blue.

NEPTUNE

Neptune dissolves existing reality the way the sea erodes the cliffs beside it. Its effects are subtle like the ringing of a buoy's bell in the fog. It suggests a reality higher than definition can usually describe. It awakens a sense of higher responsibility often causing guilt, worry, anxieties, or delusions. Neptune is associated with all forms of escape and can make things seem a certain way so convincingly that you are absolutely sure of something that eventually turns out to be quite different.

It is the planet of illusion and therefore governs the invisible realms that lie beyond our ordinary minds, beyond our simple factual ability to prove what is "real." Treachery, deceit, disillusionment, and disappointment are linked to Neptune. It describes a vague reality that promises eternity and the divine, yet in a manner so complex that we cannot really fathom it at all. At its worst Neptune is a cheap intoxicant; at its best it is the poetry, music, and inspiration of the higher planes of spiritual love. It has dominion over movies, photographs, and much of the arts.

PLUTO

Pluto lies at the outpost of our system and therefore rules finality in a horoscope—the final closing of chapters in your life, the passing of major milestones and points of development from which there is no return. It is a final wipeout, a closeout, an evacuation. It is a distant, subtle but powerful catalyst in all transformations that occur. It creates, destroys, then recreates. Sometimes Pluto starts its influence with a minor event or insignificant incident that might even go unnoticed. Slowly but surely, little by little, everything changes, until at last there has been a total transformation in the area of your life where Pluto has been operating. It rules mass thinking and the trends that society first rejects, then adopts, and finally outgrows.

Pluto rules the dead and the underworld—all the powerful forces of creation and destruction that go on all the time beneath, around, and above us. It can bring a lust for power with strong obsessions.

It is the planet that rules the metamorphosis of the caterpillar into a butterfly, for it symbolizes the capacity to change totally and forever a person's lifestyle, way of thought, and behavior.

THE MOON IN EACH SIGN

The Moon is the nearest planet to the Earth. It exerts more observable influence on us from day to day than any other planet. The effect is very personal, very intimate, and if we are not aware of how it works it can make us quite unstable in our ideas. And the annoying thing is that at these times we often see our own instability but can do nothing about it. A knowledge of what can be expected may help considerably. We can then be prepared to stand strong against the Moon's negative influences and use its positive ones to help us to get ahead. Who has not heard of going with the tide?

The Moon reflects, has no light of its own. It reflects the Sun—the life giver—in the form of vital movement. The Moon controls the tides, the blood rhythm, the movement of sap in trees and plants. Its nature is inconstancy and change so it signifies our moods, our superficial behavior—walking, talking, and especially thinking. Being a true reflector of other forces, the Moon is cold, watery like the surface of a still lake, brilliant and scintillating at times, but easily ruffled and disturbed by the winds of change.

The Moon takes about 27⅓ days to make a complete transit of the Zodiac. It spends just over 2¼ days in each sign. During that time it reflects the qualities, energies, and characteristics of the sign and, to a degree, the planet which rules the sign. When the Moon in its transit occupies a sign incompatible with our own birth sign, we can expect to feel a vague uneasiness, perhaps a touch of irritableness. We should not be discouraged nor let the feeling get us down, or, worse still, allow ourselves to take the discomfort out on others. Try to remember that the Moon has to change signs within 55 hours and, provided you are not physically ill, your mood will probably change with it. It is amazing how frequently depression lifts with the shift in the Moon's position. And, of course, when the Moon is transiting a sign compatible or sympathetic to yours, you will probably feel some sort of stimulation or just be plain happy to be alive.

In the horoscope, the Moon is such a powerful indicator that competent astrologers often use the sign it occupied at birth as the birth sign of the person. This is done particularly when the Sun is on the cusp, or edge, of two signs. Most experienced astrologers, however, coordinate both Sun and Moon signs by reading and confirming from one to the other and secure a far more accurate and personalized analysis.

For these reasons, the Moon tables which follow this section (see pages 86–92) are of great importance to the individual. They show the days and the exact times the Moon will enter each sign of the Zodiac for the year. Remember, you have to adjust the indicated times to local time. The corrections, already calculated for most of the main cities, are at the beginning of the tables. What follows now is a guide to the influences that will be reflected to the Earth by the Moon while it transits each of the twelve signs. The influence is at its peak about 26 hours after the Moon enters a sign. As you read the daily forecast, check the Moon sign for any given day and glance back at this guide.

MOON IN ARIES
This is a time for action, for reaching out beyond the usual self-imposed limitations and faint-hearted cautions. If you have plans in your head or on your desk, put them into practice. New ventures, applications, new jobs, new starts of any kind—all have a good chance of success. This is the period when original and dynamic impulses are being reflected onto Earth. Such energies are extremely vital and favor the pursuit of pleasure and adventure in practically every form. Sick people should feel an improvement. Those who are well will probably find themselves exuding confidence and optimism. People fond of physical exercise should find their bodies growing with tone and well-being. Boldness, strength, determination should characterize most of your activities with a readiness to face up to old challenges. Yesterday's problems may seem petty and exaggerated—so deal with them. Strike out alone. Self-reliance will attract others to you. This is a good time for making friends. Business and marriage partners are more likely to be impressed with the man and woman of action. Opposition will be overcome or thrown aside with much less effort than usual. CAUTION: Be dominant but not domineering.

MOON IN TAURUS
The spontaneous, action-packed person of yesterday gives way to the cautious, diligent, hardworking "thinker." In this period ideas will probably be concentrated on ways of improving finances. A great deal of time may be spent figuring out and going over schemes and plans. It is the right time to be careful with detail.

People will find themselves working longer than usual at their desks. Or devoting more time to serious thought about the future. A strong desire to put order into business and financial arrangements may cause extra work. Loved ones may complain of being neglected and may fail to appreciate that your efforts are for their ultimate benefit. Your desire for system may extend to criticism of arrangements in the home and lead to minor upsets. Health may be affected through overwork. Try to secure a reasonable amount of rest and relaxation, although the tendency will be to "keep going" despite good advice. Work done conscientiously in this period should result in a solid contribution to your future security. CAUTION: Try not to be as serious with people as the work you are engaged in.

MOON IN GEMINI

The humdrum of routine and too much work should suddenly end. You are likely to find yourself in an expansive, quicksilver world of change and self-expression. Urges to write, to paint, to experience the freedom of some sort of artistic outpouring, may be very strong. Take full advantage of them. You may find yourself finishing something you began and put aside long ago. Or embarking on something new which could easily be prompted by a chance meeting, a new acquaintance, or even an advertisement. There may be a yearning for a change of scenery, the feeling to visit another country (not too far away), or at least to get away for a few days. This may result in short, quick journeys. Or, if you are planning a single visit, there may be some unexpected changes or detours on the way. Familiar activities will seem to give little satisfaction unless they contain a fresh element of excitement or expectation. The inclination will be toward untried pursuits, particularly those that allow you to express your inner nature. The accent is on new faces, new places. CAUTION: Do not be too quick to commit yourself emotionally.

MOON IN CANCER

Feelings of uncertainty and vague insecurity are likely to cause problems while the Moon is in Cancer. Thoughts may turn frequently to the warmth of the home and the comfort of loved ones. Nostalgic impulses could cause you to bring out old photographs and letters and reflect on the days when your life seemed to be much more rewarding and less demanding. The love and understanding of parents and family may be important, and, if it is not forthcoming, you may have to fight against bouts of self-pity. The cordiality of friends and the thought of good times with them that are sure to be repeated will help to restore you to a happier frame of mind. The desire to be alone may follow minor setbacks or rebuffs at this time, but solitude is unlikely to help. Better to get on the telephone or visit someone. This period often causes peculiar dreams and upsurges of imaginative thinking which can be helpful to authors of occult and mystical works. Preoccupation with the personal world of simple human needs can overshadow any material strivings. CAUTION: Do not spend too much time thinking—seek the company of loved ones or close friends.

MOON IN LEO

New horizons of exciting and rather extravagant activity open up. This is the time for exhilarating entertainment, glamorous and lavish parties, and expensive shopping sprees. Any merrymaking that relies upon your generosity as a host has every chance of being a spectacular success. You should find yourself right in the center of the fun, either as the life of the party or simply as a person whom happy people like to be with. Romance thrives in this heady atmosphere and friendships are likely to explode unexpectedly into serious attachments. Children and younger people should be attracted to you and you may find yourself organizing a picnic or a visit to a fun-fair, the movies, or the beach. The sunny company and vitality of youthful companions should help you to find some unsuspected energy. In career, you could find an opening for promotion or advancement. This should be the time to make a direct approach. The period favors those engaged in original research. CAUTION: Bask in popularity, not in flattery.

MOON IN VIRGO

Off comes the party cap and out steps the busy, practical worker. He wants to get his personal affairs straight, to rearrange them, if necessary, for more efficiency, so he will have more time for more work. He clears up his correspondence, pays outstanding bills, makes numerous phone calls. He is likely to make inquiries, or sign up for some new insurance and put money into gilt-edged investment. Thoughts probably revolve around the need for future security—to tie up loose ends and clear the decks. There may be a tendency to be "finicky," to interfere in the routine of others, particularly friends and family members. The motive may be a genuine desire to help with suggestions for updating or streamlining their affairs, but these will probably not be welcomed. Sympathy may be felt for less fortunate sections of the community and a flurry of some sort of voluntary service is likely. This may be accompanied by strong feelings of responsibility on several fronts and health may suffer from extra efforts made. CAUTION: Everyone may not want your help or advice.

MOON IN LIBRA

These are days of harmony and agreement and you should find yourself at peace with most others. Relationships tend to be smooth and sweet-flowing. Friends may become closer and bonds deepen in mutual understanding. Hopes will be shared. Progress by cooperation could be the secret of success in every sphere. In business, established partnerships may flourish and new ones get off to a good start. Acquaintances could discover similar interests that lead to congenial discussions and rewarding exchanges of some sort. Love, as a unifying force, reaches its optimum. Marriage partners should find accord. Those who wed at this time face the prospect of a happy union. Cooperation and tolerance are felt to be stronger than dissension and impatience. The argumentative are not quite so loud in their bellowings, nor as inflexible in their attitudes. In the home, there should be a greater recognition of the other point of view and a readiness to put the wishes of the group before selfish insistence. This is a favorable time to join an art group. CAUTION: Do not be too independent—let others help you if they want to.

MOON IN SCORPIO

Driving impulses to make money and to economize are likely to cause upsets all around. No area of expenditure is likely to be spared the ax, including the household budget. This is a time when the desire to cut down on extravagance can become near fanatical. Care must be exercised to try to keep the aim in reasonable perspective. Others may not feel the same urgent need to save and may retaliate. There is a danger that possessions of sentimental value will be sold to realize cash for investment. Buying and selling of stock for quick profit is also likely. The attention turns to organizing, reorganizing, tidying up at home and at work. Neglected jobs could suddenly be done with great bursts of energy. The desire for solitude may intervene. Self-searching thoughts could disturb. The sense of invisible and mysterious energies in play could cause some excitability. The reassurance of loves ones may help. CAUTION: Be kind to the people you love.

MOON IN SAGITTARIUS

These are days when you are likely to be stirred and elevated by discussions and reflections of a religious and philosophical nature. Ideas of faraway places may cause unusual response and excitement. A decision may be made to visit someone overseas, perhaps a person whose influence was important to your earlier character development. There could be a strong resolution to get away from present intellectual patterns, to learn new subjects, and to meet more interesting people. The superficial may be rejected in all its forms. An impatience with old ideas and unimaginative contacts could lead to a change of companions and interests. There may be an upsurge of religious feeling and metaphysical inquiry. Even a new insight into the significance of astrology and other occult studies is likely under the curious stimulus of the Moon in Sagittarius. Physically, you may express this need for fundamental change by spending more time outdoors: sports, gardening, long walks appeal. CAUTION: Try to channel any restlessness into worthwhile study.

MOON IN CAPRICORN

Life in these hours may seem to pivot around the importance of gaining prestige and honor in the career, as well as maintaining a spotless reputation. Ambitious urges may be excessive and could be accompanied by quite acquisitive drives for money. Effort should be directed along strictly ethical lines where there is no possibility of reproach or scandal. All endeavors are likely to be characterized by great earnestness, and an air of authority and purpose which should impress those who are looking for leadership or reliability. The desire to conform to accepted standards may extend to sharp criticism of family members. Frivolity and unconventional actions are unlikely to amuse while the Moon is in Capricorn. Moderation and seriousness are the orders of the day. Achievement and recognition in this period could come through community work or organizing for the benefit of some amateur group. CAUTION: Dignity and esteem are not always self-awarded.

MOON IN AQUARIUS

Moon in Aquarius is in the second last sign of the Zodiac where ideas can become disturbingly fine and subtle. The result is often a mental "no-man's land" where imagination cannot be trusted with the same certitude as other times. The dangers for the individual are the extremes of optimism and pessimism. Unless the imagination is held in check, situations are likely to be misread, and rosy conclusions drawn where they do not exist. Consequences for the unwary can be costly in career and business. Best to think twice and not speak or act until you think again. Pessimism can be a cruel self-inflicted penalty for delusion at this time. Between the two extremes are strange areas of self-deception which, for example, can make the selfish person think he is actually being generous. Eerie dreams which resemble the reality and even seem to continue into the waking state are also possible. CAUTION: Look for the fact and not just for the image in your mind.

MOON IN PISCES

Everything seems to come to the surface now. Memory may be crystal clear, throwing up long-forgotten information which could be valuable in the career or business. Flashes of clairvoyance and intuition are possible along with sudden realizations of one's own nature, which may be used for self-improvement. A talent, never before suspected, may be discovered. Qualities not evident before in friends and marriage partners are likely to be noticed. As this is a period in which the truth seems to emerge, the discovery of false characteristics is likely to lead to disenchantment or a shift in attachments. However, when qualities are accepted, it should lead to happiness and deeper feeling. Surprise solutions could bob up for old problems. There may be a public announcement of the solving of a crime or mystery. People with secrets may find someone has "guessed" correctly. The secrets of the soul or the inner self also tend to reveal themselves. Religious and philosophical groups may make some interesting discoveries. CAUTION: Not a time for activities that depend on secrecy.

NOTE: When you read your daily forecasts, use the Moon Sign Dates that are provided in the following section of Moon Tables. Then you may want to glance back here for the Moon's influence in a given sign.

MOON TABLES

CORRECTION FOR NEW YORK TIME, FIVE HOURS WEST OF GREENWICH

Atlanta, Boston, Detroit, Miami, Washington, Montreal,
Ottawa, Quebec, Bogota, Havana, Lima, Santiago..Same time

Chicago, New Orleans, Houston, Winnipeg, Churchill,
Mexico City.. Deduct 1 hour

Albuquerque, Denver, Phoenix, El Paso, Edmonton,
Helena .... Deduct 2 hours

Los Angeles, San Francisco, Reno, Portland,
Seattle, Vancouver .... Deduct 3 hours

Honolulu, Anchorage, Fairbanks, Kodiak .... Deduct 5 hours

Nome, Samoa, Tonga, Midway.................... Deduct 6 hours

Halifax, Bermuda, San Juan, Caracas, La Paz,
Barbados..Add 1 hour

St. John's, Brasilia, Rio de Janeiro, Sao Paulo,
Buenos Aires, Montevideo..........................Add 2 hours

Azores, Cape Verde Islands..........................Add 3 hours

Canary Islands, Madeira, Reykjavik ....Add 4 hours

London, Paris, Amsterdam, Madrid, Lisbon,
Gibraltar, Belfast, Rabat ....Add 5 hours

Frankfurt, Rome, Oslo, Stockholm, Prague,
Belgrade...Add 6 hours

Bucharest, Beirut, Tel Aviv, Athens, Istanbul, Cairo,
Alexandria, Cape Town, Johannesburg ....Add 7 hours

Moscow, Leningrad, Baghdad, Dhahran,
Addis Ababa, Nairobi, Teheran, Zanzibar.........Add 8 hours

Bombay, Calcutta, Sri Lanka..................... Add 10 ½ hours

Hong Kong, Shanghai, Manila, Peking, Perth...... Add 13 hours

Tokyo, Okinawa, Darwin, Pusan.................... Add 14 hours

Sydney, Melbourne, Port Moresby, Guam.......... Add 15 hours

Auckland, Wellington, Suva, Wake................. Add 17 hours

1999 MOON SIGN DATES—
NEW YORK TIME

JANUARY		FEBRUARY		MARCH	
Day Moon Enters		**Day Moon Enters**		**Day Moon Enters**	
1. Cancer	3:16 am	1. Virgo	8:38 pm	1. Virgo	5:06 am
2. Cancer		2. Virgo		2. Virgo	
3. Leo	5:32 am	3. Virgo		3. Libra	1:35 pm
4. Leo		4. Libra	4:57 am	4. Libra	
5. Virgo	10:50 am	5. Libra		5. Libra	
6. Virgo		6. Scorp.	4:07 pm	6. Scorp.	0:23 am
7. Libra	7:54 pm	7. Scorp.		7. Scorp.	
8. Libra		8. Scorp.		8. Sagitt.	0:47 pm
9. Libra		9. Sagitt.	4:39 am	9. Sagitt.	
10. Scorp.	7:50 am	10. Sagitt.		10. Sagitt.	
11. Scorp.		11. Capric.	4:11 pm	11. Capric.	0:55 am
12. Sagitt.	8:24 pm	12. Capric.		12. Capric.	
13. Sagitt.		13. Capric.		13. Aquar.	10:33 am
14. Sagitt.		14. Aquar.	0:58 am	14. Aquar.	
15. Capric.	7:30 am	15. Aquar.		15. Pisces	4:31 pm
16. Capric.		16. Pisces	6:41 am	16. Pisces	
17. Aquar.	4:12 pm	17. Pisces		17. Aries	7:14 pm
18. Aquar.		18. Aries	10:07 am	18. Aries	
19. Pisces	10:41 pm	19. Aries		19. Taurus	8:10 pm
20. Pisces		20. Taurus	0:30 pm	20. Taurus	
21. Pisces		21. Taurus		21. Gemini	9:06 pm
22. Aries	3:26 am	22. Gemini	2:55 pm	22. Gemini	
23. Aries		23. Gemini		23. Cancer	11:34 pm
24. Taurus	6:53 am	24. Cancer	6:10 pm	24. Cancer	
25. Taurus		25. Cancer		25. Cancer	
26. Gemini	9:30 am	26. Leo	10:45 pm	26. Leo	4:23 am
27. Gemini		27. Leo		27. Leo	
28. Cancer	11:58 am	28. Leo		28. Virgo	11:35 am
29. Cancer				29. Virgo	
30. Leo	3:17 pm			30. Libra	8:50 pm
31. Leo				31. Libra	

Summer time to be considered where applicable.

1999 MOON SIGN DATES—
NEW YORK TIME

APRIL		MAY		JUNE	
Day Moon Enters		**Day Moon Enters**		**Day Moon Enters**	
1. Libra		1. Scorp.		1. Capric.	
2. Scorp.	7:50 am	2. Sagitt.	2:37 am	2. Capric.	
3. Scorp.		3. Sagitt.		3. Aquar.	8:38 am
4. Sagitt.	8:08 pm	4. Capric.	3:13 pm	4. Aquar.	
5. Sagitt.		5. Capric.		5. Pisces	6:02 pm
6. Sagitt.		6. Capric.		6. Pisces	
7. Capric.	8:40 am	7. Aquar.	2:41 am	7. Pisces	
8. Capric.		8. Aquar.		8. Aries	0:09 am
9. Aquar.	7:25 pm	9. Pisces	11:17 am	9. Aries	
10. Aquar.		10. Pisces		10. Taurus	2:44 am
11. Aquar.		11. Aries	3:54 pm	11. Taurus	
12. Pisces	2:36 am	12. Aries		12. Gemini	2:49 am
13. Pisces		13. Taurus	4:57 pm	13. Gemini	
14. Aries	5:47 am	14. Taurus		14. Cancer	2:15 am
15. Aries		15. Gemini	4:08 pm	15. Cancer	
16. Taurus	6:08 am	16. Gemini		16. Leo	3:08 am
17. Taurus		17. Cancer	3:40 pm	17. Leo	
18. Gemini	5:40 am	18. Cancer		18. Virgo	7:13 am
19. Gemini		19. Leo	5:38 pm	19. Virgo	
20. Cancer	6:28 am	20. Leo		20. Libra	3:11 pm
21. Cancer		21. Virgo	11:16 pm	21. Libra	
22. Leo	10:07 am	22. Virgo		22. Libra	
23. Leo		23. Virgo		23. Scorp.	2:19 am
24. Virgo	5:05 pm	24. Libra	8:30 am	24. Scorp.	
25. Virgo		25. Libra		25. Sagitt.	2:52 pm
26. Virgo		26. Scorp.	8:06 pm	26. Sagitt.	
27. Libra	2:47 am	27. Scorp.		27. Sagitt.	
28. Libra		28. Scorp.		28. Capric.	3:13 am
29. Scorp.	2:14 pm	29. Sagitt.	8:38 am	29. Capric.	
30. Scorp.		30. Sagitt.		30. Aquar.	2:20 pm
		31. Capric.	9:07 pm		

Summer time to be considered where applicable.

1999 MOON SIGN DATES—
NEW YORK TIME

JULY			AUGUST			SEPTEMBER		
Day Moon Enters			**Day Moon Enters**			**Day Moon Enters**		
1.	Aquar.		1.	Aries	11:48 am	1.	Taurus	
2.	Pisces	11:35 pm	2.	Aries		2.	Gemini	0:26 am
3.	Pisces		3.	Taurus	4:10 pm	3.	Gemini	
4.	Pisces		4.	Taurus		4.	Cancer	3:11 am
5.	Aries	6:22 am	5.	Gemini	6:58 pm	5.	Cancer	
6.	Aries		6.	Gemini		6.	Leo	6:30 am
7.	Taurus	10:23 am	7.	Cancer	8:54 pm	7.	Leo	
8.	Taurus		8.	Cancer		8.	Virgo	10:58 am
9.	Gemini	0:01 pm	9.	Leo	10:57 pm	9.	Virgo	
10.	Gemini		10.	Leo		10.	Libra	5:17 pm
11.	Cancer	0:28 pm	11.	Leo		11.	Libra	
12.	Cancer		12.	Virgo	2:23 am	12.	Libra	
13.	Leo	1:27 pm	13.	Virgo		13.	Scorp.	2:09 am
14.	Leo		14.	Libra	8:25 am	14.	Scorp.	
15.	Virgo	4:40 pm	15.	Libra		15.	Sagitt.	1:36 pm
16.	Virgo		16.	Scorp.	5:41 pm	16.	Sagitt.	
17.	Libra	11:20 pm	17.	Scorp.		17.	Sagitt.	
18.	Libra		18.	Scorp.		18.	Capric.	2:14 am
19.	Libra		19.	Sagitt.	5:33 am	19.	Capric.	
20.	Scorp.	9:31 am	20.	Sagitt.		20.	Aquar.	1:39 pm
21.	Scorp.		21.	Capric.	6:00 pm	21.	Aquar.	
22.	Sagitt.	9:49 pm	22.	Capric.		22.	Pisces	9:52 pm
23.	Sagitt.		23.	Capric.		23.	Pisces	
24.	Sagitt.		24.	Aquar.	4:50 am	24.	Pisces	
25.	Capric.	10:09 am	25.	Aquar.		25.	Aries	2:35 am
26.	Capric.		26.	Pisces	0:51 pm	26.	Aries	
27.	Aquar.	8:55 pm	27.	Pisces		27.	Taurus	4:52 am
28.	Aquar.		28.	Aries	6:10 pm	28.	Taurus	
29.	Aquar.		29.	Aries		29.	Gemini	6:22 am
30.	Pisces	5:28 am	30.	Taurus	9:42 pm	30.	Gemini	
31.	Pisces		31.	Taurus				

Summer time to be considered where applicable.

1999 MOON SIGN DATES—
NEW YORK TIME

OCTOBER		NOVEMBER		DECEMBER	
Day Moon Enters		**Day Moon Enters**		**Day Moon Enters**	
1. Cancer	8:32 am	1. Virgo	11:08 pm	1. Libra	0:30 pm
2. Cancer		2. Virgo		2. Libra	
3. Leo	0:14 pm	3. Virgo		3. Scorp.	10:36 pm
4. Leo		4. Libra	6:58 am	4. Scorp.	
5. Virgo	5:41 pm	5. Libra		5. Scorp.	
6. Virgo		6. Scorp.	4:47 pm	6. Sagitt.	10:28 am
7. Virgo		7. Scorp.		7. Sagitt.	
8. Libra	0:53 am	8. Scorp.		8. Capric.	11:15 pm
9. Libra		9. Sagitt.	4:16 am	9. Capric.	
10. Scorp.	10:02 am	10. Sagitt.		10. Capric.	
11. Scorp.		11. Capric.	5:01 pm	11. Aquar.	12:00 pm
12. Sagitt.	9:20 pm	12. Capric.		12. Aquar.	
13. Sagitt.		13. Capric.		13. Pisces	11:19 pm
14. Sagitt.		14. Aquar.	5:47 am	14. Pisces	
15. Capric.	10:05 am	15. Aquar.		15. Pisces	
16. Capric.		16. Pisces	4:22 pm	16. Aries	7:31 am
17. Aquar.	10:18 pm	17. Pisces		17. Aries	
				18. Taurus	11:46 am

1999 PHASES OF THE MOON—
NEW YORK TIME

New Moon	First Quarter	Full Moon	Last Quarter
Dec. 18 ('98)	Dec. 26 ('98)	Jan. 1	Jan. 9
Jan. 17	Jan. 24	Jan. 31	Feb. 8
Feb. 16	Feb. 22	March 2	March 10
March 17	March 24	March 31	April 8
April 15	April 22	April 30	May 8
May 15	May 22	May 30	June 6
June 13	June 20	June 28	July 6
July 12	July 20	July 28	Aug. 4
Aug. 11	Aug. 18	Aug. 26	Sept. 2
Sept. 9	Sept. 17	Sept. 25	Oct. 1
Oct. 9	Oct. 17	Oct. 24	Oct. 31
Nov. 7	Nov. 16	Nov. 23	Nov. 29
Dec. 7	Dec. 15	Dec. 22	Dec. 29

Each phase of the Moon lasts approximately seven to eight days, during which the Moon's shape gradually changes as it comes out of one phase and goes into the next.

There will be a partial solar eclipse during the New Moon phase on February 16 and August 11.

There will be a lunar eclipse during the Full Moon phase on July 28.

1999 PLANTING GUIDE

	Aboveground Crops	Root Crops
January	1-20-21-25-29	2-8-9-10-11-12-26
February	17-21-25-26	4-5-6-7-8-12-13
March	20-21-24-25-31	4-5-6-7-11-12-16
April	17-21-27-28-29	1-2-3-4-8-9-12-13
May	18-19-25-26-27-28	1-5-6-10-14
June	14-15-21-22-23-24	1-2-6-7-10-11-29
July	18-19-20-21-22-26-27	3-4-8-12-31
August	15-16-17-18-22-23	4-5-8-9-27-28-31
September	11-12-13-14-18-19-23-24	1-4-5-27-28
October	10-11-12-16-17-21	2-8-25-29-30
November	8-12-13-17-18-21-22	5-6-7-25-26
December	9-10-14-15-19	2-3-4-5-23-29-30-31

	Pruning	Weeds and Pests
January	2-11-12	4-5-6-7-13-14
February	7-8	1-2-3-9-10-14-15
March	6-7-16	2-9-10-14
April	3-4-12-13	5-6-10-11-15
May	1-10	2-3-7-8-12-30-31
June	6-7	4-5-8-9-12
July	3-4-12-31	1-2-6-10-29
August	8-9-27-28	2-6-7-10-29-30
September	4-5	2-3-7-8-9-26-30
October	2-29-30	4-5-6-7-27-31
November	7-25-26	1-2-3-23-24-27-28-29-30
December	4-5-23-31	7-25-26-27-28

MOON'S INFLUENCE OVER PLANTS

Centuries ago it was established that seeds planted when the Moon is in signs and phases called Fruitful will produce more growth than seeds planted when the Moon is in a Barren sign.

Fruitful Signs: Taurus, Cancer, Libra, Scorpio, Capricorn, Pisces
Barren Signs: Aries, Gemini, Leo, Virgo, Sagittarius, Aquarius
Dry Signs: Aries, Gemini, Sagittarius, Aquarius

Activity	Moon In
Mow lawn, trim plants	**Fruitful sign:** 1st & 2nd quarter
Plant flowers	**Fruitful sign:** 2nd quarter; best in Cancer and Libra
Prune	**Fruitful sign:** 3rd & 4th quarter
Destroy pests; spray	**Barren sign:** 4th quarter
Harvest potatoes, root crops	**Dry sign:** 3rd & 4th quarter; Taurus, Leo, and Aquarius

MOON'S INFLUENCE OVER YOUR HEALTH

ARIES	Head, brain, face, upper jaw
TAURUS	Throat, neck, lower jaw
GEMINI	Hands, arms, lungs, shoulders, nervous system
CANCER	Esophagus, stomach, breasts, womb, liver
LEO	Heart, spine
VIRGO	Intestines, liver
LIBRA	Kidneys, lower back
SCORPIO	Sex and eliminative organs
SAGITTARIUS	Hips, thighs, liver
CAPRICORN	Skin, bones, teeth, knees
AQUARIUS	Circulatory system, lower legs
PISCES	Feet, tone of being

Try to avoid work being done on that part of the body when the Moon is in the sign governing that part.

MOON'S INFLUENCE OVER DAILY AFFAIRS

The Moon makes a complete transit of the Zodiac every 27 days 7 hours and 43 minutes. In making this transit the Moon forms different aspects with the planets and consequently has favorable or unfavorable bearings on affairs and events for persons according to the sign of the Zodiac under which they were born.

When the Moon is in conjunction with the Sun it is called a New Moon; when the Moon and Sun are in opposition it is called a Full Moon. From New Moon to Full Moon, first and second quarter—which takes about two weeks—the Moon is increasing or waxing. From Full Moon to New Moon, third and fourth quarter, the Moon is decreasing or waning.

Activity	Moon In
Business: buying and selling new, requiring public support	Sagittarius, Aries, Gemini, Virgo 1st and 2nd quarter
meant to be kept quiet	3rd and 4th quarter
Investigation	3rd and 4th quarter
Signing documents	1st & 2nd quarter, Cancer, Scorpio, Pisces
Advertising	2nd quarter, Sagittarius
Journeys and trips	1st & 2nd quarter, Gemini, Virgo
Renting offices, etc.	Taurus, Leo, Scorpio, Aquarius
Painting of house/apartment	3rd & 4th quarter, Taurus, Scorpio, Aquarius
Decorating	Gemini, Libra, Aquarius
Buying clothes and accessories	Taurus, Virgo
Beauty salon or barber shop visit	1st & 2nd quarter, Taurus, Leo, Libra, Scorpio, Aquarius
Weddings	1st & 2nd quarter

TAURUS

TAURUS

Character Analysis

Of all the signs of the Zodiac, Taurus is perhaps the most diligent and determined. Taurus are hard workers and stick with something once it's begun. They are thorough people and are careful to avoid making mistakes. Patient, the Bull knows how to bide his time. If something doesn't work out as scheduled, he or she will wait until the appropriate moment comes along, then forge ahead.

The person born under this sign is far from lazy. He will work hard to achieve whatever it is he desires. He is so determined that others often think of him as being unreasonably stubborn. He'll stick to a point he believes is right—nothing can force him to give up his chosen path once his mind is made up.

Taurus takes his time in whatever he does. He wants to make sure everything is done right. At times this may exasperate people who are quick about things. Still and all, a job done by a Taurus is generally a job well done. Careful, steady, and reliable, Taurus is just the opposite of high-strung. This person can take a lot upon himself. Sometimes his burdens or worries are of such proportions that others would find them impossible to carry, but somehow Taurus manages in his silent way.

Taurus may be even-tempered, but he puts up with nonsense from no one. Others had better not take advantage of his balanced disposition. If they do, they are apt to rue the day.

The Taurus man or woman plans well before taking any one line of action. He believes in being well-prepared before embarking on any one project. Others may see him as a sort of slowpoke, but he is not being slow—just sure. He is not the sort of person who would act on a whim or fancy. He wants to be certain of the ground he is standing on.

Material things make him feel comfortable and successful. Some have a definite love of luxury and the like. This may be the result of a slight feeling of inferiority. Material goods make him feel that he is doing well and that he is just as good as the next person.

Taurus is someone who can be trusted at all times. Once he has declared himself a friend, he remains so. He is loyal and considerate of others. In his circle of friends he is quite apt to be one of the successful people. Taurus admires success; he looks up to people who have made something of themselves.

On the whole, Taurus is a down-to-earth person. He is not pretentious or lofty, but direct and earnest. Things that are a bit abstract or far-fetched may not win his immediate approval. He believes in being practical. When he makes a decision, it is generally one with a lot of thought behind it.

Health

People born under this second sign of the Zodiac generally are quite fit physically. They are often gifted with healthy constitutions and can endure more than others in some circumstances. Taurus is often vigorous and strong. At times his strength may astonish others. He can put up with more pressure than most. Pain or the threat of it generally does not frighten him.

He can be proud of his good health. Even when ill, he would rather not give in to it or admit it. But when a disability becomes such that it cannot be ignored, Taurus becomes sad and depressed. For him it is a kind of insult to be ill. When he is laid up with an illness, it generally takes awhile to recover. Although his constitution is strong, when struck down by a disease, his powers for recuperation are not very great. Getting better is a slow and gradual process for the average Taurus.

Males born under this sign are often broad and stocky. They may be wide-shouldered and powerfully built. They are seldom short on muscle. As they age, they sometimes become fat.

Females born under the sign of Taurus are often attractive and charming. They are fond of pretty things and like to see to it that they look fashionable. Although they are often beautiful when young, as they grow older some of them tend to put on a little extra weight. They often have unusually attractive eyes, and their complexions are clear and healthy.

The weakest part of the Taurus body is the throat. If ever he is sick, this part of his body is often affected. Sore throats and the like are often common Taurus complaints.

Occupation

The Taurus man or woman can do a good job—no matter what the work is. They have the ability to be thorough and accurate. They never shirk their duties. They may be looked upon as being slow, especially when they begin a task; but after they are thoroughly familiar with what they are doing, they work at an even and reasonable pace. They are methodical, which counts a good deal. They are good at detail. They seldom overlook anything.

Not all Taurus are slow. Some are quick and brilliant. In many cases, it depends on the circumstances they have to deal with. In any event, they never forget anything once they have learned it. They can be quite shrewd in business matters and are often highly valued in their place of business.

The average Taurus has plenty of get-up-and-go. He is never lazy or neglectful in his work. He enjoys working and does what he can to bring about favorable results.

In business, he will generally shy away from anything that involves what seems to be an unnecessary risk. He likes the path he trods to be a sure one, one that has been well laid out. When he has to make his own way, he sees to it that he is certain of every step of the route. This may often exasperate colleagues. His plodding ways generally pay off in the end, however. In spite of this, and because of his distrust of change, he often misses out on a good business deal. His work may become humdrum and dull due to his dislike of change in routine or schedule.

The Taurus man or woman does well in a position of authority. He is a good manager and knows how to keep everything in order. Discipline is no problem. He knows what scheme to follow and sticks to it. Because his own powers of self-control are so well developed, he has no problem in managing others. Taurus is not frightened by opposition. He knows how to forge ahead with his plans and will not stop until everything comes out according to plan.

Taurus is a stickler for detail. Every little point has to be thoroughly covered before he is satisfied. Because he is a patient person, he knows how to bide his time; he is the kind of person who will wait for the right opportunity to come along, if need be. This sort of person excels in a position where he can take his time in doing things. Any job that requires thoroughness and painstaking effort is one in which a Taurus is likely to do well. They make good managers and can handle certain technical and industrial jobs. Some Taurus are gifted with the ability to draw or design and do well in the world of architecture. Many of them are quite artistic, and it depends on the proper circumstances to bring this out. In most cases, however, Taurus is content with doing work that is sure and calculated. His creative ability may not have the proper chance to surface, and it is only through cultivation that he is able to make a broad use of it.

Although many people born under this sign work in the city, they prefer the peace and quiet of remote places to the hustle and bustle of the busy metropolis. Many of them do well in the area of agriculture. They have a way with growing things. A Taurus man or woman could easily become a successful dairy or poultry farmer. They find it easy to relate to things rural or rustic. Many of them are gifted with green thumbs.

When working with others, Taurus can be relied upon. His partner if possible should be similar in nature. The Bull may become annoyed if he works with someone who is always changing his mind or schedule. He doesn't care much for surprises or sudden changes. New ideas may not appeal to him at first; he has to have time to get used to them. Generally, he likes to think of something new as being a creation of his own. And by taking his time in approaching it, he comes to see it in that light. Taurus should be gently coaxed when working with others. He will give his consent to new ideas if his colleagues are subtle enough in their presentation.

Although the Taurus man or woman may not hold an important position in the place where he works, this does not disturb him. He doesn't mind working under others—especially if they are good and able leaders or managers. Taurus is a loyal worker. He can always be depended on to complete his tasks.

The Taurus man or woman understands the value of money and appreciates the things it can do. He may not be a millionaire, but he does know how to earn and save well enough so that he can acquire those material items he feels are important. Some people born under this sign can easily acquire a greedy streak if they don't watch out. So obsessed with material gain are some Taurus that they do not take time to relax and enjoy other things that life has to offer. Money-oriented, the ambitious Taurus sometimes turns into someone who is all work and no play. It is not surprising, then, that a great many bankers and financiers are born under this sign of the Zodiac.

The Taurus person is generally straightforward and well-meaning. If someone is in need, he will not hesitate to assist them financially. Taurus as children are sometimes stingy, but as they grow up and have enough money, they become reasonably free in their use of it. Still and all, the average Taurus will never invest all the money he has in anything. He always likes to keep a good portion of it aside for that inevitable rainy day. Although he may not be interested in taking many risks, the person born under this sign is often lucky. When he does take a chance and gambles, he quite often turns out the winner.

When a Taurus puts his best foot forward, he can achieve almost anything—even though it may take a little longer than it does with most. He has many hidden strengths and positive characteristics that help him to get ahead.

Home and Family

The Taurus person is a lover of home life. He likes to be surrounded by familiar and comfortable things. He is the kind of person who calls his home his castle. Generally, the home of a Taurus radiates comfort and hospitality. The Taurus woman knows how to decorate and arrange a house so that visitors feel immediately at home upon entering. The Taurus man is more often than not a good breadwinner. He sees to it that the members of his immediate family have everything they need.

The Taurus person usually likes the peace, quiet, and beauty of the country. If possible, he will see to it that he lives there—for part of the year if not for the whole year. The Taurus housewife has her work down to an efficient routine. She is interested in keeping everything neat and orderly. She is a very good hostess and knows how to make people feel at ease.

Being well-liked is important. Taurus likes to be surrounded by good friends. He admires important people and likes to include them in his social activities if possible. When entertaining, the Taurus woman usually outdoes herself in preparing all sorts of delicious items. She is skilled in the culinary arts. If ever she is poorly entertained or fed by others, she feels upset about it.

The Taurus man or woman usually has a tastefully furnished home. But what is more important to Taurus than beauty is comfort. His house must be a place where he can feel at home.

Taurus can be strict with their children and stand for no nonsense. They are interested in seeing that their children are brought up correctly. It is important for them that the youngsters reflect the good home they come from. Compliments from others about the behavior of their children make Taurus parents happy and proud. As the children grow older, however, and reach the teenage stage, some difficulties may occur in the beginning. The Taurus mother or father may resent the sudden change in the relationship as the child tries to assert his own individuality.

Social Relationships

Taurus generally does what he can to be popular among his friends. He is loyal and caring with people who are close to him. Because he is sincere and forthright, people generally seek him out as a friend. He makes a good talker as well as a listener. People in difficulties often turn to him for advice.

The Taurus person is genuinely interested in success, and there is nothing he admires more than someone who has achieved his goal. In making friends, it seems as though a person born under this sign gravitates toward people who have made a success of themselves or people on their way up. Influential people are admired by Taurus. Being surrounded by people who have met with some success in life makes the person born under this sign feel somewhat successful too.

The Taurus person is one who generally likes to keep his family matters to himself. He resents the meddling of friends—even close friends.

He is a person who sticks to his principles, and as a result he may make an enemy or two as he goes along.

Love and Marriage

In love matters, Taurus may go through a series of flings—many of them lighthearted—before settling down with the "right" person. By nature, Taurus is serious. In love matters, his feelings run deep; but he will take steps to guard himself against disappointment if he feels the affair won't be lasting. Taurus can be romantic. As with everything, once he has made up his mind about someone, nothing will stand in his way; he'll win the object of his affection if it's the last thing he does. Other suitors don't frighten him in the least.

Younger Taurus have nothing against light romances, but as they grow older they look for stability and deep affection in a love affair. Faithful in love as they are in most things, they look for partners who are apt to feel the way they do.

The Taurus in love does not generally attempt a coy approach. More likely than not he'll be direct in expressing his feelings. Once he has won the person he loves, the average Taurus is often possessive as well as protective.

Persons born under this sign generally do well in a marriage relationship. Matters at home go well as long as he is treated fairly by his mate. If conditions at home are not to his liking, he can be biting and mean.

There is no halfway in marriage as far as Taurus is concerned; it's a matter of two people giving themselves completely. As husbands and wives, they make ideal mates in many respects. They are usually quite considerate and generous. They like looking after the other members of their families. They are very family-oriented types, and nothing pleases them more than to be able to spend time at home with their loved ones.

Romance and the Taurus Woman

The Taurus woman has a charm and beauty that are hard to define. There is something elusive about her that attracts the opposite sex—something mysterious. Needless to say, she is much sought after. Men find her a delight. She is generally easygoing, relaxed, and good-natured. Men find her a joy to be with because they can be themselves. They don't have to try to impress her by being something they are not.

Although she may have a series of romances before actually settling down, every time she falls in love it is the real thing. She is not superficial or flighty in romance. When she gives her heart, she hopes it will be forever. When she does finally find the right person, she has no trouble in being true to him for the rest of her life.

In spite of her romantic nature, the female Taurus is quite practical, too, when it comes to love. She wants a man who can take care of her. Someone on whom she can depend. Someone who can provide her with the comforts she feels she needs. Some Taurus look for men who are well-to-do or who have already achieved success. To them, the practical side of marriage is just as important as the romantic. But most Taurus women are attracted to sincere, hardworking men who are good company and faithful in the relationship. A Taurus wife sticks by the man of her choice. She will do everything in her power to give her man the spiritual support he needs in order to advance in his career.

The Taurus woman likes pretty, gentle things. They enjoy making their home a comfortable and attractive one. They are quite artistic, and their taste in furnishings is often flawless. They know how to make a house comfortable and inviting. The Taurus woman is interested in material things. They make her feel secure and loved. Her house is apt to be filled with various objects that have an important meaning for her alone.

She is even-tempered and does what she can to get along with her mate or loved one, but once she is rubbed the wrong way she can become very angry and outspoken. The considerate mate or lover, however, has no problem with his Taurus woman. When treated well, she maintains her pleasant disposition, and is a delight to be with. She is a woman who is kind and warm when she is with the man of her choice. A man who is strong, protective, and financially sound is the sort of man who can help bring out the best in a woman born under this sign. She enjoys being flattered and being paid small attentions. It is not that she is excessively demanding, but just that she likes to have evidence from time to time that she is dearly loved.

The Taurus woman is very dependable and faithful. The man who wins her is indeed lucky. She wants a complete, comfortable, and correct home life. She seldom complains. She is quite flexible and can enjoy the good times or suffer the bad times with equal grace. Although she does enjoy luxury, if difficult times come about, she will not bicker but stick beside the man she loves. For her marriage is serious business. It is very unlikely that a Taurus woman would seek a divorce unless it was absolutely necessary.

A good homemaker, the Taurus woman knows how to keep the love of her man alive once she has won him. To her, love is a way of life. She will live entirely for the purpose of making her man happy. Men seldom have reason to be dissatisfied with a Taurus mate. Their affections never stray. Taurus women are determined people. When they put their minds to making a marriage or love relationship work, it seldom fails. They'll work as hard at romance as they will at anything else they want.

As a mother, the Taurus woman does what she can to see that her children are brought up correctly. She likes her children to be polite and obedient. She can be strict when she puts her mind to it. It is important to her that the youngsters learn the right things in life—even if they don't seem to want to. She is not at all permissive as a parent. Her children must respect her and do as she says. She won't stand for insolence or disobedience. She is well-meaning in her treatment of her children. Although the children may resent her strictness as they are growing up, in later life they see that she was justified in the way she handled them.

Romance and the Taurus Man

The Taurus man is as determined in love as he is in everything else. Once he sets his mind on winning a woman, he keeps at it until he has achieved his goal.

Women find him attractive. The Taurus man has a protective way about him. He knows how to make a woman feel wanted and taken care of. Taurus men are often fatherly, so women looking for protection and unwavering affection are attracted to them. Because of their he-man physiques, and sure ways, they have no trouble in romance. The opposite sex find their particular brand of charm difficult to resist.

He can be a very romantic person. The number of romances he is likely to have before actually settling down may be many. But he is faithful. He is true to the person he loves for as long as that relationship lasts. When he finds someone suited to him, he devotes the rest of his life to making her happy.

Married life agrees with the man born under the Taurus sign. They make good, dependable husbands and excellent, concerned fathers. The Taurus man is, of course, attracted to a woman who is good-looking and charming. But the qualities that most appeal to him often lie deeper than the skin. He is not interested in glamour alone. The girl of his choice must be a good homemaker, resourceful, and loving. Someone kind and considerate is apt to touch his heartstrings more than a pretty, one-dimensional face. He is looking for a woman to settle down with for a lifetime.

Marriage is important to him because it means stability and security, two things that are most important to Taurus. He is serious about marriage. He will do his best to provide for his family in a way he feels is correct and responsible. He is not one to shirk his family responsibilities. He likes to know that the woman he has married will stand beside him in all that he does.

The Taurus man believes that only he should be boss of the family. He may listen and even accept the advice of his spouse, but he is the one who runs things. He likes to feel that he is the king in his castle.

He likes his home to be comfortable and inviting. He has a liking for soft things; he likes to be babied a little by the woman he loves. He may be a strict parent, but he feels it is for the children's own good.

Woman—Man

TAURUS WOMAN
ARIES MAN

If you are attracted to a man born under the sign of the Ram, it is not certain as to how far the relationship would go. An Aries who has made his mark in the world and is somewhat steadfast in his outlook and attitudes could be quite a catch for you. On the other hand, Aries are swift-footed and quick-minded; their industrious manner may often fail to impress you, particularly when you become aware that their get-up-and-go sometimes leads nowhere. When it comes to a fine romance, you want a nice broad shoulder to lean on; you might find a relationship with someone who doesn't like to stay put for too long a time somewhat upsetting. Then, too, the Aries man is likely to misunderstand your interest in a slow-but-sure approach to most matters. He may see you as a stick-in-the-mud. What's more, he'll tell you so if you make him aware of it too often. Aries speak their minds, sometimes at the drop of a hat.

You may find a man born under this sign too demanding. He may give you the feeling that he wants you to be at all places at the same time. Even though he realizes that this is impossible, he may grumble at you for not at least having tried. You have a barrelful of patience at your disposal, and he may try every bit of it. Whereas you're a thorough person, he may overshoot something essential to a project or a relationship due to his eagerness to quickly achieve his end.

Being married to a Ram does not mean that you'll necessarily have a secure and safe life as far as finances are concerned. Aries are not rash with cash, but they lack the sound head that you have for putting something away for that inevitable rainy day. He'll do his best to see that you're well provided for though his efforts may leave something to be desired.

Although there will be a family squabble occasionally, you, with your steady nature and love of permanence, will learn to take it in your stride and make your marriage a success.

He'll love the children. Aries make wonderful fathers. Kids take to them like ducks to water, probably because of their quick minds and zestful behavior. Sometimes Aries fathers spoil their children, and here is where you'll have to step in. But don't be too strict with youngsters, or you'll drive most of their affection over to their father. When they reach the adolescent stage and become increasingly difficult to manage, it would perhaps be better for you to take a backseat and rely on your Aries husband's sympathy and understanding of this stage of life.

TAURUS WOMAN
TAURUS MAN

Although a man born under the same sign as you may seem like a "natural," better look twice before you leap. It can also be that he resembles you too closely to be compatible. You can be pretty set in your ways. When you encounter someone with just as much willpower or stubbornness, a royal fireworks display can be the result. When two Taurus lock horns it can be a very exhausting and totally frustrating get-together. But if the man of your dreams is one born under your sign and you're sure that no other will do, then proceed with extreme caution. Even though you know yourself well—or think you do—it does not necessarily mean that you will have an easy time understanding him. Since you both are practical, you should try a rational approach to your relationship. Put all the cards on the table, discuss the matter, and decide whether to cooperate, compromise, or call it quits.

If you both have your sights set on the same goals, a life together could be just what the doctor ordered. You both are affectionate and have a deep need for affection. Being loved, understood, and appreciated is vital for your mutual well-being.

Essentially, you are both looking for peace, security, and harmony in your lives. Working toward these goals together may be a good way of eventually attaining them, especially if you are honest and tolerant of each other.

If you should marry a Taurus man, you can be sure that the wolf will stay far away from the door. They are notoriously good providers and do everything to make their families comfortable and happy. He'll appreciate the way you make a home warm and inviting. Good food, all the comforts, and a few luxuries are essential ingredients. Although he may be a big lug of a guy, he'll be fond of gentle treatment and soft things. If you puff up his pillow and tuck him in at night, he won't complain. He'll eat it up and ask for more.

In friendships, you'll both be on even footing. You both tend to seek out friends who are successful or prominent. You admire people who work hard and achieve what they set out for. It helps to reassure your way of looking at things.

Taurus parents love their children very much and never sacrifice a show of affection even when scolding them. Since you both are excellent disciplinarians bringing up children, you should try to balance your tendency to be strict with a healthy amount of pampering and spoiling.

TAURUS WOMAN
GEMINI MAN

Gemini men, in spite of their charm and dash, may make even placid Taurus nervous. Some Twins do seem to lack the common sense you set so much store in. Their tendencies to start a half-dozen projects, then toss them up in the air out of boredom, may only exasperate you. You may be inclined to interpret their jumping around from here to there as childish if not downright psychotic. Gemini will never stay put. If you should take it into your head to try and make him sit still, he will resent it strongly.

On the other hand, he's likely to think you're a slowpoke and far too interested in security and material things. He's attracted to things that sparkle and bubble—not necessarily for a long time. You are likely to seem quite dull and uninteresting—with your practical head and feet firm on the ground—to the Gemini gadabout. If you're looking for a life of security and steadiness, then Mr. Right he ain't.

Chances are you'll be taken in by his charming ways and facile wit. Few women can resist Gemini charm. But after you've seen through his live-for-today, gossamer facade, you'll be most happy to turn your attention to someone more stable, even if he is not as interesting. You want a man who's there when you need him, someone on whom you can fully rely. Keeping track of Gemini's movements will make your head spin. Still, being a Taurus, you're a patient woman who can put up with almost anything if you think it will be worth the effort.

A successful and serious-minded Gemini could make you a very happy woman, perhaps, if you gave him half the chance. Although Gemini may impress you as being scatterbrained, he generally has a good head on his shoulders and can make efficient use of it when he wants. Some of them, who have learned the art of being steadfast, have risen to great professional heights.

Once you convince yourself that not all people born under the sign of the Twins are witless grasshoppers, you won't mind dating a few to support your newborn conviction. If you do walk down the aisle with one, accept the fact that married life with him will mean taking the bitter with the sweet.

Life with a Gemini man can be more fun than a barrel of clowns. You'll never experience a dull moment. You'd better see to it, though, that you get his paycheck every payday. If you leave the budgeting and bookkeeping to him you'll wind up behind the eight ball.

The Gemini father is apt to let children walk all over him, so you'd better take charge of them most of the time.

TAURUS WOMAN
CANCER MAN

The man born under the sign of Cancer may very well be the man after your own heart. Generally, Cancers are steady people. They share the Taurus interest in security and practicality. Despite their sometimes seemingly grouchy exterior, men born under the sign of the Crab are sensitive and kind. They are almost always hard workers and are very interested in making successes of themselves in business as well as socially. Their conservative outlook on many things often agrees with yours. He'll be a man on whom you can depend come rain or come shine. He'll never shirk his responsibilities as a provider and will always see to it that his mate and family never want.

Your patience will come in handy if you decide it's a Moon Child you want for a mate. He doesn't rush headlong into romance. He wants to be sure about love as you do. After the first couple of months of dating, don't jump to the conclusion that he's about to make his "great play."

Don't let his coolness fool you, though. Underneath his starched reserve is a very warm heart. He's just not interested in showing off as far as affection is concerned. For him, affection should only be displayed for two sets of eyes—yours and his. If you really want to see him warm up to you, you'd better send your roommate off, then bolt the doors and windows—to insure him that you won't be disturbed or embarrassed. He will never step out of line—he's too much of a gentleman for that, but it is likely that in such a sealed off atmosphere, he'll pull out an engagement ring (that belonged to his grandmother) and slip it on your finger.

Speaking of relatives, you'll have to get used to the fact that Cancers are overly fond of their mothers. When he says his mother's the most wonderful woman in the world, you'd better agree with him—that is, if you want to become his wife. It's a very touchy area for him. Say one wrong word about his mother or let him suspect that your interest in her is not real, and you'd better look for husband material elsewhere.

He'll always be a faithful husband; Cancers seldom tomcat around after they've taken that vow. They take their marriage responsibilities seriously. They see to it that everything in their homes runs smoothly. Bills will always be paid promptly. He'll take out all kinds of insurance policies on his family and property. He'll see to it that when retirement time rolls around, you'll both be very well off.

The Cancer father is patient, sensitive, and understanding, always protective of his children.

TAURUS WOMAN
LEO MAN

To know a man born under the sign of the Lion is not necessarily to love him—even though the temptation may be great. When he fixes most girls with his leonine double-whammy, it causes their hearts to throb and their minds to cloud over. But with you, the sensible Bull, it takes more than a regal strut and a roar to win you. There's no denying that Leo has a way with women, even practical Taurus women. Once he's swept you off your feet it may be hard to scramble upright again. Still, you're no pushover for romantic charm if you feel there may be no security behind it. He'll wine you and dine you in the fanciest places and shower you with diamonds if he can. Still, it would be wise to find out just how long the shower's going to last before consenting to be his wife.

Lions in love are hard to ignore, let alone brush off. Your "no" will have a way of nudging him on until he feels he has you completely under his spell. Once mesmerized by this romantic powerhouse, you will most likely find yourself doing things you never dreamed of. Leos can be like vain pussycats when involved in romance; they like to be cuddled and pampered and told how wonderful they are. This may not be your cup of tea, exactly. Still when you're romancing a Leo, you'll find yourself doing all kinds of things to make him purr. Although he may be sweet and gentle when trying to win you, he'll roar if he feels he's not getting the tender love and care he feels is his due. If you keep him well supplied with affection, you can be sure his eyes will never stray and his heart will never wander.

Leo men often turn out to be leaders. They're born to lord it over others in one way or another. If he is top banana in his firm, he'll most likely do everything he can to stay on top. And if he's not number one yet, then he's working on it, and will see to it that he's sitting on the throne before long.

You'll have more security than you can use if he's in a position to support you in the manner to which he feels you should be accustomed. He's apt to be too lavish, though. Although creditors may never darken your door, handle as much of the household bookkeeping as you can to put your mind at ease.

He's a natural-born friend-maker and entertainer. At a party, he will try to attract attention. Let him. If you allow him his occasional ego trips without quibbling, your married life will be one of warmth, wealth, and contentment.

When a little Lion or Lioness comes along, this Baby Leo will be brought up like one of the landed gentry if Papa Leo has anything to say about it.

TAURUS WOMAN
VIRGO MAN

Although the Virgo man may be a fussbudget at times, his seriousness and common sense may help you overlook his tendency to be too critical about minor things.

Virgo men are often quiet, respectable types who set great store in conservative behavior and levelheadedness. He'll admire you for your practicality and tenacity, perhaps even more than for your good looks. He's seldom bowled over by glamour. When he gets his courage up, he turns to a serious and reliable girl for romance. He'll be far from a Valentino while dating. In fact, you may wind up making all the passes. Once he does get his motor running, however, he can be a warm and wonderful fellow—to the right woman.

He's gradual about love. Chances are your romance with him will most likely start out looking like an ordinary friendship. Once he's sure you're no fly-by-night flirt and have no plans of taking him for a ride, he'll open up and rain sunshine over your heart.

Virgo men tend to marry late in life. He believes in holding out until he's met the right one. He may not have many names in his little black book; in fact, he may not even have a little black book. He's not interested in playing the field; leave that to men of the more flamboyant signs. The Virgo man is so particular that he may remain romantically inactive for a long period. His girl has to be perfect or it's no go. If you find yourself feeling weak-kneed for a Virgo, do your best to convince him that perfect is not so important when it comes to love. Help him to realize that he's missing out on a great deal by not considering the near-perfect or whatever you consider yourself to be. With your surefire perseverance, you'll make him listen to reason and he'll wind up reciprocating your romantic interests.

The Virgo man is no block of ice. He'll respond to what he feels to be the right feminine flame. Once your love life with a Virgo starts to bubble, don't give it a chance to fall flat. You may never have a second chance at romance with him.

If you should ever separate for a while, forget about patching up. He'd prefer to let the pieces lie scattered. Once married, though, he'll stay that way—even if it hurts. He's too conscientious to try to back out of a legal deal.

A Virgo man is as neat as a pin. He's thumbs down on sloppy housekeeping. An ashtray with even one used cigarette is apt to make him see red. Keep everything bright, neat, and shiny. Neatness goes for the children, too, at least by the time he gets home from work. But Daddy's little girl or boy will never lack for interesting playthings and learning tools.

TAURUS WOMAN
LIBRA MAN

Taurus may find Libra men too wrapped up in a dream world ever to come down to earth. Although he may be very careful about weighing both sides of an argument, that does not mean he will ever make a decision about anything. Decisions large and small are capable of giving Libra the willies. Don't ask him why. He probably doesn't know, himself. As a lover, you—who are interested in permanence and constancy in a relationship—may find him a puzzlement. One moment he comes on hard and strong with "I love you", the next moment he's left you like yesterday's mashed potatoes. It does no good to wonder "What did I do now?" You most likely haven't done anything. It's just one of Libra's ways.

On the other hand, you'll appreciate his admiration of harmony and beauty. If you're all decked out in your fanciest gown or have a tastefully arranged bouquet on the dining room table, you'll get a ready compliment—one that's really deserved. Libras don't pass out compliments to all and sundry. Generally, he's tactful enough to remain silent if he finds something disagreeable.

He may not be as ambitious as you would like your lover or husband to be. Where you do have drive and a great interest in getting ahead, Libra is often content to drift along. It is not that he is lazy or shiftless, it's just that he places greater value on aesthetic things than he does on the material. If he's in love with you, however, he'll do anything in his power to make you happy.

You may have to give him a good nudge now and again to get him to see the light. But he'll be happy wrapped up in his artistic dreams when you're not around to remind him that the rent is almost due.

If you love your Libra don't be too harsh or impatient with him. Try to understand him. Don't let him see the stubborn side of your nature too often, or you'll scare him away. Libras are peace-loving people and hate any kind of confrontation that may lead to an argument. Some of them will do almost anything to keep the peace—even tell little white lies, if necessary.

Although you possess gobs of patience, you may find yourself losing a little of it when trying to come to grips with your Libra. He may think you're too materialistic or mercenary, but he'll have the good grace not to tell you, for fear you'll perhaps chew his head off.

If you are deeply involved with a Libra, you'd better see to it that you help him manage his money. It's for his own good. Money will never interest him as much as it should, and he does have a tendency to be too generous when he shouldn't be.

Although Libra is a gentle and understanding father, he'll see to it that he never spoils his children.

TAURUS WOMAN
SCORPIO MAN

In the astrological scheme of things Scorpio is your zodiacal mate, but also your zodiacal opposite. If your heart is set on a Scorpio, you must figure him out to stay on his good side.

Many people have a hard time understanding a Scorpio man. Few, however, are able to resist his fiery charm. When angered, he can act like a nestful of wasps, and his sting is capable of leaving an almost permanent mark. Scorpios are straight to the point. They can be as sharp as a razor blade and just as cutting.

The Scorpio man is capable of being very blunt, and he can act like a brute or a cad. His touchiness may get on your nerves after a while. If it does, you'd better tiptoe away from the scene rather than chance an explosive confrontation.

It's quite likely that he will find your slow, deliberate manner a little irritating. He may misinterpret your patience for indifference. On the other hand, you're the kind of woman who can adapt to almost any sort of situation or circumstance if you put your mind and heart to it. Scorpio men are perceptive and intelligent. In some respects, they know how to use their brains more effectively and quicker than most. They believe in winning in everything; in business, they usually achieve the position they desire through drive and intellect.

Your interest in your home is not likely to be shared by him. No matter how comfortable you've managed to make the house, it will have very little influence on him as far as making him aware of his family responsibilities. He doesn't like to be tied down, generally. He would rather be out on the battlefield of life, belting away at what he feels is a just and worthy cause, than using leisure time at home.

He is passionate in his business affairs and political interests. He is just as passionate—if not more so—in romance. Most women are easily attracted to him—and the Taurus woman is no exception, that is, at least before she knows what she might be getting into. Those who allow their hearts to be stolen by a Scorpio man soon find that they're dealing with a cauldron of seething excitement.

Scorpio likes fathering a large family. He gets along well with children and is proud of them, but often he fails to live up to his responsibilities as a parent. When he takes his fatherly duties seriously, he is adept with youngsters. Whenever you have trouble understanding the kids, Scorpio's ability to see beneath the surface of things will be invaluable.

TAURUS WOMAN
SAGITTARIUS MAN

The Taurus woman who has her cap set for a Sagittarius man may have to apply large amounts of strategy before being able to make him pop that question. When visions of the altar enter the romance, Sagittarius are apt to get cold feet. Although you may become attracted to the Archer, because of his positive, winning manner, you may find the relationship loses some of its luster when it assumes a serious hue. Sagittarius are full of bounce—perhaps too much bounce to suit you. They are often hard to pin down and dislike staying put. If ever there's a chance to be on the move, he'll latch on to it post haste. They're quick people, both in mind and spirit. And sometimes because of their zip, they make mistakes. If you have good advice to offer, he'll tell you to keep it.

Sagittarius like to rely on their own wit whenever possible. His up-and-at-'em manner about most things is likely to drive you up the wall occasionally. Your cautious, deliberate manner is likely to make him impatient. And he can be resentful if you don't accompany him on his travel or sports ventures. He can't abide a slowpoke. At times, you'll find him too breezy and kiddish. However, don't mistake his youthful demeanor for premature senility.

Sagittarius are equipped with first-class brain power and know well how to put it to use. They're often full of good ideas and drive. Generally they're very broad-minded people and are very much concerned with fair play and equality.

In romance, he's quite capable of loving you wholeheartedly while treating you like a good pal. His hail-fellow well-met manner in the arena of love is likely to scare a dainty damsel off. However, a woman who knows that his heart is in the right place won't mind his bluff, rambunctious style.

He's not much of a homebody. He's got ants in his pants and enjoys being on the move. Humdrum routine, especially at home, bores him to distraction. At the drop of a hat he may ask you to whip off your apron and dine out for a change instead. He's fond of coming up with instant surprises. He'll love to keep you guessing. His friendly, candid nature gains him many friends.

When it comes to children, you may find that you've been left holding the bag. Sagittarius feel helpless around little shavers. When children become older, he will develop a genuine interest in them.

TAURUS WOMAN
CAPRICORN MAN

A Taurus woman is often capable of bringing out the best in a Capricorn man. While other women are puzzled by his silent and slow ways, Taurus, with her patience and understanding, can lend him the confidence he perhaps needs in order to come out from behind the rock.

Quite often, the Capricorn man is not the romantic kind of lover that attracts most women. Still, behind his reserve and calm, he's a pretty warm guy. He is capable of giving his heart completely once he has found the right girl. The Taurus woman who is deliberate by nature and who believes in taking time to be sure will find her kind of man in a Capricorn. He is slow and deliberate about almost everything—even romance. He doesn't believe in flirting and would never let his heart be led on a merry chase. If you win his trust, he'll give you his heart on a platter. Quite often, it is the woman who has to take the lead when romance is in the air. As long as he knows you're making the advances in earnest he won't mind. In fact, he'll probably be grateful.

Don't think that he's all cold fish; he isn't. Although some Goats have no difficulty in expressing passion, when it comes to displaying affection, they're at sea. But with an understanding and patient Bull, he should have no trouble in learning to express himself, especially if you let him know how important affection is to you, and for the good of your relationship.

The Capricorn man is very interested in getting ahead. He's ambitious and usually knows how to apply himself well to whatever task he undertakes. He's far from a spendthrift and tends to manage his money with extreme care. But a Taurus woman with a knack for putting away money for that rainy day should have no trouble in understanding this.

The Capricorn man thinks in terms of future security. He wants to make sure that he and his wife have something to fall back on when they reach retirement age.

He'll want you to handle the household efficiently, but that's no problem for most Taurus. If he should check up on you from time to time about the price of this and the cost of that, don't let it irritate you. Once he is sure you can handle this area to his liking, he'll leave it all up to you.

Although he may be a hard man to catch when it comes to marriage, once he's made that serious step, he's quite likely to become possessive. Capricorns need to know that they have the support of their women in whatever they do, every step of the way. Your Capricorn man, because he's waited so long for for the right mate, may be considerably older than you.

Capricorn fathers never neglect their children and instinctively know what is good for them.

TAURUS WOMAN
AQUARIUS MAN

The Aquarius man in your life is perhaps the most broad-minded you have ever met. Still, you may think he is the most impractical. He's more of a dreamer than a doer. If you don't mind putting up with a man whose heart and mind are as wide as the sky but his head is almost always up in the clouds, then start dating that Aquarius man who somehow has captured your fancy. Maybe you, with your Taurus good sense, can bring him down to earth before he gets too starry-eyed.

He's no dumbbell; make no mistake about that. He can be busy making complicated and idealistic plans when he's got that out-to-lunch look in his eyes. But more than likely, he'll never execute them. After he's shared one or two of his progressive ideas with you, you may think he's a nut. But don't go jumping to any wrong conclusions. There's a saying that the Water Bearer is a half-century ahead of everybody else. If you do decide to say yes to his will-you-marry-me, you'll find out how right some of his zany whims are on your golden anniversary. Maybe the waiting will be worth it. Could be that you have an Einstein on your hands—and heart.

Life with an Aquarius won't be one of total despair for you if you learn to balance his airiness with your down-to-brass-tacks practicality. He won't gripe if you do. Being the open-minded man he is, the Water Bearer will entertain all your ideas and opinions. He may not agree with them, but he'll give them a trial airing out, anyway.

Don't tear your hair out when you find that it's almost impossible to hold a normal conversation with your Aquarius friend. He's capable of answering your how-do-you-do with a running commentary on some erudite topic. Always keep in mind that he means well. His broad-mindedness extends to your freedom and individuality, a modern idea indeed.

He'll be kind and generous as a husband and will never lower himself by quibbling over petty things. You take care of the budgeting and bookkeeping; that goes without saying. He'll be thankful that you do such a good job of tracking all the nickels and dimes that would otherwise burn a hole in his pocket.

In your relationship with a man born under Aquarius you'll have plenty of opportunities to put your legendary patience to good use. At times, you may feel like tossing in the towel and calling it quits, but try counting to ten before deciding it's the last straw.

Aquarius is a good family man. He's understanding with children and will overlook a naughty deed now and then or at least try to see it in its proper perspective.

TAURUS WOMAN
PISCES MAN

The Pisces man could be the man you've looked for high and low and thought never existed. He's terribly sensitive and terribly romantic. Still, he has a very strong individual character and is well aware that the moon is not made of green cheese. He'll be very considerate of your every wish and will do his best to see to it that your relationship is a happy one.

The Pisces man is great for showering the object of his affection with all kinds of gifts and tokens of his love.

He's just the right mixture of dreamer and realist; he's capable of pleasing most women's hearts. When it comes to earning bread and butter, the strong Pisces will do all right in the world. Quite often they are capable of rising to very high positions. Some do extremely well as writers or psychiatrists. He'll be as patient and understanding with you as you will undoubtedly be with him. One thing a Pisces man dislikes is pettiness. Anyone who delights in running another into the ground is almost immediately crossed off his list of possible mates. If you have any small grievances, don't tell him about them. He couldn't care less and will think less of you if you do.

If you fall in love with a weak Pisces man, don't give up your job before you get married. Better hang on to it a long time after the honeymoon; you may still need it. A funny thing about the man born under this sign is that he can be content almost anywhere. This is perhaps because he is inner-directed and places little value on material things. In a shack or in a palace, the Pisces man is capable of making the best of all possible adjustments. He won't kick up a fuss if the roof leaks and if the fence is in sad need of repair. He's got more important things on his mind, he'll tell you. At this point, you're quite capable of telling him to go to blazes. Still and all, the Pisces man is not shiftless or aimless, but it is important to understand that material gain is never an urgent goal for him.

Pisces men have a way with the sick and troubled. It's often his nature to offer his shoulder to anyone in the mood for a good cry. He can listen to one hard-luck story after another without seeming to tire. He often knows what's bothering a person before the person knows it himself.

As a lover, he'll be attentive. You'll never have cause to doubt his intentions or sincerity. Everything will be aboveboard in his romantic dealings with you.

Children are often delighted with the Pisces man because he spoils and pampers them no end.

Man—Woman

TAURUS MAN
ARIES WOMAN

The Aries woman may be a little too bossy and busy for you. Generally, Aries are ambitious creatures and can become impatient with people who are more thorough and deliberate than they are—especially when they feel it's taking too much time. Unlike you, the Aries woman is a fast worker. In fact, sometimes she's so fast, she forgets to look where she's going. When she stumbles or falls, it's a nice thing if you're there to grab her. She'll be grateful. Don't ever tell her "I told you so" when she errs.

Aries are proud and don't like people to naysay them. That can turn them into blocks of ice. And don't think that an Aries woman will always get tripped up in her plans because she lacks patience. Quite often they are capable of taking aim and hitting the bull's-eye. You'll be flabbergasted at times by their accuracy as well as by their ambition. On the other hand, because of your interest in being sure and safe, you're apt to spot many a mistake or flaw in your Aries friend's plans before she does.

In some respects, the Aries-Taurus relationship is like that of the tortoise and the hare. Although it may seem like plodding to the Ram, you're capable of attaining exactly what she has her sights set on. It may take longer but you generally do not make any mistakes along the way.

Taurus men are renowned lovers. With some, it's almost a way of life. When you are serious, you want your partner to be as earnest and as giving as you are. An Aries woman can be giving when she feels her partner is deserving. She needs a man she can look up to and be proud of. If the shoe fits, slip into it. If not, put your sneakers back on and tiptoe out of her sight. She can cause you plenty of heartache if you've made up your mind about her but she hasn't made up hers about you. Aries women are very demanding, or at least they can be if they feel it's worth their while. They're high-strung at times and can be difficult if they feel their independence is being restricted.

If you manage to get to first base with the Ram of your dreams, keep a pair of kid gloves in your back pocket. You'll need them for handling her. Not that she's all that touchy; it's just that your relationship will have a better chance of progressing if you handle her with tender loving care. Let her know that you like her for her brains as well as for her good looks. Don't even begin to admire a woman sitting opposite you in the bus. When your Aries date sees green, you'd better forget about a rosy future together.

Aries mothers believe in teaching their children initiative at a very early age. Unstructured play might upset your Taurus notion of tradition, but such experimentation encouraged by your Aries mate may be a perfect balance for the kids.

TAURUS MAN
TAURUS WOMAN

Although two Taurus may be able to understand each other and even love each other, it does not necessarily hold true that theirs will be a stable and pleasant relationship. The Taurus woman you are dating may be too much like you in character to ever be compatible. You can be set in your ways. When you encounter someone with just as much willpower or stubbornness, the results can be anything but pleasant.

Whenever two Bulls lock horns it can be a very exhausting and unsatisfactory get-together. However, if you are convinced that no other will do, then proceed—but with caution. Even though you know yourself well—or, at least, think you do—it does not necessarily mean that you will have an easy time understanding your Taurus mate. However, since both of you are basically practical people, you should try a rational approach to your relationship:

put your cards on the table, talk it over, then decide whether you should or could cooperate, compromise, or call it a day. If you both have your sights set on the same goal, life together could be just what the doctor ordered.

Both of you are very affectionate people and have a deep need for affection. Being loved, understood, and appreciated are very important for your well-being. You need a woman who is not stingy with her love because you're very generous with yours. In the Taurus woman you'll find someone who is attuned to your way of feeling when it comes to romance. Taurus people, although practical and somewhat deliberate in almost everything they do, are very passionate. They are capable of being very warm and loving when they feel that the relationship is an honest one and that their feelings will be reciprocated.

In home life, two Bulls should hit it off very well. Taurus wives are very good at keeping the household shipshape. They know how to market wisely, how to budget, and how to save. If you and your Taurus wife decide on a particular amount of money for housekeeping each month, you can bet your bottom dollar that she'll stick to it right up to the last penny.

You're an extremely ambitious person—all Bulls are—and your chances for a successful relationship with a Taurus woman will perhaps be better if she is a woman of some standing. It's not that you're a social climber or that you are cold and calculating when it comes to love, but you are well aware that it is just as easy to fall in love with a rich or socially prominent woman as it is with a poor one.

Both of you should be careful in bringing up your children. Taurus has a tendency to be strict. When your children grow up and become independent, they could turn against you as a result.

TAURUS MAN
GEMINI WOMAN

The Gemini woman may be too much of a flirt ever to take your honest heart too seriously. Then again, it depends on what kind of a mood she's in. Gemini women can change from hot to cold quicker than a cat can wink its eye. Chances are her fluctuations will tire you after a time, and you'll pick up your heart—if it's not already broken into small pieces—and go elsewhere.

Women born under the sign of the Twins have the talent of being able to change their moods and attitudes as frequently as they change their party dresses. They're good-time gals who like to whoop it up and burn the candle to the wick. You'll always see them at parties, surrounded by men of all types, laughing gaily or kicking up their heels at every opportunity. Wallflowers they're not. The next day you may bump into her at the library, and you'll hardly recognize her. She'll probably have five or six books under her arms—on five or six different subjects. In fact, she may even work there. Don't come on like an instant critic. She may know more about everything than you would believe possible. She is one smart lady.

You'll probably find her a dazzling and fascinating creature— for a time, at any rate—just as the majority of men do. But when it comes to being serious, sparkling Gemini may leave quite a bit to be desired. It's not that she has anything against being serious, it's just that she might find it difficult trying to be serious with you. At one moment she'll praise you for your steadfast and patient ways, the next moment she'll tell you in a cutting way that you're an impossible stick-in-the-mud.

Don't even try to fathom the depths of her mercurial soul—it's full of false bottoms. She'll resent close investigation, anyway, and will make you rue the day you ever took it into your head to try to learn more about her than she feels is necessary. Better keep the relationship fancy-free and full of fun until she gives you the go-ahead sign. Take as much of her as she's willing to give and don't ask for more. If she does take a serious interest in you and makes up her fickle mind about herself and you, then she'll come across with the goods.

There will come a time when the Gemini girl will realize that she can't spend her entire life at the ball and that the security and warmth you offer is just what she needs in order to be a happy, fulfilled woman.

Don't try to cramp her individuality; she'll never try to cramp yours.

A Gemini mother enjoys her children, which can be the truest form of love. Like them, she's often restless, adventurous, and easily bored. She will never complain about their fleeting interests because she understands the changes the youngsters will go through as they mature.

TAURUS MAN
CANCER WOMAN

The Cancer woman needs to be protected from the cold, cruel world. She'll love you for your masculine yet gentle manner; you make her feel safe and secure. You don't have to pull any he-man or heroic stunts to win her heart; that's not what interests her. She's will be impressed by your sure, steady ways—the way you have of putting your arm around her and making her feel that she's the only girl in the world. When she's feeling glum and tears begin to well up in her eyes, you have that knack of saying just the right thing. You know how to calm her fears, no matter how silly some of them may seem.

The Moon Child is inclined to have her ups and downs. You have the talent for smoothing out the ruffles in her sea of life. She'll most likely worship the ground you walk on or put you on a terribly high pedestal. Don't disappoint her if you can help it. She'll never disappoint you. She will take great pleasure in devoting the rest of her natural life to you. She'll darn your socks, mend your overalls, scrub floors, wash windows, shop, cook, and do just about anything short of murder in order to please you and to let you know that she loves you. Sounds like that legendary good old-fashioned girl, doesn't it? Contrary to popular belief, there are still a good number of them around—and many of them are Cancers.

Of all the signs in the Zodiac, the women under Cancer are the most maternal. In caring for and bringing up children, they know just how to combine the right amount of tenderness with the proper dash of discipline. A child couldn't ask for a better mother. Cancer women are sympathetic, affectionate, and patient with children.

While we're on the subject of motherhood, there's one thing you should be warned about: never be unkind to your mother-in-law. It will be the only golden rule your Cancer wife will probably expect you to live up to. No mother-in-law jokes in the presence of your mate, please. With her, they'll go over like a lead balloon. Mother is something special for her. She may be the crankiest, nosiest old bat, but if she's your wife's mother, you'd better treat her like royalty. Sometimes this may be difficult. But if you want to keep your home together and your wife happy, you'd better learn to grin and bear it.

Your Cancer wife will prove to be a whiz in the kitchen. She'll know just when you're in the mood for your favorite dish or snack, and she can whip it up in a jiffy.

Treat your Cancer wife fairly, and she'll treat you like a king.

TAURUS MAN
LEO WOMAN

The Leo woman can make most men roar like lions. If any woman in the Zodiac has that indefinable something that can make men lose their heads and find their hearts, it's the Leo woman. She's got more than her share of charm and glamour, and she knows how to put them to good use. Jealous men either lose their sanity or at least their cool when trying to woo a woman born under the sign of the Lion.

She likes to kick up her heels quite often and doesn't care who

knows it. She often makes heads turn and tongues wag. You don't
necessarily have to believe any of what you hear—it's most likely
just jealous gossip or wishful thinking.

This vamp makes the blood rush to your head, and you mo-
mentarily forget all of the things that you thought were important
and necessary in your life. When you come back down to earth
and are out of her bewitching presence, you'll conclude that although this vivacious creature can make you feel pretty wonderful,
she just isn't the kind of girl you'd planned to bring home to
mother. Although Leo will certainly do her best to be a good wife
for you, she may not live up to your idea of what your wife should
be like.

If you're planning on not going as far as the altar with that Leo
woman who has you flipping your lid, you'd better be financially
equipped for some very expensive dating. Be prepared to shower
her with expensive gifts, take her dining and dancing in the
smartest nightspots in town. Promise her the moon, if you're in a
position to go that far. Luxury and glamour are two things that
are bound to lower a Leo's resistance. She's got expensive tastes,
and you'd better cater to them if you expect to get to first base
with this gal.

If you've got an important business deal to clinch and you have
doubts as to whether it will go over well or not, bring your Leo
partner along to that business luncheon. It will be a cinch that
you'll have that contract—lock, stock, and barrel—in your pocket
before the meeting is over. She won't have to say or do anything—
just be there at your side. The grouchiest oil magnate can be trans-
formed into a gushing, obedient schoolboy if there's a
charm-studded Leo woman in the room.

Easygoing and friendly, the Leo mother loves to pal around
with the children and proudly show them off. She can be so proud
of her kids that she sometimes is blind to their faults. Yet when
she wants the children to learn and to take their rightful place in
society, the Leo mother is a strict but patient teacher.

TAURUS MAN
VIRGO WOMAN

The Virgo woman is particular about choosing her men friends.
She's not interested in just going out with anybody. She has her
own idea of what a boyfriend or prospective husband should be,
and it's possible that image has something of you in it. Generally,
Virgo is quiet and refined. She doesn't believe that nonsense has
any place in a love affair. She's serious and will expect you to be.
She's looking for a man who has both of his feet on the ground—
someone who can take care of himself as well as take care of her.

She knows the value of money and how to get the most out of a dollar. She's far from being a spendthrift. Throwing money around unnerves her, even if it isn't her money that's being tossed to the winds.

She'll most likely be very shy about romancing. Even the simple act of holding hands may make her blush—on the first couple of dates. You'll have to make all the advances, which is how you feel it should be. You'll have to be careful not to make any wrong moves. She's capable of showing anyone who oversteps the boundaries of common decency the door. It may even take a long time before she'll accept that goodnight kiss. Don't give up. You're exactly the kind of man who can bring out the woman in her. There is warmth and tenderness underneath Virgo's seemingly frigid facade. It will take a patient and understanding man to bring her enjoyment of sex to full bloom.

You'll find Virgo a very sensitive partner, perhaps more sensitive than is good for her. You can help her overcome this by treating her with gentleness and affection.

When a Virgo has accepted you as a lover or mate, she won't stint on giving her love in return. With her, it's all or nothing at all. You'll be surprised at the transformation your earnest attention can bring about in this quiet kind of woman. When in love, Virgos only listen to their hearts, not to what the neighbors say.

Virgo women are honest in love once they've come to grips with it. They don't appreciate hypocrisy, particularly in romance. They believe in being honest to their hearts, so much so that once they've learned the ropes and they find that their hearts have stumbled on another fancy, they will be true to the new heartthrob and leave you standing in the rain. But if you're earnest about your interest in her, she'll know and reciprocate your affection. Do her wrong once, however, and you can be sure she'll snip the soiled ribbon of your relationship.

The Virgo mother encourages her children to develop practical skills in order to stand on their own two feet. If she is sometimes short on displays of affection, here is where you come in to demonstrate warmth and cuddling.

TAURUS MAN
LIBRA WOMAN

It is a woman's prerogative to change her mind. This is a woman born under the sign of Libra. Her changeability, in spite of its undeniable charm, could actually drive even a man of your patience up the wall. She's capable of smothering you with love and kisses one day, and the next day she's apt to avoid you like the plague. If you think you're a man of steel nerves, perhaps you can tolerate her sometimeness without suffering too much. However, if you own up to the fact that you're only a mere mortal of flesh and blood, then you'd better try to fasten your attention on someone more constant.

But don't get the wrong idea: a love affair with a Libra is not all bad. In fact, it has an awful lot of positives. Libra women are soft, very feminine, and warm. She doesn't have to vamp in order to gain a man's attention. Her delicate presence is enough to warm the cockles of any man's heart. One smile and you're a piece of putty in the palm of her hand.

She can be fluffy and affectionate, things you like in a girl. On the other hand, her indecision about what dress to wear, what to cook for dinner, or whether or not to redo the house could make you tear your hair out. What will perhaps be more exasperating is her flat denial that she can't make a simple decision when you accuse her of this. The trouble is she wants to be fair and thinks the only way to do this is to weigh both sides of the situation before coming to a decision. A Libra can go on weighing things for days, months, or years if allowed the time.

The Libra woman likes to be surrounded with beautiful things. Money is no object when beauty is concerned. There'll always be plenty of flowers around her apartment. She'll know how to arrange them tastefully, too. Women under this sign are fond of beautiful clothes and furnishings. They'll run up bills without batting an eye, if given the chance, in order to surround themselves with luxury.

Once she's cottoned to you, the Libra woman will do everything in her power to make you happy. She'll wait on you hand and foot when you're sick, bring you breakfast in bed, and even read you the funny papers if you're too sleepy to open your eyes. She'll be very thoughtful about anything that concerns you. If anyone dares suggest you're not the grandest man in the world, your Libra wife will give him or her a good talking to.

The Libra woman, ruled by the lovely planet Venus as you are, will share with you the joys and burdens of parenthood. She works wonders in bringing up children, although you most always will come first in her affections. The Libra mother understands that youngsters need both guidance and encouragement. Her children will never lack anything that could make their lives easier and richer.

TAURUS MAN
SCORPIO WOMAN

Scorpio is the true zodiacal mate and partner for a Taurus, but is also your zodiacal opposite. The astrological link between Taurus and Scorpio draws you both together in the hopes of an ideal part-nership, blessed by the stars. But the Taurus man with a placid disposition and a staid demeanor may find the woman born under the sign of Scorpio too intense and moody.

When a Scorpio woman gets upset, be prepared to run for cover. There is nothing else to do. When her temper flies, so does everything else that's not bolted down. On the other hand, when she chooses to be sweet, she can put you in a hypnotic spell of romance. She can be as hot as a tamale or as cool as a cucumber, but whatever mood she happens to be in, it's for real. She doesn't believe in poses or hypocrisy. The Scorpio woman is often seduc-tive and sultry. Her femme fatale charm can pierce through the hardest of hearts like a laser ray. She doesn't have to look like Mata Hari—many resemble the tomboy next door—but once you've looked into those tantalizing eyes, you're a goner.

The Scorpio woman can be a whirlwind of passion, perhaps too much passion to suit even a hot-blooded Taurus. Life with a girl born under this sign will not be all smiles and smooth sailing. When prompted, she can unleash a gale of venom. If you think you can handle a woman who purrs like a pussycat when treated correctly but spits bullets once her fur is ruffled, then try your luck. Your stable and steady nature will have a calming effect on her. But never cross her, even on the smallest thing. If you do, you'll be in the doghouse.

Generally, the Scorpio woman will keep family battles within the walls of your home. When company visits, she's apt to give the impression that married life is one great big joyride. It's just her way of expressing loyalty to you, at least in front of others. She may fight you tooth and nail in the confines of your living room, but at the ball or during an evening out, she'll hang on your arm and have stars in her eyes. She doesn't consider this hypoc-risy, she just believes that family quarrels are a private matter and should be kept so. She's pretty good at keeping secrets. She may even keep a few from you if she feels like it.

By nature, you're a calm and peace-loving man. You value de-pendability highly. A Scorpio may be too much of a pepperpot for your love diet; you might wind up a victim of chronic heart-burn. She's an excitable and touchy woman. You're looking to settle down with someone whose emotions are more steady and reliable. You may find a relationship with a Scorpio too draining.

Never give your Scorpio partner reason to think you've be-trayed her. She's an eye-for-an-eye woman. She's not keen on forgiveness when she feels she's been done wrong.

If you've got your sights set on a shapely Scorpio siren, you'd better be prepared to take the bitter with the sweet.

The Scorpio mother secretly idolizes her children, although she will never put them on a pedestal or set unrealistic expectations for them. She will teach her children to be courageous and steadfast. Astrologically linked, the Taurus-Scorpio couple make wonderful parents together. Both of you will share the challenges and responsibilities for bringing up gracious yet gifted youngsters.

TAURUS MAN
SAGITTARIUS WOMAN

The Sagittarius woman is hard to keep track of. First she's here, then she's there. She's a woman with a severe case of itchy feet. She'll win you over with her hale-fellow-well-met manner and breezy charm. She's constantly good-natured and almost never cross. She will strike up a palsy-walsy relationship with you, but you might not be interested in letting it go any further. She probably won't sulk if you leave it on a friendly basis. Treat her like a kid sister, and she'll love you all the more for it.

She'll probably be attracted to you because of your restful, self-assured manner. She'll need a friend like you to rely on and will most likely turn to you frequently for advice.

There's nothing malicious about the female Archer. She'll be full of bounce and good cheer. Her sunshiny disposition can be relied upon even on the rainiest of days. No matter what she'll ever say or do, you'll know that she means well. Sagittarius are often short on tact and say literally anything that comes into their heads, no matter what the occasion. Sometimes the words that tumble out of their mouths seem downright cutting and cruel. She never meant it that way, however. She is capable of losing her friends, and perhaps even yours, through a careless slip of the lip. On the other hand, you will appreciate her honesty and good intentions.

She's not a date you might be interested in marrying, but she'll certainly be a lot of fun to pal around with. Quite often, Sagittarius women are the outdoor type. They're crazy about hiking, fishing, white-water canoeing, and even mountain climbing. She's a busy little lady, and no one could ever accuse her of being a slouch. She's great company most of the time and can be more fun than a three-ring circus when treated fairly. You'll like her for her candid and direct manner. On the whole, Sagittarius are very kind and sympathetic women.

If you do wind up marrying this girl-next-door type, you'll perhaps never regret it. Still, there are certain areas of your home life that you'll have to put yourself in charge of just to keep matters on an even keel. One area is savings. Sagittarius often do not have heads for money and as a result can let it run through their fingers like sand before they realize what has happened to it.

Another area is children. She loves kids so much, she's apt to spoil them silly. If you don't step in, she'll give them all of the freedom they think they need. But the Sagittarius mother trusts her youngsters to learn from experience and know right from wrong.

TAURUS MAN
CAPRICORN WOMAN

You'll probably not have any difficulty in understanding the woman born under the sign of Capricorn. In some ways, she's just like you. She is faithful, dependable, and systematic in just about everything that she undertakes. She is concerned with security and sees to it that every penny she spends is spent wisely. She is very economical in using her time, too. She doesn't believe in whittling away her energy in a scheme that is bound not to pay off.

Ambitious themselves, they're often attracted to ambitious men—men who are interested in getting somewhere in life. If a man of this sort wins her heart, she'll stick by him and do all she can to see to it that he gets to the top. The Capricorn woman is almost always diplomatic and makes an excellent hostess. She can be very influential with your business acquaintances.

She's not the most romantic woman of the Zodiac, but she's far from being frigid when she meets the right man. She believes in true love and doesn't appreciate getting involved in flings. To her, they're just a waste of time. She's looking for a man who means business—in life as well as in love. Although she can be very affectionate with her boyfriend or mate, she tends to let her head govern her heart. That is not to say that she is a cool, calculating cucumber. On the contrary, she just feels she can be more honest about love if she consults her brains first. She'll want to size up the situation first before throwing her heart in the ring. She wants to make sure that it won't get crushed.

A Capricorn woman is concerned and proud about her family tree. Relatives are important to her, particularly if they've been able to make their mark in life. Never say a cross word about her family members. That can really go against her grain, and she won't talk to you for days on end.

She's generally thorough in whatever she undertakes: cooking, cleaning, entertaining. Capricorn women are well-mannered and gracious, no matter what their background. They seem to have it in their natures always to behave properly.

If you should marry a Capricorn, you need never worry about her going on a wild shopping spree. The Goat understands the value of money better than most women. If you turn over your paycheck to her at the end of the week, you can be sure that a good hunk of it will go into the bank and that all the bills will be paid on time.

With children, the Capricorn mother is both loving and correct. She will teach the youngsters to be polite and kind, and to honor tradition as much as you do. The Capricorn mother is very ambitious for the children. An earth sign like you, she wants the children to have every advantage and to benefit from things she perhaps lacked as a child.

TAURUS MAN
AQUARIUS WOMAN

The woman born under the sign of the Water Bearer can be odd and eccentric at times. Some say that this is the source of her mysterious charm. You may think she's nutty, and you may be fifty percent right. Aquarius women have their heads full of dreams, and stars in their eyes. By nature, they are often unconventional and have their own ideas about how the world should be run. Sometimes their ideas may seem pretty weird, but more likely than not they are just a little too progressive for their time. There's a saying that runs: the way Aquarius thinks, so will the world in fifty years.

If you find yourself falling in love with an Aquarius, you'd better fasten your safety belt. It may take some time before you really know what she's like and even then you may have nothing more to go on but a string of vague hunches. She can be like a rainbow, full of dazzling colors. She's like no other girl you've ever known. There's something about her that is definitely charming, yet elusive; you'll never be able to put your finger on it. She seems to radiate adventure and magic without even half trying. She'll most likely be the most tolerant and open-minded woman you've ever encountered.

If you find that she's too much mystery and charm for you to handle—and being a Taurus, chances are you might—just talk it out with her and say that you think it would be better if you called it quits. She'll most likely give you a peck on the cheek and say you're one hundred percent right but still there's no reason why you can't remain friends. Aquarius women are like that. And perhaps you'll both find it easier to get along in a friendship than in a romance.

It is not difficult for her to remain buddy-buddy with someone she has just broken off with. For many Aquarius, the line between friendship and romance is a fuzzy one.

She's not a jealous person and, while you're romancing her, she'll expect you not to be, either. You'll find her a free spirit most of the time. Just when you think you know her inside out, you'll discover that you don't really know her at all. She's a very sympathetic and warm person. She can be helpful to people in need of assistance and advice.

She's a chameleon and can fit in anywhere. She'll seldom be suspicious even when she has every right to be. If the man she loves slips and allows himself a little fling, chances are she'll just turn her head the other way and pretend not to notice that the gleam in his eye is not meant for her.

The Aquarius mother is generous and seldom refuses her children anything. You may feel the youngsters need a bit more discipline and practicality. But you will appreciate the Aquarius mother's wordly views, which prepare the youngsters to get along in life. Her open-minded attitude is easily transmitted to the children. They will grow up to be respectful and tolerant.

TAURUS MAN
PISCES WOMAN

The Pisces woman places great value on love and romance. She's gentle, kind, and romantic. Perhaps she's that girl you've been dreaming about all these years. Like you, she has very high ideals; she will only give her heart to a man who she feels can live up to her expectations.

Many a man dreams of an alluring Pisces woman. You are no exception. She's soft and cuddly and very domestic. She'll let you be the brains of the family; she's contented to play a behind-the-scenes role in order to help you achieve your goals. The illusion that you are the master of the household is the kind of magic that the Pisces woman is adept at creating.

She can be very ladylike and proper. Your business associates and friends will be dazzled by her warmth and femininity. Although she's a charmer, there is a lot more to her than just a pretty exterior. There is a brain ticking away behind that soft, womanly facade. You may never become aware of it—that is, until you're married to her. It's no cause for alarm, however, she'll most likely never use it against you, only to help you and possibly set you on a more sucessful path.

If she feels you're botching up your married life through careless behavior or if she feels you could be earning more money than you do, she'll tell you about it. But any wife would really.

She will never try to usurp your position as head and breadwinner of the family.

No one had better dare say one uncomplimentary word about you in her presence. It's likely to cause her to break into tears. Pisces women are usually very sensitive beings. Their reaction to adversity, frustration, or anger is just a plain, good, old-fashioned cry. They can weep buckets when inclined.

She can do wonders with a house. She is very fond of dramatic and beautiful things. There will always be plenty of fresh-cut flowers around the house. She will choose charming artwork and antiques, if they are affordable. She'll see to it that the house is decorated in a dazzling yet welcoming style.

She'll have an extra special dinner prepared for you when you come home from an important business meeting. Don't dwell on the boring details of the meeting, though. But if you need that grand vision, the big idea, to seal a contract or make a conquest, your Pisces woman is sure to confide a secret that will guarantee your success. She is canny and shrewd with money, and once you are on her wavelength you can manage the intricacies on your own.

If you are patient and kind, you can keep a Pisces woman happy for a lifetime. She, however, is not without her faults. Her sensitivity may get on your nerves after a while. You may find her lacking in practicality and good old-fashioned stoicism. You may even feel that she uses her tears as a method of getting her own way.

Treat her with tenderness, and your relationship will be an enjoyable one. Pisces women are generally fond of sweets, so keep her in chocolates (and flowers, of course) and you'll have a very happy wife. Never forget birthdays, anniversaries, and the like. These are important occasions for her. If you ever let such a thing slip your mind, you can be sure of sending her off in a huff.

Your Taurus talent for patience and gentleness can pay off in your relationship with a Pisces woman. Chances are she'll never make you sorry that you placed that band of gold on her finger.

There is usually a strong bond between a Pisces mother and her children. She'll try to give them things she never had as a child and is apt to spoil them as a result. She can deny herself in order to fill their needs. But the Pisces mother will teach her youngsters the value of service to the community while not letting them lose their individuality.

TAURUS
LUCKY NUMBERS 1999

Lucky numbers and astrology can be linked through the movements of the Moon. Each phase of the thirteen Moon cycles vibrates with a sequence of numbers for your Sign of the Zodiac over the course of the year. Using your lucky numbers is a fun system that connects you with tradition.

New Moon	First Quarter	Full Moon	Last Quarter
Dec. 18 ('98) 7 4 6 0	Dec. 26 ('98) 4 8 5 2	Jan. 1 1 9 5 7	Jan. 9 7 8 3 9
Jan. 17 9 6 6 9	Jan. 24 9 0 7 5	Jan. 31 1 0 3 4	Feb. 8 4 8 5 2
Feb. 16 6 3 7 1	Feb. 22 0 1 8 4	March 2 6 6 7 2	March 10 2 8 5 9
March 17 3 7 0 3	March 24 1 1 6 8	March 31 8 9 4 1	April 8 1 7 2 5
April 15 0 6 3 7	April 22 7 3 5 6	April 30 9 0 7 4	May 8 4 8 2 0
May 15 6 9 7 6	May 22 2 4 5 9	May 30 4 6 3 7	June 6 7 1 5 8
June 13 8 6 6 2	June 20 4 0 9 6	June 28 0 9 4 7	July 6 7 2 5 3
July 12 3 3 8 1	July 20 1 2 5 2	July 28 7 3 6 1	August 4 0 1 4 2
August 11 2 7 9 0	August 18 1 5 6 3	August 26 2 1 0 5	Sept. 2 8 6 6 2
Sept. 9 2 4 5 9	Sept. 17 9 6 3 8	Sept. 25 5 0 6 9	Oct. 1 7 7 3 5
Oct. 9 5 6 1 7	Oct. 17 4 8 2 5	Oct. 24 0 6 3 1	Oct. 31 1 6 8 9
Nov. 7 9 4 1 7	Nov. 16 2 5 0 3	Nov. 23 3 4 4 9	Nov. 29 9 2 3 7
Dec. 7 7 4 1 5	Dec. 15 5 8 3 6	Dec. 22 0 9 5 7	Dec. 29 7 2 8 3

TAURUS
YEARLY FORECAST 1999

Forecast for 1999 Concerning Business
and Financial Affairs, Job Prospects,
Travel, Health, Romance and Marriage
for Those Born with the Sun
in the Zodiacal Sign of Taurus.
April 21–May 20

For those born under the influence of the Sun in the zodiacal sign of Taurus, ruled by Venus, planet of taste and harmony, this promises to be a year of healing old wounds and moving ahead with personal ambitions. Burdens and stumbling blocks hanging over you from the past are likely to be released this year, leaving you free to start out in a new direction. The need to be constantly making sacrifices should be passing you by, with more opportunities for greater self-fulfillment coming your way. It is likely that you will make a series of long-term commitments this year, which should enhance your sense of security in the long run. There may be an overall sense of life moving onto a more even keel. Where business matters are concerned, your intuition is likely to play a big part in your decisions no matter what specific business you are involved in. It can benefit you to be more willing to adapt to changing circumstances. In relation to money matters, a lack of invested funds may mean that you have to rely increasingly on whatever you can earn from your main skills and talents. Opportunities to improve your financial status will not fall into your lap; you will need to work for them. Keep a watchful eye on spending in relation to your social life. With routine occupational affairs you are likely to experience a series of short periods all during the year when you can achieve a great deal by linking up with other people. Teamwork is one of your main keys to success. There may be more reasons to journey long distances this year. Some trips will probably be intensely personal. Taurus health requires greater vigilance. This is one of those years when any emotional traumas you experience tend to take their toll on your physical well-being. Making more of an effort to release your emotions is likely to benefit you, helping to prevent the onset of minor but nevertheless aggravating illness. Your romantic life is likely to be highly charged. You may waver between faith and doubt, trying constantly to keep your feet on the ground without putting a damper on your dreams.

For professional Taurus people, this is a year when you can benefit from trusting your intuition rather than relying solely on your intellect. It is not in the Taurus nature to make rash moves. You tend to plan any departure from the norm slowly and gradually. However, an increasing sense of life being unsettled is likely to prompt you to take a few more risks than usual. Greater flexibility in your overall attitude is your ally; situations around you can change overnight, with little warning. New discoveries and innovations are likely to open up a whole range of business options for you. There is money to be made through ideas and opportunities toward which other people may hold a cynical attitude but which you have a sixth sense about. Try to avoid the natural Taurus tendency to dig your heels in and stay put amidst the waves of change around you. Guard against refusing to move with the times. There is much more to be gained through going with the flow of change and recognizing new possibilities as they arise. For Taurus people involved in the commercial and financial fields, it is likely to be advantageous to consolidate business interests. Concentrate on developing one particular area which seems sound rather than scattering your interests far and wide. If you are intent on moving into a branch of your current business, the soundest opportunities are likely to arise during the first quarter of the year. Monies invested in training are likely to give you a good return. You will probably experience much quicker profits from investments made this year than you initially expect. Strengthening your network of contacts, both from previous and new business, is one of the main keys to success. The prime time for working to establish a new business is between March 2 and August 29.

Financially, it is in your best interests to work harder at saving this year. If you have little in the bank at the start of the year, you are likely to feel the pinch at key periods during the rest of the year. Cutting back temporarily on social spending may be necessary in order to meet priority costs and bills. Since you may have to rely on a higher income to ease your financial situation, you may want to take on extra work, even doing two jobs at a time. In so doing you are likely to be consolidating skills and perhaps even discovering talents you did not know you had. These could help you tremendously in the job market in the future. It is unlikely that opportunities to improve your financial situation will come your way easily. Instead, you will benefit from taking a different perspective and looking for new kinds of opportunities which you have not considered before. Aim to keep your focus fixed on long-term gains. Get-rich-quick schemes are unlikely, and even if you do track down one or two, they will probably not be as profitable as claims may suggest. Your natural skepticism is sure to be a help in rooting out the fake from the valuable. Be extra careful during the periods between January 1 and 26 and again from May 6 to July 5. At those times you are prone to be impetuous in relation to spending due to increased romantic and social interests.

In routine occupational affairs there is much to be gained by making a special effort to cooperate even with individuals who irritate you. While you may not condone their points of view, it is in your interests to allow room for compromise. If involved in any legal proceedings in relation to work matters, there could be much dispute about the situation this year. Expect a series of delays, particularly around summertime. What is finally negotiated is likely to leave you on much better terms with a number of key individuals. You can expect to move from strength to strength in both work and personal relationships as you increase mutual cooperation. For Taurus people bored with a particular aspect of work, the likelihood is that this component will disappear or at least diminish before the year is through. There should be more overall opportunities to develop creative skills and artistic talents in the world of work and in your general everyday life. The very start of the year, between January 1 and 26, is apt to be an especially busy, fast-moving period.

Where travel is concerned, you may be making more long-distance journeys this year than last. At least one of the trips that you make is likely to be related to a strong personal ambition which you wish to fulfill. This will probably be part of your overall drive to achieve much more on a personal level. Travel in relation to the past is also likely. You could be revisiting a locale that has a lot of deep memories for you. Any excursion which you have anxieties about beforehand is likely to turn out much better than you expect, particularly if taken between February 14 and June 28. If you do not have the time or money to take a proper vacation this year, weekend breaks with your partner or with a good friend during the summer could compensate. The period between July 6 and September 2 is especially favorable for a getaway.

Greater care is needed this year not to become overly stressed. As a Taurus you have a tendency to allow your energy to drain down before you strive to replenish it. Pay more attention to diet, concentrating on foods which will keep you going over long periods. Bottling up your emotions is not smart. If you do not express your feelings, do not be surprised if you have more than your fair share of physical symptoms as a result. You can help to prevent the onset of minor health conditions by finding ways to release your pent-up emotions. Aggressive sports when you are angry, and more gentle exercise such as yoga if you are merely upset, should help you.

All through the first half of the year you are likely to experience much stronger feelings in relation to your mate or partner. Do not allow occasional but intense irritations to develop into long-term resentments. As a Taurus you prefer peace and harmony, but sparks could be flying this year. Intense conflict once aired with your partner can easily turn into moments of intense passion when your deeper feelings of love become more obvious to you both. For Taurus singles, opportunities to meet someone new are good this year. Although you may have doubts about the long-term prospects of one particular liaison, this union is likely to have quite a profound effect upon you.

TAURUS DAILY FORECAST

January–December 1999

JANUARY

1. FRIDAY. Mixed. This quiet New Year gives you an excellent opportunity to review your finances. Your position is likely to be healthier than you realize. Consider starting an investment fund, even if it means making a small sacrifice in another area; it could reap real rewards. You need plenty of time to think carefully about your New Year resolutions. There is a chance you have been a little unrealistic. Friends may drop by unexpectedly, but you may not be in any mood for socializing. A retreat into a stubborn silence can cause offense; try to be congenial. Guard against taking sides in a dispute between friends; you risk losing one of them over a matter that does not directly concern you.

2. SATURDAY. Unsettling. News from someone at a distance could put a problem in a new light. What was started a couple of weeks ago may come to a head today, especially if it concerns contractual or legal matters. You may be pressured to name a price or to sign a document before you are ready. Routine chores may be a source of irritation for those close to you, causing some sharp exchanges over them. Consider visiting someone who is close as a way of letting tempers cool. If you have been thinking about new financial investments, guard against the soft sell or gimmicky offer. If you work, the worries of what the coming week may bring could begin to crowd in on you. Avoid becoming outraged by someone else's apparent bigotry or unthoughtfulness.

3. SUNDAY. Frustrating. Even the best-laid plans can fall apart. If you are feeling that yours are being thwarted at every turn, you would be wise to just let things be and make the most of the last day of the holiday season. Attached Taurus people may have to spend the day apart from a loved one who has been called away at short notice. A family outing you have organized may have to be postponed because of confusion over the arrangements. Guard against letting your frustration show. No matter how careful you have been, sometimes people can still fail to understand or to follow through. Avoid retreating into your own world to brood. Later, try not to let an argument over TV viewing become a full-scale row.

4. MONDAY. Satisfactory. The workweek begins rather slowly. You will probably have to deal with more than your fair share of interruptions. Try not to plan too far ahead this week; conditions are changing rapidly. Any new ideas you have been mulling over during the festive season should be aired. A person in authority is likely to be impressed with the way you have carefully reasoned out your case. What you hear via the grapevine probably has a kernel of truth. Any suspicions or doubts you might have about someone's trustworthiness will probably be confirmed. You are apt to be very pleased with the work of a professional, especially if it is connected with a home improvement project. You are likely to benefit from a quiet time spent alone this evening.

5. TUESDAY. Manageable. Although you have plenty to do early today, consider volunteering for a task that others appear reluctant to take on. Guard against appearing too enthusiastic, however; you may arouse suspicion. If you are working, a colleague may reveal some confidential information. Verify all the facts before you make a move. This is the ideal time to finish off outstanding tasks. Enlisting the help of others with a knotty problem can lead to finding the solution. Otherwise, you risk wasting time by going down some blind alleys. Later, look forward to a romantic evening with your date or your loved one away from crowds or even other family members.

6. WEDNESDAY. Rewarding. Creative work of all kinds is favored. However, guard against wasting money on what may turn out to be just a fad. If you have invested money, you are likely to see some satisfying returns today. If you have children, consider signing them up for a drama or singing class, especially if they show a certain talent. If you go out shopping, resist any temptation to buy on impulse. You could make an expensive purchase you regret. You are likely to receive news of a new addition to the family through birth or marriage. Taurus people who are single can impress a date by pulling out all the stops. This is a good time to book your summer holiday, especially a cruise.

7. THURSDAY. Sensitive. You are very sensitive to the mood of others. Watch for any tendency for people to take advantage of your goodwill. An interest in occult or paranormal subjects is heightened. Seeking out someone to talk with about your daydreams might reveal a hidden message. A seemingly glamorous opportunity might require more work from you than you realize. People are apt to be charmed by your charisma but may ask unrealistic favors of you. Friends could turn up unexpectedly, trying to cajole you into dropping everything to go out on the town with them. There is a possibility you might party into the small hours, but avoid eating or drinking too much. Do not take a flirtatious friend seriously.

8. FRIDAY. Favorable. Confusion over a routine task is likely to be resolved. Someone at a distance may have some disturbing news. A woman in authority will probably help you advance your cause. Taurus people are known for good organizational skills. You may be asked to put them to use in an important new business venture. Financial deals struck today should prove lucrative, especially if you bring your partner in. However, be sure to read the small print before investing any of your hard-earned money. An unexpected opportunity at work may result in one of your ideas being used. Consider taking up a new hobby that involves eating or drinking. Attending a cheese and wine party could encourage you to develop an interest in wine tasting or even wine making at home.

9. SATURDAY. Cautious. The usual Saturday routine is unlikely to run smoothly. Even though Taurus people are usually very cautious, you are at risk of being involved in an accident. Take extra care when using sharp instruments or hot appliances. This is not a good time for doing any odd jobs around the home. If you are working today you may have to deal with an unpleasant person. Allow for the possibility that you have your wires crossed and are jumping to the wrong conclusion. Although you have plenty of energy, a shopping expedition is likely to leave you feeling exhausted and grumpy. A good workout in the gym is more likely to dispel your frustrations and raise your spirits.

10. SUNDAY. Difficult. Any unresolved difficulties that arose yesterday are likely to continue. However, it appears that the heat of anger has been replaced by a chilling of relations. Taurus people are apt to put up and shut up, but keeping quiet is only likely to leave you feeling out of sorts. You would be wise to spend some time alone to think about what is really bothering you. However, guard against any tendency to retreat into your own corner. If you are attached, your partner may wish to share plans for the future although you are not quite ready for this. Curb a tendency to react instantaneously; it could be misinterpreted as pessimism, or you may be accused of pouring cold water over their dreams.

Enjoy an evening with your loved one that includes a walk in the moonlight.

11. MONDAY. Variable. You may be taken by surprise as you realize that others do not appear to be in tune with you. People in authority seem especially remote. This is not a good time to discuss promotion or career prospects. Taurus people working in the financial sector will probably find out about a clever fraud or confidence trick. Or you may receive a solicitation letter from a distant place; consider carefully any business proposition it contains. Tensions on the domestic front are likely to erupt. You would be wise to face the music now rather than sweeping everything under the rug. Because you find it difficult to concentrate, there is a chance you will overlook important points of detail. If you work with computers, familiarize yourself with some new technology that could save time and money.

12. TUESDAY. Fortunate. An acquaintance may be glad of the opportunity to talk over a personal problem with you. Let them do most of the talking; it appears that they want a shoulder to cry on rather than practical advice. Take this to be your good deed for the day, even though you will probably find it emotionally draining. Joint financial interests are strongly favored. Your sustained efforts are apt to pay off handsomely. If you are responsible for other people's money, you may be required to delve back into the history of a particular account. Your Taurus capacity for persistence is likely to yield the result you want. Keeping a close watch on your long-term interests will probably reveal an exciting new opportunity to turn a speedy profit.

13. WEDNESDAY. Tricky. Conditions indicate that you should move quickly on surprising new developments in your joint financial ventures. Now is a good time to lay the foundations for a new project you have been thinking about. You instinctively know the right moves to make. However, there is a risk of confusion arising. You would be wise to double-check each move. Guard against neglecting your home life as you pursue your ambitions. A person in authority appears to be in an irritable mood. Avoid sensitive issues; you could be shocked by their reaction. The day is apt to be peppered with interruptions. You may even be asked to attend to a minor crisis at work. A cash-flow problem will probably mean that you cannot afford to buy a luxury item just yet. Wait until you can pay with cash, not credit.

14. THURSDAY. Buoyant. You should be feeling more able to cope with the world. Winning friends and influencing people will probably come easily. You have plenty of energy and will probably want to put it to work. This is a good time to resolve any difficulties you may be having with someone close to you. A diplomatic approach is indicated; a confrontation is unlikely to be worth it in the long run. Channeling your energies into a real estate deal appears favored. Even though the week is drawing to a close, you are likely to achieve a lot. An old pal may look you up. If they live at a distance, consider accepting an invitation to visit. You may be asked to contribute to a worthy cause or to sign a petition for a vital change.

15. FRIDAY. Changeable. If a friend or acquaintance has been taking liberties recently, today appears to be the right time to bring the problem out into the open. A request for a favor could be the cause of a misunderstanding. Attached Taurus people would be wise to check your joint account before making any new financial transaction. This is a good time for catching up on neglected chores or routine tasks. Others appear very capable of continuing the work in hand. A confrontation with a subordinate over a principle appears inevitable. Stick to your guns, especially if you know you are in the right. Take care when lifting heavy items; you risk pulling a muscle or causing an injury if the item drops.

16. SATURDAY. Cautious. Stress is likely to be the cause of any headache you are suffering. Make this weekend as stress-free as possible. Avoid arguing over routine; there is not anything that is so important that it cannot wait. If you are thinking about holidays, this is a good time to look through some travel brochures. However, postpone making definite plans until another day. You do not appear to have the reserves of energy you think you have. Avoid driving yourself too hard. Watch for symptoms of mild burnout. Stick to tried-and-tested methods. Taurus people in adult education are likely to have a productive day, whether taking a class or teaching one. Be open to new ideas of all kinds.

17. SUNDAY. Difficult. Acting rashly could land you in hot water. An argument with a friend can easily be settled if you give in a little and accept their apology. Avoid indulging in highly spiced foods or alcohol. This is the ideal time to begin any legal negotiations, or you may learn of an important development if you have already started them. This is also a good time to consider switching to a new legal adviser if you are unhappy with your present one. Taurus people often prefer to stay at home. Friends and family members will probably find it especially difficult to get you out and about today. You would be wise to compromise rather than retreating into a stubborn silence. Try to find ways to entertain the family at home, such as renting a video, playing a card game, or preparing a special meal.

18. MONDAY. Deceptive. Although this is a busy and productive start to the week, you could be in for a chaotic time. If you are hoping for a promotion, make sure you record the details of any conversation you have with your superiors, especially if you are thinking of trying something new that is not covered by company policy. What you hear via the grapevine could work to your advantage. Most rumors have a kernel of truth; but check them out with an independent source. You appear to be in a good position to try out unknown talents. Taurus people tend to stick to what is known and familiar. However, today's fast-changing conditions call for flexible, quick responses. You are likely to receive an unexpected dividend from a recent investment of your time or money.

19. TUESDAY. Lucky. If you have more on your schedule than you can cope with, a woman is likely to offer to help you out. But lighten up a little. Being able to laugh at yourself can keep things in perspective. You may even find that your sense of fun could be contagious. New business ventures are especially favored; you appear to be especially ambitious for yourself and others. Any recent efforts to consolidate your position should help you now move forward with confidence. Routine matters demand attention. Try not to let your eagerness to forge ahead make you overlook them. A visit to your doctor for a routine medical checkup appears to be long overdue, or you may need to see your dentist.

20. WEDNESDAY. Slow. Today's lull in your busy routine is likely to enable you to air problems with those close to you. Take the opportunity to reconcile recent differences with a friend. If you are in a position of authority, this appears to be a good time to take an informal tour of the workplace. Try to get your staff's honest opinion about the business. Be receptive to their ideas. If someone confides in you about a personal matter, look beneath the surface to see what is really bothering them. A review of shared finances is indicated. Conditions also favor sustained concentration. If you are involved in research of any kind, getting help from your associates will probably enable you to make steady progress. Consider inviting a friend for dinner this evening.

21. THURSDAY. Useful. This is a good time for entering into negotiations. If you are thinking of taking out a loan, shop around to get the best deal. You can be confident that offers are genuine. Your mind appears to be buzzing with ideas for future security. Check out all the practical angles before you make your move. You may receive a surprise gift from a friend. A travelog could make stimulating reading. If you have a talent for writing, news from abroad could inspire you to write a short story. If you are in business, you will probably be asked to travel on very short notice. Make sure your passport is still valid if you are traveling to a foreign country. A conversation about other people's customs and habits could prove highly illuminating and save you from embarrassment.

22. FRIDAY. Misleading. Be on guard against getting into a heated discussion with a friend about social or political matters. There is a chance you might begin to take what they say too personally. Indications are that your instincts and intuition cannot be completely relied upon. Consider using some of your Taurus sense of realism. Otherwise, there is a risk of confusion and disappointment. You will probably receive some inside knowledge about a public scandal. However, keep what you learn under wraps. Others appear to be attracted to you, but you would be wise to stick to what directly concerns you. No good is likely to come from meddling in other people's affairs or trying to get them to accept your views.

23. SATURDAY. Easygoing. New ideas that seem to come out of nowhere appear to be sound. You are unlikely to have any trouble convincing others of their worth. If you are in work, try to overcome any tendency to stay in the background. Consider taking your ideas directly to the person in charge. He or she will probably be impressed by your initiative. Make it a priority to finish off outstanding tasks. There are likely to be few distractions to prevent you from making good progress. You can act on confidential information now. There is a chance you will bump into an old friend if you are shopping. Their good news will probably show that you were in the right place at the right time. Enjoy an evening get-together with friends.

24. SUNDAY. Changeable. You are unlikely to be able to put your feet up for long as conditions are constantly changing. Although your preference appears to be to hole up in your private den, others may have different ideas. Going with the flow will probably mean that you will be able to cope with the demands being placed on you. Chatting with an older woman is likely to keep you on an even keel. If you are asked to look after an older relative for the day, guard against being impatient with them; otherwise you risk hurting their feelings. If you are planning a long trip, there is a possibility that you have misunderstood directions that were given to you. Double-check the route before you start, and confirm the day and date.

25. MONDAY. Demanding. Unexpected responsibility that is foisted on you today could prove a little daunting at first. Guard against being too self-effacing if others are looking to you for guidance. Any chance to shine will probably ensure the promotion you are seeking, but avoid saying anything out of turn to your next in command. New information you receive may tempt you into revealing a secret of your own. However, it is still too early to make your intentions known. An older relative may express some extreme views. You would do well not to get drawn into an argument with them as you are unlikely to change their opinions. Make the most of any lull in the day. You will probably not get many opportunities to relax.

26. TUESDAY. Fair. A fond wish could materialize if you put in the effort needed to make it happen. Guard against doing anything that radically changes your appearance, such as changing your hairstyle. Information received by telephone or fax is likely to put the bounce back in your step. However, you would be wise to postpone contacting distant relatives until another day. Otherwise you are apt to end up in a disagreement. This is a good time to look into adult education courses. In the afternoon, the emphasis switches to financial matters. Taurus people who are working may receive news of an increase in salary. This evening, an older person close to you may have a secret to share with you alone.

27. WEDNESDAY. Changeable. Career and financial matters continue to be highlighted. Your boss will probably have a surprising proposal to make. Taurus people are often cautious. Try not to be pressured into making a hasty decision. If you are thinking about ways of earning some extra cash, this is a good day for discussing your ideas. You may have to use all your powers of persuasion before others are convinced. Later you may experience confusion over paperwork. A document may not be where you expect it to be, or something you have written may appear ambiguous. Ask someone to read what you have written before you distribute it. Be wary of someone's apparently good credentials; check them out for yourself to verify them.

28. THURSDAY. Unsettling. You would be wise to refuse a friend a loan. Although this will probably mean a minor tiff, it is ultimately for the best. This is a good day for catching up on routine payments; there is probably a bigger backlog than you realize. Guard against worrying about your financial position. Any fears are apt to have more to do with your own sense of insecurity. Now is a good time to let your feelings be known; consider writing them in a letter. You may get a visit from a new neighbor. They will probably appreciate it if you suggest a walk around the area. If you are attached, your partner may be in the mood for some adventure. Guard against letting your natural sense of Taurus caution dampen spirits of those you are with.

29. FRIDAY. Exciting. This is an especially auspicious day for unattached Taurus people. It appears that a good friend may have deep feelings for you. This could be the start of something very special. For those who are attached, your partner appears determined to get what they want and prepared to use all their charm to get it. Taurus people often wait for a sign before making their intentions known. You are unlikely to receive many clearer signals than those you get today. Put aside any thoughts about future security and enjoy what the present moment has to offer. Consider a candlelit dinner with that special person in your life to round off this very special day.

30. SATURDAY. Variable. Taurus people involved in the community may be asked to distribute leaflets for a good cause or collect donations. This is a good day for bargain hunting. The money you spend on an expensive item will probably turn out to be a sound investment. Check the oil and water in your car if you are going out. Remember to keep a close eye on your shopping bags; you may forget to pick them up after you put them down. Guard against speaking hastily to a family member; indications are that they are all too willing to take your words the wrong way. Your loved one may be concerned about money; discussing joint finances will probably reassure them. Enjoy a quiet evening at home with a blockbuster novel to help you unwind.

31. SUNDAY. Disquieting. Today is unlikely to go according to plan. Although Taurus people are often reassured by what is familiar, today you should expect the unexpected. A family gathering will probably go well enough, but you would be wise to steer clear of sensitive subjects; there is a risk that some bickering will break out. You can often appear calm in difficult situations, which can do much to smooth ruffled feathers. You are likely to feel emotionally drained by the day's events. Make sure that you get a short time alone with your partner, who should be very supportive. An evening out is likely to boost your morale. Consider going to see a play staged by an amateur group or a school musical production.

FEBRUARY

1. MONDAY. Fair. Although you should be less pressured today, you may still feel the need to withdraw a little to reflect on recent events. You may have to account for someone else's error. Try to keep your cool, even though others lose theirs. You risk infuriating others if you appear too aloof or patronizing. An old adversary may suddenly reappear on the scene. What you say on first meeting might be just the thing to make them think twice. You would be wise to keep your checkbook separate from your credit cards. For Taurus people working in the media, this is a good day for trying out radical new ideas. A catchy new tune or jingle could turn out to be a big money-maker.

2. TUESDAY. Unsettling. Your leisure plans are likely to be disrupted because of a friend. This is a favored time to settle any differences with a friend from whom you have become alienated. Indications are that they will gladly accept your peace offering. Children appear to be exceptionally unruly. You may have to resort to firm disciplinary measures to get them under control. Taurus people who earn a living through the written word are unlikely to make much progress. A brisk walk around the block could be just the tonic you need. If you are employed, be prepared to attend to a rush job that requires urgent completion. You may have to work late to get it finished. Sudden inspiration can help you see the way through a difficult problem to a satisfying conclusion.

3. WEDNESDAY. Rewarding. As a Taurus you are known to have a conservative nature. But today, all indications are that you will surprise both yourself and others with the bright, innovative ideas that seem to be bubbling up. If you have been eyeing a more responsible position at work, you may be shocked to find that a younger person has gotten the promotion. The best policy is to accept it gracefully; your reaction to this setback will be noted by those who matter. Be aware of any tendency to rub people the wrong way. Others are probably a little bemused by your apparent need to disrupt the normal routine. Guard against taking matters into your own hands if a public scene turns ugly; inform the police or seek legal advice. Think before issuing any ultimatums; you will probably be required to carry them through even if you are only bluffing.

4. THURSDAY. Variable. You risk causing offense if you refuse an invitation to a friend's party without giving a clear reason. If you have been low on energy recently, make sure you are not depending on stimulants such as tea, coffee, or alcohol to give you a boost. This is a good time to reassess your diet and the effect it could be having on your sense of well-being. If you need to lose some weight, be sure a slick advertisement does not lure you into spending money unnecessarily on gimmicky dieting aids. This is a good day for airing any of yesterday's creative ideas with a person in authority. Taurus people are known for pragmatism and organizational skills. You should have no trouble convincing others if you have prepared your case well in advance.

5. FRIDAY. Mixed. The cause of a recurrent health problem is likely to come to light. You will probably have to reconsider certain aspects of your lifestyle as a result. Taurus people often lead a sedentary life. Consider including some gentle exercise as part of your regular routine. If you are unemployed, there is a chance of a lucky break; a job that appeals may be offered. If you are already in work, avoid letting the apparent indecisiveness of others stop you from forging ahead with your own plans. If extra cash has come your way, do not blow all of it on a spending spree. Keep at least some of it in reserve for that proverbial rainy day. You may realize how important a friend has been to you only after they abruptly leave the scene.

6. SATURDAY. Inactive. Because Taurus people often need peace and quiet, this uneventful day is just the thing for you. Attend to the essentials; the rest can wait. If you are working, a steady pace is favored. Guard against being a little aloof with a subordinate or co-worker. Remember to exercise some of that healthy Taurus skepticism when looking into any financial proposition, especially if it involves a cash outlay up front. What appears to be a sound investment is likely to turn into a millstone around your neck. You would be wise to keep quiet about confidential information. You could inadvertently make a bad situation worse if you let the cat out of the bag. Guard against snacking on junk food as a way of coping with stress.

7. SUNDAY. Deceptive. With today's developments you will probably come down to earth with a bump. Be prepared to part with some fond illusions. A difference of opinion is likely to reveal a previously unknown side to the character of a friend or loved one. Even though the honeymoon may be over, this is actually an opportunity to put the relationship on a more realistic footing. A woman friend is likely to call. If you are entertaining today, consider a traditional Sunday roast. This is a good time to join a group of like-minded people. Or, if you are already a member of an active group, get involved in raising funds in a surprising new way. Consider an invitation to meet up with an old associate; they may have an intriguing offer to make to you.

8. MONDAY. Frustrating. Personal relationships continue to be highlighted. You may be feeling upset after the rough treatment you have been given. Consider the possibility that any resentment you have appears to go back awhile. Resist the temptation to retreat into hurt silence; your partner may not know what is paining you. If you are in a business partnership, avoid any confrontation for the time being. Your rocking the boat is unlikely to be appreciated. You can be easily misled by others and may even get the feeling that people in authority are trying to cross you. Make every effort to remain objective. You will probably have to retreat for a while in order to regain your perspective. Only then are you likely to be able to stand your ground.

9. TUESDAY. Successful. Things should run much more smoothly than yesterday. A friend will probably jolly you out of an introspective mood. Consider an invitation to go and see a new comedy. This is a good day for finding out what is really going on. Do your own digging rather than relying on someone else's say-so. This is a good time to update your home insurance policy; so seek the advice of an expert. If you are about to make any news public, be sure you have checked all your facts, especially anything that is in print. If you are employed, this is a good time to review your long-term objectives with your boss, especially if there is some confusion over your role. Check out what the competition is doing and what salary they are paying for your line of work.

10. WEDNESDAY. Disquieting. Any difficulties you have been experiencing with your mate or partner are likely to come to a head. What is said needs to come into the open. What begins as an exchange of home truths could well turn into a heart-to-heart talk. Taurus people are usually gentle and can be easily hurt. Try to put any hurtful words behind you so that you can begin your relationship on a new footing. Conditions at work are changeable. You often prefer to stick to what you know. However, any surprises your boss springs on you could work to your advantage. Guard against sharing a confidence with a friend; it is likely that you will only cause offense to a third party.

11. THURSDAY. Satisfactory. This is an excellent day for clinching a financial deal, especially one involving real estate or shared resources. Any foundations you are laying for the future appear to be solid. Conforming is the best policy if you are working as part of a team. However, do not be afraid to gently assert your point of view if necessary. Looking for the solution to a problem from a manual will probably save you having to call in an expert. An old fair-weather friend may cross your path once more. Your boss may ask you to keep things ticking over at work. The way you handle a tricky situation that crops up is unlikely to go unnoticed. An old forgotten document may resurface just when you give up on ever finding it.

12. FRIDAY. Rewarding. The way is clear to begin something new. Your recent efforts to consolidate your position are likely to give you the confidence you need to move forward. A new proposition will probably fire you up. A fond wish even has the chance of coming true. You can rely on promises others make to you; they have your best interests at heart. Relations with your loved one should be happy and relaxed. Consider some sporting or competitive activity together; being just pals for a while can strengthen ties. Guard against being drawn into political discussions; other people's apparently aggressive stance could leave you a little bewildered. Enjoy dinner at a favorite restaurant.

13. SATURDAY. Easygoing. Come up with ways to spend some happy hours with friends this weekend. Indications are that a weekend away will work out very well. Others are likely to find unattached Taurus people quite attractive; a new romance could begin with someone who lives at a distance. You should be able to overcome the practical difficulties a situation like this often brings. If you are attached, plan a romantic interlude with your loved one. This is a good time to discuss plans for redecorating the home; consider taking out a home improvement loan to spread the cost. A woman's point of view could provide the key to solving a long-standing problem.

14. SUNDAY. Confusing. An awkward exchange with someone from a distance may stir up some unfinished business. Indications are that this will happen in the morning; guard against this minor upset souring your mood for the rest of the day. Do not be tempted to blow a lot of money on an extravagant impulse purchase. Although you are sensitive to other people's mood, guard against letting any forthright opinions they might express unnerve or upset you. You may want to retreat into your shell, but you are unlikely to get the peace and solitude you are looking for. Your loved one could see red over a misunderstanding with an older relative. Try to pour some oil on the troubled waters. A long soak in a hot bath can help you ease the day's tensions.

15. MONDAY. Variable. Today is unlikely to go according to plan. Let matters unfold rather than trying to force them to your will. You have the Midas touch, which can work in unexpected and unusual ways for you. Your instincts about a financial situation can be trusted. You will probably come up with an innovative and radical new idea. If you deal in stocks or bonds, consider investing in technological industries. You may get an unexpected dividend from shares you already own. Take care to keep a sense of realism about your own worth. Taurus people are not inclined to promote themselves; any such attempts are likely to backfire. Consider using a computer to help you in your work at home.

16. TUESDAY. Challenging. A new phase in your life is about to begin. You will probably be asked to take on more responsibility. Taurus people in work are likely to be promoted. Or you may be asked to take on a role that will raise your profile in the community. This opportunity to change direction may prompt you to take stock of your life. Seek the opinion of a trusted friend whose dispassionate but concerned point of view should help you make the right decisions. You are unlikely to change your mind once it is made up. Guard against neglecting your loved one in favor of pursuing your ambitions. New developments on any deals you are conducting should be promptly acted upon; delay can be costly.

17. WEDNESDAY. Mixed. In the morning the emphasis is on social activities. Consider inviting friends on an outing. Later, financial work requiring close negotiation may be trickier than you anticipate. Confidential activities need very careful handling. Plenty of discretion is also needed. Try not to get drawn into heated exchanges; otherwise you may make some new enemies. If you feel vulnerable, you will probably get the support you need from a close colleague. This is a good time to broach the subject of a pay raise or promotion. Do not be afraid to push forward. Someone is waiting for you to prove yourself. If you are looking for work, you could get a lucky break today as the result of a new application with an old company.

18. THURSDAY. Fair. If you are working, look for ways to mix business with pleasure. You could entertain a customer or colleagues with an expenses-paid meal, or suggest an extended lunch break to your teammates. Someone you trust has sound advice to offer about your career ambitions. Seek this person out if you are feeling a little confused. Conditions favor sustained concentration. If you are studying for exams you should make excellent progress. If your work requires original thinking, spend some time researching what others have already done. You may experience some difficulty contacting a friend, probably because of a technical glitch and not because they want to avoid you.

19. FRIDAY. Exciting. This is a very good time to start laying the foundation for a new project. Thorough groundwork now will help you cope with any unexpected setbacks much more readily. An exciting career opportunity is likely to present itself. This is no time to exercise that caution Taurus people are known for; strike while the iron is hot. A public announcement or news item is likely to surprise you. A fascinating new interest will probably grab your attention and could provide a refreshing break from routine. Indications are that you may become so absorbed that you end up being an expert on the subject. Try to make full use of computer technology to help you with any creative new idea you might be toying with. Avoid the obvious.

20. SATURDAY. Tricky. You may be in the mood for changing your appearance in some way, such as changing your hair style or wearing flashy jewelry. However, you may have an unrealistic view of what suits you and are likely to be disappointed by the results. If you are looking for bargains, keep a sharp eye out for scams. Guard against being tempted by slick advertising campaigns. Taurus people looking for work would be wise to avoid overstating your capabilities. Be sure you can prove you are experienced; you are in for some tough questioning at any interviews. If you are planning a family gathering this weekend, make sure you have not inadvertently missed inviting someone who lives at a distance or is visiting from out of town.

21. SUNDAY. Stressful. Any awkward situations you dealt with yesterday may color this usually relaxing day. Taurus people who are attached will probably be dismayed to find a loved one in a particularly touchy mood. To add insult to injury, anything you say may just add fuel to the fire. Retreat is often the best policy in these situations. However, do not make things worse by retreating into stubborn silence. A friend will probably break the apparent deadlock in a surprising way. Make sure you talk to an older relative before deciding what you want to do; you risk offending them if you do not ask their opinion first. Taurus people who work may get an unexpected call from the boss. You could even be asked to spend a few hours sorting out a problem that cannot be put off until tomorrow.

22. MONDAY. Buoyant. It will probably be a relief for you that the weekend is finally over. This is an excellent day for those in jobs connected with money. A combination of good luck and the influence of friends in high places can put you in an ideal position to further your cause. Some spadework on your part is indicated if you want to turn your golden opportunity into reality. Your mind may be buzzing with ideas on how to invest for your future security. Be guided by your instincts; they appear to be sound. Your creative abilities are likely to be stimulated. Consider trying your hand at poetry or composing music or words to a tune.

23. TUESDAY. Pleasant. Cash transactions and all that is associated with your comfort and security are highlighted. Others appear to be taking a long time to make up their minds about joint financial agreements. Now is a good time to encourage them to make a final decision. If a friend asks for a loan and you have some spare funds, give them the money without expecting it to be returned. That way your friendship is less likely to be compromised when the time comes for them to repay. Those who work can look forward to an unexpected proposal to earn more money. This is an auspicious time for Taurus people considering taking up a new interest in the occult or space travel.

24. WEDNESDAY. Productive. All that glitters is not gold. A seemingly ideal opportunity to make money may not be all it seems. Look into all the angles before you make your move. There is a possibility that someone is not telling you the whole truth. Loose ends need attention; there may be a bigger backlog than you think. This is a good time to discuss any sensitive subject with an older relative. You appear to be in an especially creative frame of mind. Brainstorming ideas should come easily. Taurus people working in advertising or the film and TV industry are particularly favored. Listen to music to help you unwind at home this evening.

25. THURSDAY. Changeable. Now appears to be a good time to make your feelings known. Consider writing them down in a letter. An old friend will probably appreciate a word from you. Showing that they are in your thoughts could give them the boost they need. If you can stop worrying about a particular problem for a while the answer is likely to come to you out of the blue. Double-check your appointments, especially if you have to travel to keep them. You are likely to hear some exaggerated rumors, probably not based on fact. A neighbor may reveal that someone has been talking about you behind your back. Make absolutely sure that you set the record straight to avoid having your reputation damaged.

26. FRIDAY. Useful. Rehearse ahead of time for any important interview. Ask a friend to perform the role of the interviewer.

Encourage them to give you as hard a time as possible so that you are well prepared for the real thing. A show put on locally may prompt you to join up. A friend may have some good news to tell. Teamwork of all kinds is strongly favored. Guard against a tendency to be complacent about a deadline; it appears that you have less time than you realize. A business lunch may go on for longer than expected. Do not object too strongly if someone offers to pick up the tab. Later, enjoy listening to some harmless gossip, then passing it along.

27. SATURDAY. Sensitive. You may be feeling especially sensitive about others. Guard against letting their opinions upset or unnerve you. Keep any promises that you have made; otherwise you risk disappointing a close family member. During the day the emphasis switches to domestic matters. You appear to be in a sentimental mood, but attend to routine chores before retreating into your dream world. If you have been neglecting your lover recently because of other concerns, they will probably express their discontent today. Dinner in a restaurant might be just the thing to launch a romantic evening together.

28. SUNDAY. Disconcerting. Any resentments that have been simmering under the surface will probably erupt today. Guard against taking a stubborn line, especially if you find yourself in an argument with an older relative. You are unlikely to achieve much if you are depending on other people's help. Indications are that they may have to change their plans at the last moment. Consider a family outing somewhere that offers something for everyone. Avoid a tendency to organize everyone's day for them. The best policy is one of live and let live; otherwise you risk getting disappointed. Someone you thought you could depend on may let you down. By the end of the day, you will probably know who to trust and who to avoid.

MARCH

1. MONDAY. Enjoyable. This is a good day to spend with children. You will probably have good reason to be proud of their accomplishments. Guard against being too stern with them; instead, give plenty of encouragement by showing your appreciation. An acquaintance will be glad of the opportunity to talk through a personal problem with you. Your circle of friends may change as a new interest begins to take up more of your time. An old pal will probably make contact. If you decide to meet, invite your current mate or partner to come also. Chances are that they will get along fine together. Make sure you can cover the cost of any large donation. There is a possibility you have overlooked something in your budget that comes due later this month.

2. TUESDAY. Fortunate. Conditions put you in a good position to make the best use of your skills and inventiveness. Your enthusiasm, combined with carefully laid out plans, should win over any reluctant helpers or investors. Any leisure plans you have made for today are unlikely to turn out as you expect. Consider an impromptu outing with your loved one. Try not to let a child bully you into giving them more money than they need. A new gadget or technological innovation may cause some problems. Scour the manual before you call an expert. Unattached Taurus people will probably find that other singles are particularly attracted to you. Because you are exuding charm and charisma, you are likely to start a new romance.

3. WEDNESDAY. Disconcerting. There is more to what is going on than you realize, especially in the workplace. You are unlikely to get the information you need. Allow for the possibility that you may have been deliberately misinformed. Someone could be trying to undermine you. The best policy is to rise above any gossip and trust that all will come clear in time. Taurus people often endure in silence. A reluctance to say what is on your mind may be the cause of nervous headaches or digestive problems you might be suffering. Try to be up front about any recent mistake you may have made. Covering your own tracks will probably result in more work later on and a tarnished reputation.

4. THURSDAY. Variable. Exaggerated rumors may cause a little confusion at first. Later on, however, a surprising development will probably give you the clue you need. This is a good time to publicize your work. An imaginatively thought out presentation may be just the thing to get your point across. Guard against over-doing. You may not have as much energy as you think. Avoid using stimulants such as coffee or tobacco as a way of keeping going. You may have to deal with a tricky situation at work in-volving a subordinate and some missing money. Maintain that calm exterior that Taurus people are famous for. Help from an unexpected quarter is at hand if you ask for it.

5. FRIDAY. Stressful. As a Taurus you are usually very down to earth and pragmatic. However, a rather disconcerting coincidence may prompt an interest in the occult or esoteric. You could be asked to join in an exciting new enterprise or group activity. Guard against your natural tendency to play it safe; it could pre-vent you from seeing that a bold stroke can pay off. Reconsider a social engagement that you would not normally accept; you are apt to be pleasantly surprised by the experience and may even shed some old misconceptions. Taurus people usually prefer what is known and familiar, but you may want to break out of your usual routine. Consider throwing an impromptu party tonight just to see who attends and what develops.

6. SATURDAY. Confusing. This could turn out to be a confusing and frustrating day. You are likely to be easily misled or overly influenced by others. You will probably feel that you are power-less to stop others from blocking you. They could be echoing doubts you might be secretly harboring. Spending some time to do an extra check of work you have just completed. If you look at it with fresh eyes, chances are you will discover a significant mistake. Seek the advice of an expert before starting anything. Your relative inexperience can result in confusion and disappoint-ment. Play things close to your chest; others are likely to try to take advantage of your step-by-step approach.

7. SUNDAY. Sensitive. Although you should be calmer and more sure of yourself today, others seem to be edgy and out of sorts. Make allowances for the way they react. Try to discuss a long-standing problem with someone who has been a thorn in your side. You may not reach an amicable conclusion straight away, but just acknowledging the problem can lead to an improved sit-uation. A family outing promises to be successful even though there is a surprise in store. The day could be marred by a row with your loved one. Try not to aggravate matters by withdrawing emotionally. Your apparent indifference could be very hurtful. You will probably both come to realize that the relationship may be rather claustrophobic and needs to be expanded to include other people.

8. MONDAY. Quiet. The emphasis continues to be on relationships. However, things are much calmer today. If you are married, this could be the right time to discuss your partner's feelings about the relationship. Try to be supportive. Rocking the boat is not going to be appreciated. If you are in business, this is a good time to discuss the future with your partner. Try to listen carefully to what they have to say. Taurus people at work should take the opportunity to discuss the workload, especially if you feel it has been distributed unevenly. This is a good day for working as part of a team or on work that requires cooperative effort. You have to fit in with other people's plans despite your misgivings.

9. TUESDAY. Fair. Some golden opportunities may arise. However, you will probably be required to put in plenty of work to make them a reality. If you are involved in any confidential negotiations, the need for discretion is paramount. A certain individual will probably have to be reminded of this or they might put a spanner in the works. This is a favorable time for house hunters. Read between the lines of property descriptions to avoid wasting time on pointless viewings. This is a good time for installing new computer equipment, both at the workplace and at home. Taurus people about to close a financial deal can expect to be very satisfied with the outcome. Get to bed early tonight.

10. WEDNESDAY. Mixed. This is a good day for consolidating plans and catching up on administrative chores. You may also find yourself quite in demand as people want favors of you. Although refusing can be difficult, you may have to do so; otherwise you could wind up spreading yourself too thin. A friend or acquaintance may demand your undivided attention. If you need peace and quiet to get on with your work, do not be afraid to say so. Try to find someplace where you will not be disturbed. A little knowledge can be a dangerous thing, especially if you have received it from a fax machine or by telephone. Keep the matter under wraps for the moment or you risk your chances of long-term success.

11. THURSDAY. Slow. Although this should be a productive day for Taurus people, you might be making more work for yourself than necessary. Be selective in your reading. Your work schedule might need some improvements. Last-minute delays because of an earlier oversight will probably occur for Taurus people traveling a long distance. Be sure to check that you have all necessary travel documents with you. Try to allow plenty of time to get to the airport or train station. Legal matters are emphasized. Some new information could come to light that will probably work to your advantage before the end of the month.

12. FRIDAY. Lucky. This is a good time to make arrangements for a vacation, especially if you are planning it with your mate or partner. If you are in business, your partner may decide to force a showdown. Taurus people are not known to react when provoked. Today, however, you will probably surprise your partner by giving as good as you get. Make sure you protect your own interests. The signs are good for finalizing confidential negotiations, but exercise some healthy skepticism, especially where it looks as if some easy money is to be made. A new job prospect may appear too good to be true. Consider all your options carefully before burning bridges with your current employer.

13. SATURDAY. Frustrating. This could turn out to be a confusing and frustrating day. Taurus people are reassured by the familiar. You are likely to become disgruntled by events that appear to be out of your control, even a little unsure about what the next step ought to be. Others will probably interpret your hesitancy as that stubbornness for which Taurus people are well known. If you are single, you may have to cope with an unwelcome old flame who pops up from the past. You may discover that things have not been quite as they seem. For instance, you could be let down by a friend who has not been able to keep a promise. You would be wise to avoid a confrontation.

14. SUNDAY. Changeable. A sermon or a Sunday newspaper article will probably give you plenty of food for thought. Consider spending more time in community activity, or making a donation to a worthy cause. Your partner may be very concerned with finances although reluctant to talk about it. If you adopt a soft approach, chances are you can make a start on discussing the matter. This could be at the root of why your partner seems to be acting out of character. If you are in business, your normal Sunday routine may be disrupted by an urgent request for you to do some extra work. Show that you are willing, but try to negotiate some time off to make up for today's extra effort.

15. MONDAY. Buoyant. Start the workweek with a spring in your step. Recent upsets and inconveniences appear to be over for the time being. This is a good day for consolidating your position and catching up on neglected duties. You should then be able to move forward with confidence. If you work in a commercial environment, ideas you come up with today will probably prove popular and lucrative. Taurus people in the fashion or cosmetic industry are likely to have a particularly productive day. Love interest is also emphasized. You could look at an old acquaintance or colleague in a new light. Expect a windfall of some kind, such as a dividend, a bonus, or news of an inheritance.

16. TUESDAY. Rewarding. You are apt to be asked to accept an official role in a charity or community organization. Taurus people need to be certain of their position. Do not hesitate to question what the work involves. Avoid making purchases or withdrawals against a joint account without checking it out with a partner first. There may be less available than you realize. Your loved one may be in an adventurous mood. Go along with any suggestion they make, however outrageous it seems to you. Indications are that you will have a lot of fun together. You may uncover a forgotten bill that requires immediate payment.

17. WEDNESDAY. Useful. Community and group activities are in even sharper focus today. Your contributions can help bring about a much needed change. This is an auspicious time to make new beginnings and forge new friendships. You are likely to be stimulated by debate and discussion. Others will probably be intrigued by your unusual viewpoint. If an old friend comes calling, you should have plenty to talk about. If you are attached, make sure you involve your partner in the conversation. If you are single, you may be introduced to an interesting person within your circle of friends; it could blossom into a romantic involvement. Consider an outing to somewhere you have never visited before.

18. THURSDAY. Successful. Conditions are excellent for digging behind the scenes to find out what is really going on. What you learn could give you a clearer idea about possible trends and put you in a good position to decide your own future plans. A forgotten letter or document could contain the answer to a prayer. Your instincts appear to be working well. Do not hesitate to act on a friend's advice concerning an investment if you have a good feeling about it too. Let your daydreams surface. You will probably find that they contain a solution to a problem that has been troubling you. Later, someone of importance may be instrumental in getting you in touch with someone you lost touch with recently. An interest in the occult or paranormal is likely to be especially heightened.

19. FRIDAY. Manageable. Check over any written work you have prepared in the past few days. A fresh look may reveal some errors. What was started last Wednesday is likely to gather pace. Someone will make contact with you, probably by telephone, to discuss the matter further. If you are looking for work, a seemingly glamorous opportunity has more to it than meets the eye. Guard against overcommitting yourself. Take advantage of any lull in your busy routine to talk over concerns with your superior. He or she may have a surprise for you, but you will probably be reassured by the news. A meeting between like-minded people can elicit the solution to a tricky problem that has been thwarting your progress.

20. SATURDAY. Demanding. Many Taurus people like to take it easy on the weekend. However, indications for today are that the more you do, the longer your list of things to do seems to become. There simply are not enough hours in the day. Guard against letting the pressure lead to an argument with your mate or partner. It is likely to result in a frosting of relations. Resist being put upon by others. You are often very easygoing; others may want to take advantage of that. Someone will probably try to meddle in your personal affairs. A firm stance is indicated, but guard against losing your patience completely. Enjoy a relaxing evening at home. Curl up with your loved one to watch a romantic film together, or listen to a favorite musical group.

21. SUNDAY. Unsettling. You may be feeling a little under the weather after yesterday's hectic scene. A family outing may not come up to expectations. Keep a close eye on any youngsters if you are out; there is a chance that they will wander off. Taurus people are not known to chafe against the familiar. However, you may be feeling the need to rebel. This is an indication for a need to change. If you are unsettled about your work life, a good friend will probably have the sound advice you need to hear. Change is likely to be forced on you. Accepting it and going with the flow is likely to be far less painful than trying to resist. Guard against sudden decisions; they will probably backfire. Take things more slowly than usual and pick your moment.

22. MONDAY. Fair. Conditions are bringing financial matters into focus. You are likely to make good choices with investment decisions. This is especially true if you are investing your own money rather than other people's. This is a good time to discuss a pay raise or promotion. You will probably have an opportunity to improve or expand your skills. A short course in accounting or financial management could be just the ticket. As a Taurus you know your own worth. There is no reason you should hesitate to tell others about it. Consider switching policies that are not working for you. Old possessions may be accumulating. Use any spare time to sift through them to see what is really of value and what should be given away.

23. TUESDAY. Variable. Work that has been running late is gathering pace now. If you are involved in the planning stages of a project, do not be afraid to voice your ideas however outlandish they seem to be. Others in authority are likely to be intrigued and impressed. You will probably be asked to keep things ticking over if a higher-up has to leave for a while. Consider making something with your own hands; the result will probably be unusual and rewarding. Guard against being deceived by what appears to be an easy money-making scheme. As the saying goes, there is no such thing as a free lunch. You may be tempted to rush through tasks, but checking out your assumptions now will probably save you expensive corrective work later on.

24. WEDNESDAY. Productive. This is a good day for catching up with your correspondence. If you are out and about, exchange news and views. Listening to other people's points of view will help you see things in a fresh light. Stick to your schedule in spite of possible transportation or communication delays. Indications are that if you are delayed, you can make up for the lost time. A neighbor is likely to be a source of irritation, possibly over boundary lines. Staying cool and collected should diffuse the situation. If you are meeting a brother or sister, check that there is no confusion over the meeting arrangements. Discuss any creative ideas you have with an associate before putting them into practice. Teamwork is favored over independent action.

25. THURSDAY. Profitable. If you are traveling, conditions seem just right for a very productive day. Working with a partner is likely to bring extra rewards. This is a good time to set the record straight, especially if you are in a business partnership. Your opposite number may be a little hostile at first. However, using some of that patience for which Taurus people are famous will probably win them around. A short business trip might provide the opportunity to mix business and pleasure. Even if it just is for the day, consider inviting your loved one along. There will probably be enough spare time for you to spend together. Taking extra care when noting your expenses will avoid problems later on when you request reimbursement.

26. FRIDAY. Changeable. Domestic concerns are likely to be uppermost in your mind as the workweek draws to a close. Take the opportunity to clear your chores as quickly as possible. This is a good day for making minor repairs or doing odd jobs around the home. If you are working, tried-and-tested methods will probably work best for you. The day could be marred by an argument with an older friend or relative. They may have got hold of incorrect information or been told an untrue rumor. Guard against making matters worse by laying down the law. Avoid withdrawing emotionally. Later you need some time alone. An evening curled up listening to your favorite music or reading a best-selling novel will help relieve some of the week's tensions and put you in a relaxed frame of mind.

27. SATURDAY. Unsettling. Things may not go according to plan. The best policy is to expect the unexpected. Keep your routine flexible. Although you appear to be in a generous mood, guard against succumbing to an impulse to buy, especially an expensive item for the home. If you wait a little longer it may become available at a bargain price. Family bickering is likely, probably because everyone wants to do their own thing. Keeping a level head might be difficult for you at times, but seeing the funny side of life might help avoid any major blowups. Taurus people who are separated or divorced will probably have to face some extra demands. If you decide to contest, you could be in for a long battle that exhausts you emotionally.

28. SUNDAY. Enjoyable. This is a good day to be around children. Consider letting them do what they want and following their lead. Although they are likely to become a little unruly in their enthusiasm, guard against laying down the law too heavily or you might dampen their spirits. A romantic involvement might turn into something lasting. You may have mixed feelings. Taking it one step at a time is the best policy, even though your loved one seems anxious to move forward. If you are attached, tread warily. Your partner may be edgy and too hasty to think the worst. They could be expecting you to satisfy their every whim. They may insist you lend a hand when you would rather do nothing. Take a short walk together to air your grievances and get back in each other's good graces.

29. MONDAY. Challenging. Your creative instincts are apt to be bursting through. Ideas will probably come so fast that you may find it hard to keep up. Consider using a tape recorder instead of jotting down notes to help you catch everything. Using a new computer software package will probably inspire you, especially if you are in graphic design or advertising. Your partner may be very ambitious for you and will probably try to push you forward. Sometimes Taurus people do not like to be hurried along, but act sooner rather than later. Unattached Taurus people are likely to embark on an especially passionate affair. Even if it is a brief one, the signs are that it will transform your outlook on life.

30. TUESDAY. Easygoing. Normally placid Taurus people will probably welcome the chance to pause for breath after recent events. Conditions are much quieter than they have been. You now have time to ponder what has been happening. A promise made to you recently should not be counted on. Try to think of an alternative just in case the other party does not deliver. After yesterday's creative brainstorm, you may feel completely blocked now. This appears to be a backlash from yesterday's excesses. There is a possibility of a disagreement erupting with a friend. A prompt apology from you will probably restore good feeling, even if you are not completely to blame. Include some exercise in your agenda, but guard against overdoing it if you are not in the best shape.

31. WEDNESDAY. Rewarding. After all the recent creative activity, conditions are now right for making them a reality. Sift through your ideas to separate the wheat from the chaff. Plenty of hard work is now required and could take some time, but this will probably not deter you; Taurus people are usually methodical and systematic. Others may want to hurry you along, but insist on taking as much time as you need and the results will be that much better. Review any projects you began or commitments you made a couple of weeks ago. There is a risk that you have been neglecting your obligations in certain areas. This is a good time to catch up on routine tasks. A certain confusion will probably be cleared up, or a secret may be revealed to you by a friend.

APRIL

1. THURSDAY. Fortunate. Taurus people who are working may be asked to fill in for a superior who will be away for a short time. This should send your self-confidence soaring. Accept any help that is offered, even though you might believe you can cope alone. If you are looking for a job, an exciting opportunity may present itself. This is an excellent day for sustained, concentrated effort, especially if you are studying for exams or are in research. Taurus people are well known for organizational skills and a steady approach to work. Rethinking the way you do your work will probably help you overcome a major obstacle. Do not take no for an answer from anyone.

2. FRIDAY. Confusing. The more you disagree with a family member, the more you should be listening carefully to what is being said. Guard against telling others how to think, especially those nearest and dearest to you. Avoid raising your voice in anger or frustration. This is not a good time to confront others about their behavior. Indications are that you have probably jumped to the wrong conclusion. Taurus people often show great resilience. However, you could be dissipating your energies to no good purpose. Think things over in your mind before acting. Later, you will probably discover that someone you thought you could trust is trying to undermine your reputation among colleagues or neighbors.

3. SATURDAY. Frustrating. Although you may still lack a spark of vitality, others appear to be bouncing around like firecrackers. You are likely to feel at the mercy of their whims because you do not have the energy or inclination to resist. Guard against retreating into a sullen mood. Someone who has been avoiding you recently appears ready to talk now. Make time for them, even though you have a busy schedule. Be ready to forgive and forget the past so that you can get on with the future. Holding a grudge can only hurt you in the long run. There is little doubt that you are on the track of a breakthrough. Stick to your idea even if others pour cold water on it. You deserve a pat on the back even if you have to give it to yourself.

4. SUNDAY. Variable. Recent events may have left you feeling emotionally drained. However, you still need to reach out to others. Pamper yourself and your mate or partner. Go for a meal in a top restaurant, or buy yourselves some beautiful new clothes. You would be wise, however, not to overindulge. If you are short of cash, take a long walk arm in arm with your loved one. A friend bearing good news will probably call unexpectedly. Seek out the company of younger but like-minded people. Their fresh approach can help you regain your perspective. This is not a favored time to criticize a younger member of the family, especially if you object to the company they keep. Let them work out their own strategies for success in life.

5. MONDAY. Successful. Both your intuition and your sound Taurus sense of pragmatism are working well. If you are in business you will probably have an unerring instinct for the right deal. If you are house hunting you are likely to find the home of your dreams. This is a good time to discuss any work problems with your boss, especially if you think the workload has been distributed unfairly. Conditions are right to iron out final wrinkles in plans for the future. A problem you thought had been cleared up once and for all is likely to resurface, leaving you feeling rather disappointed or confused. You would be wise to heed the advice a friend offers, even though you may be reluctant to listen to it.

Your pal's intentions are genuine enough and their judgment excellent, but do not feel bound by all of their ideas.

6. TUESDAY. Tricky. You should be in a very optimistic frame of mind. If you are looking for ways to make money, read between the lines of a slick advertisement. Although it seems to be above-board, you could miss important points of detail. Taurus people who are single should avoid trying to buy someone's heart. Your generosity may be misplaced. An apparent injustice will probably make you feel indignant, but control a tendency to overdramatize; your emotionally charged reactions are unlikely to accomplish much. There is a chance that a domestic crisis such as a burst water pipe could disrupt your routine. Seek expert help urgently to correct the problem. Stay in touch with a friend who recently moved.

7. WEDNESDAY. Manageable. Conditions return to a much more even keel today. Your sense of optimism remains strong, although tempered with a more realistic perspective. Your mental horizons are likely to be broadened. You may encounter an old friend who has tales to tell of faraway places. Or a travelog is likely to prove stimulating reading. This is a good day for booking a vacation, especially if you are thinking of going on a cruise or a safari. You are likely to get the best deal available. If you are in business, consider taking a training course to improve your marketing skills. It may seem to you that a meeting has been a waste of time, but indications are that relations are being cemented for the future. Someone who has been difficult to work with in the past seems to be making an effort to cooperate now.

8. THURSDAY. Mixed. Free yourself of any excess energy in a physical way. For instance, opt to walk rather than taking a ride, or visit others rather than waiting for them to come knocking at your door. You could be drawn into a heated exchange. If you get involved, remain neutral without seeming indifferent. Staying with what you know will probably turn out to be too limiting. Consider venturing into a new field even though you have little or no experience. A challenging opportunity is likely to have a revitalizing effect. Pleasant memories may be stirred by a long-distance telephone call or letter. A well-blended combination of imagination and persuasion is likely to bring a plan to fruition.

9. FRIDAY. Uncertain. If you are planning a visit to old friends, allow for the possibility of traffic holdups. Consider taking a different route. Any difficulties you have been having with an authority figure is likely to come out into the open. Backing down may be the best policy, even though you know you are in the right. Seek the opinion of a trusted friend. This is a starred day to volunteer your services. Giving your time is more important than making a donation. Accept a request to help out at a bazaar or organize a sale. Roping in help from others in your circle will ensure a good time for everyone. Later you should be in the mood for romance with that special person in your life.

10. SATURDAY. Demanding. Be prepared for all-day friction. You may have to deal with someone at work who is nursing an old grudge and needs the opportunity to vent their anger. Try not to become impatient with them, especially if it is a subordinate. Allow for the possibility that you are not seeing the broader picture. You are likely to be disappointed by a business deal that does not go through as planned. Time will probably reveal, however, that it would not have delivered its promise. Be prepared to part with some fond illusions about your opposite number. A difference of opinion is likely to show a previously unknown side of their character. The honeymoon appears to be over for you Taurus people who recently began a new partnership of any kind. Reality can be an eye-opener.

11. SUNDAY. Changeable. An impromptu family outing should be the ideal way of spending the day. Consider playing the role of tourist by visiting local places of interest that others travel miles to see. This time together is also likely to help heal any rift that might be developing. If there are any outstanding chores to do, get everyone to pitch in so that they can be cleared in double-quick time. Stifle an urge to blurt out what is on your mind. Right now there is unlikely to be a right time or place. Give further thought to a cause you fervently believe in; you just might come up with some ideas that could be of practical use. If you are in business, your partner will probably ask you to drop everything to help meet an urgent deadline. An afternoon nap can give you renewed energy this evening.

12. MONDAY. Useful. Do not put pleasure before business. Play it safe. Resist the temptation to take a longer lunch break than usual, and guard against frittering away your time. Taurus people in business would be wise to curb optimism about budgets. A new project is unlikely to reward you as richly as you hope. Treat yourself to a gift only if you are sure you can afford it. Consider entertaining business associates at home. Although your ideas seem to be sound, you are likely to be disappointed if you unveil them now. The signs are that others will be skeptical. Simple mistakes are likely; make sure you check your work thoroughly at every stage and take nothing for granted.

13. TUESDAY. Disquieting. You may have no choice but to distance yourself from a former friend who appears to have been a strong influence in your life. Guard against being caught up in the hype of a new group. Although you may sympathize with a friend's point of view, you would be wise not to be drawn into their sphere. Avoid pushing through any ideas by sheer force of will. Others need time to catch up with your thinking. Your partner may not be ready to tell you about something that is bothersome. Let them pick their moment to bring the matter out into the open. An acquaintance may be glad of the opportunity to talk over a personal problem with you. Guard against showing any shocked reaction or voicing your own opinion. They are probably looking for support rather than advice from you.

14. WEDNESDAY. Buoyant. A letter or postcard from a friend visiting at a distance will probably lift your spirits. If you are in business, take careful note of the day's events; you may need to refer back to them at a future date. Work not needing physical effort is favored. Teamwork is apt to be especially rewarding. Conditions will become much quieter by late morning. Take the opportunity to catch up with neglected chores. This is also a favored time for reflecting on how well you are balancing your own desires against your duty to others. Taurus people usually have a great sense of responsibility and can often forget a duty to self as well. Decisions requiring a consensus should be made in the open; otherwise someone may claim to detect a hidden agenda.

15. THURSDAY. Good. A surprising new development could vindicate your position. A shock announcement might expose your hidden enemies. Good luck accompanies good planning. Signs are that you should be flexible in your working methods but firm in your long-term goals. You would be wise to let others do the talking. The less you say now, the less can be used against you in the future. What you learn via the grapevine or network could prove beneficial to your cause in the long run. More is likely to be revealed if you continue to adopt a passive stance. A confidential promise made by a higher-up today can be counted on. An authority figure will probably approach you for some advice or a favor; be totally truthful.

16. FRIDAY. Stressful. You should keep any new ideas you are thinking of publicizing under wraps for just a little while longer. Anything new that is started today is likely to fail in the early stages. The best policy appears to be to carry on quietly in the background, even though it seems that everything is falling apart around you. Taurus people often remain stubbornly resolute. You are likely to need all the resoluteness you can muster to resist the pressure to move forward. Use what remains of the week to finish up outstanding tasks. Guard against getting meeting arrangements confused or you may have some awkward explaining to do to a higher-up or to a loved one. Evening socializing should be low-key and alcohol-free.

17. SATURDAY. Tricky. Although you may be in the mood for changing your appearance, try out your ideas first before making any permanent changes. For instance, use a hair color that washes out, or try on some wigs to see if a new hairstyle suits you. Guard against buying expensive clothing on impulse. What you believe looks great today could turn out to be a regrettable mistake. A duty visit to an older relative might spark a disagreement. Do not let your irritation show, as this is likely to result in a serious upset. Consider indulging their whim, even though you both know that they are being selfish and unreasonable. Curb any temptation to cut corners in your eagerness to make progress on a new task. Shortcuts are likely to come back to haunt you at a later time or could damage your reputation.

18. SUNDAY. Unsettling. Financial concerns may be uppermost in your mind. Consider switching policies if some are not maturing as you had hoped. You are likely to uncover a forgotten bill that requires immediate payment. If you are out, keep your checkbook separate from your credit card. Take ready money only if you need it. A cut-price store that has just opened could lead to bargains without compromising your standard of living. Consider buying a beautiful item for the home. Spending time with a family member who is unlikely to make demands on you should help you unwind this evening and prepare for the hectic workweek ahead.

19. MONDAY. Fair. Get up earlier than usual in order to get a head start on the work awaiting you. You will probably clear your administrative chores in double-quick time. You seem to know instinctively the right moves to make. You should be able to respond quickly and positively to a fast-changing situation. Take every opportunity to show off your talents. A good way to enlist help from others is to explain what they stand to gain. Keep fully abreast of any possible initiatives. Playing the impartial observer is unlikely to further your cause. You have more to gain if you do not publicize your detailed intentions just yet. Consider investing spare cash in a promising new company or product.

20. TUESDAY. Tense. Possibly your calendar is incomplete. Double-check all your appointments, especially if you have to travel to them. You would be wise to defer important decisions;

indications are that you are not able to think clearly enough about them. You will probably hear news on the grapevine that is just rumors. A neighbor may reveal that someone has been trying to undermine you. Make absolutely sure they have their story right before you make a move. You should be able to handle any confrontation very effectively. Others are likely to respect your forthrightness, but you may end up feeling disillusioned. Comfort yourself with the thought that things often appear worse than they are. Have confidence in the long-term future.

21. WEDNESDAY. Variable. Yesterday's mood continues. You are more likely to want to spend time alone. There is a risk of disappointment when you discover that something you own is not as valuable as you thought. Younger people in your family will probably look to you for encouragement in their endeavors. Try to be as supportive as possible. If you are thinking of investing some spare cash, be sure to read the small print. You risk being misled by the general tone of what is on offer. Resist the temptation to spend money simply because you want to make an instant impression. Speculation or gambling is not favored. Consider making an anonymous donation to a favorite charity or cause.

22. THURSDAY. Frustrating. Try not to intervene in a dispute that does not directly concern you. Your peacemaking attempts are unlikely to be appreciated. Someone close to you appears to be deliberately misunderstanding you. The best policy is to let the matter drop rather than rising to the bait. You would be wise to wait for official confirmation before taking action on a rumor. Guard against feeling sorry for yourself. The effect of alcohol is especially potent at this time. Avoid taking an aggressive stance in your dealings with powerful people. You may be a little rundown; consider taking a vitamin booster. If you are going through a rocky period with your loved one, make an effort to discuss some of the deeper reasons for the rift.

23. FRIDAY. Exciting. It is said that the early bird catches the worm. Taurus people will have to get up quite early indeed to make the most of this action-packed day. Conditions are changing fast; flexibility and quick thinking are required. Matters concerning real estate or property are emphasized. If your work is connected in any way with housing, lucrative deals may simply fall into your lap. Your instinct and luck appear to be working well together. Domestic concerns are also highlighted. A long weekend break to take your loved ones on a mystery tour or adventure trip is indicated. Consider doing something all the family can enjoy. There is only one problem you will probably have to overcome:

a tendency that many Taurus people have to be a little too cautious. Lighten up and enjoy your birthday period.

24. SATURDAY. Disruptive. You may be at odds with yourself this morning. A turbulent day awaits you. Signs are that you are about to begin a new phase in your life. Any tendency to conservatism will probably make change quite painful. In particular, you may have to face the possibility that a relationship is ending. If you are going through a rocky period with your loved one, you may have both been hurt and confused by each other's actions and words. A strenuous workout or playing a competitive sport will probably help dissipate some of your aggressive feelings. You are then likely to be in a much better position to talk things over. Taurus people who are single should not wait to be asked out tonight. New romance is about to blossom with a newcomer on the scene.

25. SUNDAY. Fair. If you are involved in artistic work, ideas are likely to flow thick and fast. Try not to be too discouraged if you do not actually achieve very much in practical terms. Someone who seeks your support will probably appreciate your ability to see their point of view. You would be wise not to throw good money after bad in attempts to recover a financial loss. A leisure activity may turn out to be more expensive than you first thought. Children could be a little unruly. As a consequence, a disagreement may develop over how children should be disciplined or brought up. Consider getting together with others who share a sporting interest. Guard against stretching a muscle or provoking a mild strain when exercising.

26. MONDAY. Disconcerting. A cash-flow crisis may prevent you from buying a large household item you really want. Or leisure plans are likely to be canceled because of an unforeseen expenditure. Indications are that you are likely to be the loser if you follow advice to place a bet, but consider taking action on financial advice given earlier this week. Guard against investing too large an amount up front in your eagerness to get rich quick. Even if you only invest a small sum, your nest egg is likely to show excellent returns. Children may expect you to join in their boisterous games. However, you may be a little low on energy. Consider renting a family video packed with exciting adventure as a compromise. News concerning the prospects of someone close to you could dash your hopes, especially if it is an older person.

27. TUESDAY. Mixed. Others are likely to ask small favors of you. Try not to overload yourself in the effort to please. This is a good day for attending to routine transactions such as paying your monthly bills. You may have to juggle your payments based on your current bank balance. Renting out a spare room could be a good way of earning some extra cash. Conditions are ideal for hosting a highly successful family get-together. All your hard work is likely to be appreciated. Offering your services and talents freely will probably make you feel very good about yourself. You are most likely to benefit from physical exercise that involves water, such as swimming or canoeing. Consider buying a small dog or other pet.

28. WEDNESDAY. Variable. The motto of the day for Taurus people should be to strike while the iron is hot. This is not a day for consolidating your plans or performing routine tasks. Conditions favor clinching deals and cultivating new contacts. Leave your answer machine or pager on if you are going to spend time away from your telephone. Guard against any tendency toward self-effacement, especially when dealing with those in authority. Any responsibility that is foisted upon you is likely to appear a little daunting at first. Keep a sense of perspective by reminding yourself of your own worth. There is likely to be a golden opportunity to make a financial killing. The trick is to recognize the opportunity the moment it arises.

29. THURSDAY. Frustrating. Because you have plenty of energy there is a possibility that you might overdo. Do not tackle everything at once. Take extra care of anything that has been loaned to you; there is a risk of loss or damage. Although quite determined to have your way, consider switching your strategy if you are trying to win over others to your way of thinking. Guard against any tendency to ride roughshod over other people's feelings. The urge to freely express yourself is strong. Make a point of choosing your words carefully, whether they are written or spoken. Otherwise you may have to explain yourself at a later time. You are likely to do better in a leadership position; being just another teammate will probably leave you feeling thwarted or frustrated.

30. FRIDAY. Changeable. Nothing has been cast in stone. Enjoy what life brings you rather than trying to plan every detail in advance. What comes to light today will probably provide a clue for your future strategy. Look for clues to figure out who is really in charge. Take steps to cultivate your relationships with those who are in the know. You can afford to take a calculated risk. Consider modifying any behavior patterns you know are not helpful. Teaming up with a more experienced person will probably help you hone your own skills. If you are recruiting a new employee, check out their credentials thoroughly before hiring them. This is a good day for going through your wardrobe. Get rid of out of date clothes or those that no longer fit and treat yourself to a new outfit.

MAY

1. SATURDAY. Stressful. Your weekend plans are likely to be disrupted because of a sudden demand at work. This is apt to cause conflict between you and your partner. Try to think of an inventive solution to clear the air. Alternatively, your partner might not be where you had planned to meet due to being called away at short notice rather than any thoughtlessness on their part. Conditions change during the day. You will probably find yourself in an introspective frame of mind. An article about those less fortunate than you is likely to stir sympathetic feelings. Write a letter to your local representative or other influential person expressing your views about what should be done.

2. SUNDAY. Mixed. Your reflective mood is continuing; conditions are ideal for pondering and planning. Focus on all things fantastic, such as the paranormal or the occult. If you are attached, or have family, your desire to withdraw from everyday concerns could cause friction and disappointment. Conflicting rumors will probably reach your ears. The best policy is to stay cool; there appears to be little point in trying to push for more information just yet. Signs are that all will become clear soon enough. Allow for the possibility that someone is trying to use you as a scapegoat in an attempt to cover up their own mistakes. Guard against blowing your top when defending your actions. Playing the role of peacemaker is unlikely to get much thanks. You may have to back down in the face of an older relative's unreasonableness.

3. MONDAY. Routine. This is a subdued start to the workweek. The events of the weekend probably remain at the front of your mind. Those of you who are in business would be wise to guard against any continuing tendency to introspection. You could miss an important financial opportunity. If you are moving, this is an ideal time for agreeing on mortgage terms. However, beware a tendency to be overoptimistic. Consider reviewing your calculations to make sure you can afford the initial outlay. If you are buying for the first time, there might be ways to get help with attorney fees or with the down payments. An exciting job offer is indicated, probably prompting you to consider a career move. Signs are good for considering entering the caring professions, such as nursing, social work, or even coaching.

4. TUESDAY. Variable. Read through the small print when making any financial commitment. Chances are you have overlooked something or have misunderstood what is being proposed. Likewise, details of any new business propositions should be checked out. You still need some privacy; other people's company and their demands could leave you feeling disgruntled. Taurus people in a leadership position have to tread warily with subordinates. One-to-one is likely to be more productive than group effort. Consider putting off buying an expensive or luxury item; otherwise you could run short of cash before next payday. Taurus students are likely to be fired up by a substitute teacher or visiting speaker. Consider finding somewhere quiet to work as a way of avoiding interruptions.

5. WEDNESDAY. Useful. Someone at a distance needs your expertise. This is likely to leave you feeling very positive about yourself. You have plenty of patience and energy in reserve and are likely to take any difficulties you encounter in your stride. Stick to the tried and tested methods that you know work best for you, especially in your dealings with people in far-off places. Responsibility could be weighing a little more heavily than usual, but you are more than able to cope. Allow for any tendency to hold back and wait for the right moment. People are looking to you for guidance and action now. Consider running for an elected office, even though you believe your chances of winning may be remote. The experience alone should make the campaign worthwhile.

6. THURSDAY. Disconcerting. Check your travel documents if you are taking a trip abroad. There is a chance you have overlooked an important item. A little knowledge can be dangerous. Review any new information, especially if you get it by fax or telephone. Conditions provide plenty of chances for you to shine, but be low-key about your confidence in your own abilities. Otherwise there is a chance you could appear overbearing or bombastic. A heavy workload is indicated, but your bullish mood and optimism should get you through. If you are entertaining this evening, an informal occasion should be more fun for you as well as your guests.

7. FRIDAY. Demanding. If you are feeling a little washed out after the strenuous efforts of recent days, this is apt to be mental rather than physical tiredness. A good workout in the gym or a leisurely swim should help restore the balance. Guard against overstretching yourself; you risk tearing a ligament or sustaining a sprain. Your boss could have some disappointing news which leaves you feeling let down. This is not a good time to discuss the matter; it is only likely to lead to confusion and further delay. You may have to stay sober while those around you make merry. No one is likely to think the less of you if you decide to leave a party early. Someone's remarks about your appearance might shock and surprise you.

8. SATURDAY. Tricky. Although this is usually a day for routine activities such as shopping or catching up on household chores, conditions appear very unstable. As a consequence, the day will probably not be smooth. It seems that there are not enough hours in the day. Relations with those close to you are intense. What you say or do could bring about a deeper understanding of your hidden motivations. What comes to light could well be a shock, but probably beneficial in the end. This is a good day for bargain hunting. You will probably have to scour the shops a little longer, but it will be worth it. Conditions are good for starting a new home improvement project; both your stamina and your wallet will be better for it.

9. SUNDAY. Excellent. This promises to be a much more harmonious day. You can afford to relax and enjoy it. You should have plenty of physical energy; a game of ball could be a great tonic. If you are in the mood for romance, let your feelings show. Tell your loved one how much you appreciate the little things that are done for you. Springtime is best for lovers. A day trip together could turn into a memorable interlude. Leisure pursuits are indicated, such as reading for entertainment or visiting a local exhibition. Surrounding yourself with beautiful things can give you a special glow.

10. MONDAY. Cautious. News you get from a friend or co-worker will probably make you realize that you have been deliberately ignored or even misinformed. You would be wise to check out the facts with a trusted ally before you make your move. If you think it is necessary, do not hesitate to get an expert second opinion on any financial transactions, especially if you feel a little out of your depth. If you have been putting off creating a workable budget, now is a good time to tackle it. Consider spending some time discussing joint finances with your opposite number. You will probably be able to spot some areas where you can economize, perhaps even save a little. Books on self-improvement or career advancement are likely to prove fascinating reading.

11. TUESDAY. Disquieting. A garbled message will probably leave you feeling a little disgruntled. You may be finding it a little difficult to remain objective about a matter close to your heart. You could be accused of clouding the issue as a result. The best policy is to take a back seat; you will have a chance to say your piece at a later time. A situation at work needs to be smoothed over. You risk making matters worse if you jump to the wrong conclusion. Taurus people who are embarking on a new romance could be in for a disappointment. Your date may cancel at the last moment. An intriguing advertisement appears to be so much hype with no substance; you would be wise not to make a purchase on the strength of it.

12. WEDNESDAY. Fair. Conditions are ideal for telling your loved one just how you feel. Consider writing a long love letter. Conditions are also good for indulging yourself. Consider a visit to the health club for a massage or opt for a manicure and pedicure. You may find an unusual piece of jewelry that people will notice. Your partner could be feeling a little suffocated. Taurus people are caring and sensitive; this is a good time to encourage your partner to air their feelings. You may be feeling a little anxious. An intriguing new leisure pursuit could turn into a grand passion, especially if it is connected with the past in some way, such as local history or family genealogy.

13. THURSDAY. Unsettling. This is a good day for catching up on neglected or overdue tasks. A recent decision may have to be rescinded or modified. You would be wise to tread carefully with family members, especially an older relative; they are apt to think they know better than you, no matter what your age. Any high aspirations you are holding are likely to be dashed in the cold light of day. But this is a good day for using your creative talents to the fullest. If you are trying to dream up some new ideas, consider doodling on paper instead of using technology. You can rely on your own imagination to come up with some good inspiration. Allow for the possibility of a falling out with someone whose views are diametrically opposed to yours. Guard against digging your heels in; neither of you are likely to back down.

14. FRIDAY. Manageable. Do not listen to rumor or gossip, even if it casts you in a good light. You would be wise to wait for official confirmation before moving forward. Take quick advantage of any new opportunities coming your way. Your track record will stand you in good stead with your superiors. It would do no harm to remind them what you can do and what you hope to do in the future. Taurus people are well known for sound common sense and a pragmatic approach. A meeting is unlikely to be very productive but should pave the way for future good relations. If you are traveling, a different route than normal could save you time and aggravation.

15. SATURDAY. Sensitive. Do not be too disconcerted if it seems that a chapter in your life is closing. Recent events have been leading up to this turning point. A bolt from the blue concerning work matters may force you to reevaluate your personal ambitions; give yourself all the time you need before burning your bridges. You should look to the future rather than dwelling on the past. Consider taking on a job no one else seems to want; it could turn out to be a showcase for your special talents. An old colleague may be put in a position of authority over you. The best policy is to establish the relationship on a new footing rather than continuing as if nothing had changed. Any new starts are likely to be thwarted.

16. SUNDAY. Satisfactory. Conditions favor reviewing your personal spending habits. There is a possibility you are losing track of current expenditure. You will probably find you have overextended yourself. If you are having difficulty repaying a loan, seek professional advice sooner rather than later. Burning the candle at both ends may begin to catch up with you now. Taurus people often need to take things at a slow pace. Sleeping late or taking an afternoon nap might be just what the doctor ordered. A misunderstanding with a family member can be cleared up in a surprising and amusing way. Later, you may be inspired to pursue an intellectual activity, especially if it is concerned with technology or other scientific endeavor. Go out of your way to praise a family member for recent achievement.

17. MONDAY. Demanding. Guard against boasting or exaggerating your achievements. Good results often speak for themselves. Work may be coming in faster than you can cope with it. An enthusiastic co-worker or junior staff member may be only too willing to be of assistance; consider giving them the chance. Resist the urge to work late. Concentrate on priority work; the rest can wait until later in the week. If you are romantically involved, your loved one may be keen to put the relationship on a more permanent footing. Taurus people are unlikely to be easily pushed into a decision, but you will probably feel reassured and flattered by their interest. Electronic equipment is likely to malfunction, forcing you to redo a job.

18. TUESDAY. Profitable. Conditions favor any business that is combined with short journeys. Taurus salespeople are likely to have an especially constructive day. If you do not work in a paying position, consider lending a hand in the local community. Socializing is favored. Mixing business and pleasure should result in a rewarding day. A shopping trip for something special will probably be successful, but you are likely to have to shop a little longer than you anticipate. If you live alone, this is a good time for visiting neighbors or inviting friends or family members for dinner. Work requiring close negotiation will probably run very smoothly; a highly satisfactory outcome is indicated.

19. WEDNESDAY. Disquieting. A colleague who is a thorn in your side is likely to be particularly prickly today. You would be wise to avoid a confrontation at all costs. This is not a time when you can afford to make enemies. Support from an unexpected quarter is likely to prove invaluable. You may encounter difficulties while finishing outstanding tasks. The information you have could be incorrect. Using some of that steady persistence Taurus people are famous for will probably help you finish in good time. You are likely to cross swords with an aggressive official. There is little point in being drawn into a public scene, especially if it is over a minor matter. Allow for the possibility of extended routine travel time, especially if you have to rely on public transportation.

20. THURSDAY. Misleading. Nothing is certain. Change appears to be happening all around, but you are unlikely to notice until it begins to impact on you directly. A flexible approach is more likely to get you ahead; making elaborate plans is a waste of time and inappropriate. Taking steps to protect what you own would be a wise move. Be sure your home insurance coverage is adequate. This is a good time for safeguarding personal possessions that you want to pass on to the next generation. The closing stages of a project appear problematic, but do not throw in the towel. It seems that others are envious of your achievements and want to do all they can to frustrate you. Keeping a level head while ignoring gossip will probably help you win the day and enhance your reputation.

21. FRIDAY. Changeable. You should bide your time until the right opportunity presents itself. The best policy is to stick to approved guidelines; any departure from established procedure could backfire on you. There is a possibility of a domestic crisis unexpectedly developing. Turning to someone you would not normally think of will probably help you resolve the difficulty. Taurus people are often described as the strong, silent type, but the indications are that you should try to open up as much as possible with those close to you. Otherwise there is a possibility that they may misconstrue your quietness as a sign of discontent. If you are thinking of following an exercise regime, consider how much of it can be done at home. Any equipment you need can probably be easily obtained secondhand at a significant saving.

22. SATURDAY. Challenging. It is said that a fool and his money are soon parted. Although this would not normally apply to cautious Taurus types, indications are that you need to take more care than usual when spending money. There is a possibility of making an expensive purchase you later regret. Neither do conditions favor signing loans; such a commitment could drain your resources more quickly than you thought. However, this is a good day for working hard at play. Consider splurging out on some entertainment that will bring out the child in you, such as a trip to the zoo or an afternoon at a fair. If you are around children today, a fine balance needs to be struck between indulging their whims and restricting their demands so that you do not go broke.

23. SUNDAY. Pleasant. The emphasis continues to be on leisure activities. This looks like a fine day for going out and having lots of fun. Taurus people appreciate the good things in life. Conditions are right for spoiling both yourself and your loved ones. A day trip will probably prove to be more expensive than you anticipate, but worth it. Children especially are likely to be delighted. Your energy level may not be enough to join in their games, but you should be content to be an enthusiastic spectator. Unattached Taurus people can look forward to an especially romantic interlude. Whether unattached or not, consider a candlelit dinner at a favorite restaurant this evening as a prelude to an exciting night.

24. MONDAY. Good. Your energy level should be high enough to achieve some of your wildest dreams. For Taurus people who are in business, this is coupled with an uncanny sense for the right deal. You may sign a very lucrative contract before the day is out. Your creative intellect is stimulated; consider trying your hand at writing or composing music. A visit to a place of culture such as the opera or a famous museum is favored. Working Taurus people may well be involved in a decision-making process that requires team consensus. Allow for the possibility that some of your teammates have their own agenda. As a Taurus you are a hearty eater, but you could wind up with indigestion if you overdo food and drink even at your regular mealtimes. Stick with fruit and vegetables and nonalcoholic drinks.

25. TUESDAY. Fortunate. A combination of good luck and sound business sense ensure that you build on yesterday's successes. Taurus people who have been pounding the sidewalk looking for work will probably get a breakthrough today. The job is apt to have excellent promotion prospects and a good financial package. Consider giving all your dealings the personal touch. If the company you work for is thinking of improving its image, your contributions could result in a substantial prize or bonus payment. If you have time on your hands, update your resume. Even if you are not actively seeking new employment, there is no harm in testing the current market to see what you are worth. This is an auspicious day for launching a new friendship or romance with someone from out of town.

26. WEDNESDAY. Unsettling. After the heady events of the past few days, it probably seemed as if there were no limit to what you could do. Today's conditions, however, indicate that the bubble is about to burst. A row with a co-worker or subordinate may bring you back to earth with an unpleasant bump. Guard against taking any setbacks out on those around you. You may be suffering the consequences of any overindulgence in food or drink; getting on the scales this morning will probably leave you a little unhappy with your weight. Taurus people often have a sweet tooth. Cutting out desserts and snacks is usually enough to eliminate any excess pounds. If you are thinking of going on a strict diet, consult your doctor first. There is a possibility that such a regime could do more harm than good in the long run.

27. THURSDAY. Frustrating. Making friends and influencing people will not come easily to you today. Indications are that you are being a little too heavy-handed. Consider lightening your touch with some diplomacy; it can be a far more effective weapon than trying to bulldoze your way through. A garbled message may mean you are unable to make contact with those who matter. A dispute with an older person is likely. Common sense will probably prevail if you take one step at a time. You might have to back down gracefully; otherwise you risk having your opponents dig in their heels completely. You will probably have to rearrange your schedule if a housebound person depends on you. You would be wise to keep any new ideas to yourself for a while longer. Although they appear sound, others are likely to be skeptical.

28. FRIDAY. Demanding. Dealing with others should be easier today, but allow for their eccentricities. A conversation with someone in authority is apt to begin smoothly enough. Then a chance remark from them could throw a spanner in the works. Keep alert in order to keep up with what they have to say. Property deals are unlikely to be as good as they look on paper. You will have to use that stubborn Taurus streak if you want to resist a hard-sell technique. You have the right to insist on taking time to think things over before signing on the dotted line. Any financial papers you receive should be carefully filed away to avoid loss or damage.

29. SATURDAY. Inactive. You may be feeling a little frayed around the edges. You can afford to put your feet up now and be lazy for a while. You probably need some time alone to mull over the week's events; conditions are favorable for this. Even if Saturday is just another busy day for you, allow yourself some quiet moments to let your thoughts and feelings come to the surface. A heart-to-heart talk with your loved one is indicated. This does not have to be a heavy scene; making time and space for each other can keep a relationship special. You may receive a surprise gift from your partner for no other reason than that they want to show their affection for you. A cozy dinner for two followed by a visit to the theater or movies is favored.

30. SUNDAY. Variable. The results of what you began a couple of weeks ago will probably start to bear fruit. This is a good time to review your position and make necessary adjustments before moving forward. You would be wise not to plan too far ahead; the signs are that more will come to light. Conditions favor thinking about your future security and that of your family. Consider taking out a life insurance policy if you do not already have one. However, be careful to choose the right deal; if you keep shopping around, you will probably find the one you want. You may receive some surprising news about a new addition to the family or the news of a pending move. You should keep strenuous exercise to a minimum. There is a possibility of pulling a muscle or straining your back.

31. MONDAY. Mixed. Financial security continues to be high-lighted. A few telephone calls to various insurance companies should get the result you want. If you are looking for ways to make money, avoid falling victim to a scam or confidence trick. Indications are that you will lose out on any investments if you do not do your homework first. Others are likely to find unattached Taurus people especially attractive; you seem to be exuding appeal to the opposite sex. If someone makes their intentions known, consider taking the plunge even if it looks as if it is only going to be a fling. Your apparent eagerness to resolve a long-standing problem is likely to tempt you into making a bold move. A good idea out of the blue could be the answer to your prayer.

JUNE

1. TUESDAY. Calm. Thinking can be the best way to travel. Let your thoughts run free today. You are likely to have lots of fun dreaming up some new schemes. Double-check your hotel booking if planning a trip which involves an overnight stay. Someone may make a surprise announcement that they are moving away or changing jobs. This is a good day for legal matters; the best policy is to spend some time gathering and organizing your information. If you are involved in any overseas deal, there is no reason for becoming concerned over an apparent lack of progress. A trip to a distant friend or relative can be an enjoyable interlude for the weekend; plan ahead.

2. WEDNESDAY. Successful. Today's conditions give you opportunities to turn yesterday's ideas into reality. Your only dilemma appears to be which ideas you should keep and which you should discard. Bringing your experience together with your sound Taurus pragmatism should benefit you. If you are preparing for higher education, a knowledgeable person is likely to be able to advise you on your future career, indicating which subjects you need to study. This is a good day for delving into the lessons of the past. If you are in research, help is likely to come from abroad. If you are traveling you may have to deal with touchy officials. You would be wise to abide by local customs so that you are less likely to cause offense as an unwelcome visitor.

3. THURSDAY. Disconcerting. Contacting people at a distance can be difficult. You might get cut off during a telephone call, or you might not be able to make a connection at all. Avoid any depressing or negative entertainment. Indications are that you may feel a little lethargic or dragged down. Starting the day with light exercise can get the adrenaline flowing. If you are away from your loved one, there is a possibility that you are in for a slight disappointment; a letter might not arrive as you had expected. Because an interfering in-law is determined to have their say, there seems to be little point in avoiding a confrontation despite your attempts to do so. Give yourself a treat this evening by visiting your favorite ethnic restaurant with your mate or a date.

4. FRIDAY. Manageable. Things are beginning to open up for you once more. Your thoughts are likely to turn toward your personal aspirations. What you hear via the grapevine will probably help further your cause. Do not assume someone else will automatically take over if you decide to let go of the reins a little. If a problem has been needling you, it is unlikely to get any worse if you do not think about it until after the weekend. A surprise opening should help you see your way clear; after that you should be able to move forward with confidence. There is a possibility that someone is trying to snoop into your affairs. By varying your routine you should be able to keep them guessing. An off-the-cuff remark might be taken the wrong way, forcing you to apologize.

5. SATURDAY. Satisfactory. Career matters are moving forward in the fast track. Your superior organizational skills are likely to get noticed; you might be being groomed for a managerial position. If you do not normally work on the weekend, any willingness to do so is likely to reap more rewards than just overtime pay. Make the most of today's opportunities; you do not need permission to modify your schedule. You seem to have ample energy to cope with all that the world throws at you. But guard against a tendency to overextend yourself; you could wind up feeling a little frayed around the edges. Consider learning a practical skill; you will probably take to it like a duck to water, and there is even a chance of turning it into a money-making sideline.

6. SUNDAY. Mixed. A visit to a friend's house could turn a little sour. If you want to continue this friendship, avoid raking up the past or airing any grievances. Tread carefully around those close to you; giving orders rather than making requests will probably only result in them resisting you. Guard against crossing the fine line between close friendship and intimacy; indications are that it will cost you the friendship in the long run. You may have to get the support of like-minded people if you want action from your local representative. This is a good time to lay down a plan of attack; group action has its own special power. Conforming to a group's ideals is indicated, but do not be afraid to voice your own views in a low-key way.

7. MONDAY. Exciting. Neither be a lender nor a borrower is the motto to remember today, especially if requests involve friends. If they ask for something from you, a refusal now might offend for a short time but is unlikely to cause permanent damage. If you are out and about in a group, you may get more than your fair share of a bill. Work will probably be slowed down because of the absence of a co-worker. Someone is telling you only what they want you to hear; you would be wise to get all the information you can before making your next move. Otherwise there is a risk of your plans coming unstuck. Seek the help of an expert if you are dealing with a tricky problem affecting your long-term future.

8. TUESDAY. Rewarding. You would probably prefer to stay home today. Likely delays on public transportation only serve to increase that feeling; leave travel until later in the day if you can. Taurus people are often most comfortable in familiar surroundings. This is an excellent day for puttering around the house or doing minor improvements to the home. If you are thinking of redecorating, conditions are just right for dreaming up a new color scheme. Take some time out to review your own situation. Look at current progress to see if you are still on track with your long-term goals. A little imagination can go a long way. Consider searching for a better way of tackling your daily routine. Aim for a practical solution; good results do not always require perfection.

9. WEDNESDAY. Variable. A last-minute hitch to a project nearing completion might stress you. You need to act quickly and decisively to restore the situation. Although you may be feeling a little unsure, the signs are that you can move your plan forward with confidence. You would be wise to pace yourself carefully; otherwise there is a risk of running out of time. A spirit of co-operation and trust is indicated. Constantly checking up on others to see if they are doing what you want is likely to produce negative results. You may have to question an official over a point of procedure. If they are adamant, let the matter drop before you blow a gasket. You are closer to a goal than you realize; continuing to plug on should ensure that you achieve your ambition in due time.

10. THURSDAY. Happy. Finish up mundane chores as early as possible; soon the emphasis will switch to more immediate concerns. Indications are that you should not take life too seriously. Conditions are just right for those of you who are in a flirtatious mood. Someone who operates close to your own base appears only too happy to play along. Treat it as the lighthearted interlude it seems to be. A new outfit will probably catch your eye and may be just the thing to catch the eye of others, too. If you are working, you may hear of an office love affair, probably involving your boss or another higher-up. Try writing a love letter, especially if you want to enliven an existing relationship.

11. FRIDAY. Challenging. Conditions have abruptly changed to a more subdued note. You will probably have to shoulder the responsibility for someone who is absent. If you are in business, a new project may be starting off too slowly for your comfort.

Allow for the possibility that you have underestimated the work-load. You could be biting off a little more than you can chew. A quick review of the schedule combined with the experience of problems encountered so far should help you come up with a more realistic deadline. It's a good time to start a diet or exercise regime. However, keep in mind that there is no shortcut to getting back into shape.

12. SATURDAY. Fair. A shopping trip is likely to be enjoyable. Using your imagination could help your finances stretch that much further. If you do not have much cash to spare, scour local flea markets for bargains. If you are entertaining this evening, buy food that is available in abundance; fresh produce which is in sea-son is often best. Another look at your monthly budget will prob-ably reveal that there are more effective ways of paying certain bills. Paying by direct debit each month instead of a lump sum each quarter can help spread the load. If you need money, a visit to your bank or other reputable loan company is indicated; avoid any dealings with loan sharks. Also avoid borrowing on your credit card at high interest.

13. SUNDAY. Useful. Although this is usually a day of rest, you may have a lot of practical concerns to attend to. This is an ex-cellent time to go through your personal accounts. You have some opportunities to make necessary economies. It is unlikely that money-conscious Taurus do not keep some kind of accounting system. If not, now is the ideal time to start one. Your energy level is high. Proceed with any odd jobs or routine home main-tenance tasks. Lethargy is not part of your vocabulary, but guard against exhausting yourself. Later, catch up on your correspon-dence. A long letter to a close relative may be way overdue to let them know all that you have been doing.

14. MONDAY. Fortunate. Higher-ups may want to make use of your talents. Indications are that you should give your time freely. Dealing with others who are less experienced than you can be gratifying; it does no harm to remind yourself from time to time how much you do know. You appear to be in a generous mood. Look for opportunities where you can be of use or assistance. Consider making a donation to your favorite charity, or give money to someone less fortunate than yourself. At home, you are apt to be in a very romantic mood. Expressing your deeper feel-ings for your loved one will probably come very easily. If you are single, chances are that you will embark on an intense love affair, probably with someone who is already a familiar face.

15. TUESDAY. Enjoyable. This is a good day for visiting people who live close. Consider going on foot rather than using the car or public transportation. Traffic is likely to be particularly heavy. If you are a parent, this is a good time to think about your children's long-term education. Look into all the options available. Gather as much information as possible. It might be a good idea to check your calendar for important dates; there is a chance you have overlooked someone's birthday or anniversary. This is a particularly productive day for Taurus people in sales. However, there is a chance orders are delayed because of a communication problem; get back to base before the close of the day to sort it out. New contacts are a valuable source of information.

16. WEDNESDAY. Demanding. The first part of the day is likely to be taken up with getting out and about or visiting people who live nearby. But your excursions may be stressful. Allow for the possibility of a vehicle breakdown. If you own a car, you would be wise to take along the telephone number of your car service. Confirming any loose arrangements before you travel probably means you will not have a wasted journey. In the afternoon, the emphasis switches to domestic matters. Stay at home if you can. If you are looking for somewhere to live, guard against being dazzled by the apparent charm of an old house; it could well become a liability. There is a risk of a family disagreement that stalls your plans.

17. THURSDAY. Changeable. You may find it hard to overcome any sense of lethargy or inertia. You want to let everyone else do the running around; others are likely to accuse you of being lazy. Domestic concerns are restrictive. You will probably have to pay a duty visit to an older relative. Taurus people often have a kind and sympathetic nature; a good visit will lift both their spirits and yours. Taurus singles will probably be flattered by someone's obvious interest, probably someone met through family connections. Conditions are excellent for real estate negotiations. However, guard against becoming a little complacent; otherwise, you could be in for a rude awakening.

18. FRIDAY. Buoyant. You should be bouncing back from yesterday's laidback mood. You seem to be full of energy and ready to tackle anything. This is a good day for doing heavy cleaning. Your energy coupled with that determination Taurus people are famous for will probably get you through your tasks in double-quick time. If you work, you might have to deal with an aggressive associate. Surprise them by giving as good as you get. Allow for the possibility of a minor accident in the home. Do not leave a hot pan unattended; make sure new electrical appliances are properly grounded. Consider buying something beautiful for the home, but only if your budget can stretch to include paying for it in cash.

19. SATURDAY. Unsettling. Children are apt to be boisterous and difficult to control. Take the opportunity to let go of adult concerns by entering into the spirit of children's games rather than getting worked up over their behavior. Otherwise you risk a sharp exchange of words you may have cause to regret. Use that Taurus capacity for holding your peace. Consider taking your frustrations out by playing a sport. Guard against making a tasteless joke at someone else's expense. Feelings are running high. A new romance may be coming to an early end. Remembering the good times is often much better than bitter recriminations. Resist the temptation to throw good money after bad in an attempt to recoup any recent financial loss. Budget strictly for the week ahead.

20. SUNDAY. Rewarding. Consider any opportunity to work as part of a group. Your special talents will be put to full use; you will probably quickly find a niche that no one else can fill. The grapevine is likely to produce some interesting news, especially involving a concern close to your heart. If you are romantically involved, your loved one may need time to sort out their feelings before making a commitment. Let events run their natural course rather than trying to push them too soon. If you have children, allow some extra time to take an interest in what they are doing. They may be looking to you for specific advice and help. Joining forces with a relative could result in a productive new partnership.

21. MONDAY. Easygoing. Routine chores should run like clockwork. You will probably have some time to spare as a result. Consider putting some extra work into a project; that way you are more likely to meet an important deadline. Taurus people are not known for an inability to keep secrets, but resist any urge to blurt out confidential information. You may not have all the facts. Health matters are highlighted. Minor aches and pains could be evidence that you are run-down or stressed. Look into alternative healing remedies or changing your diet. However, consult your doctor first. If you own a pet, a routine visit to the vet may be overdue.

22. TUESDAY. Sensitive. Any work you finish around the home is likely to be a job well done. If you are in the mood for socializing, indications are that you will prefer the company of serious-minded people. Invite some people connected with work to your home. Your creative intellect is likely to be stimulated, especially if you are brainstorming ideas for a new project. A bad eating habit may be the cause of a recurrent but minor health problem. By abstaining from a particular kind of food your system should be able to purge itself of any impurities. Business dealings require a combination of keen negotiating skills and sustained work if they are to be successful in the long run.

23. WEDNESDAY. Exciting. Conditions are changing rapidly. Act swiftly on the advice of someone in the know. Deals should be clinched early in the day. What was within your grasp in the morning may elude you in the afternoon. Later, the emphasis switches to relationships. If you are feeling unsettled, discuss your problem with someone close; they appear to be in a good position to advise you. If you are in business, you may want to force radical change, but you would be wise to get the full support of your associates before making your next move. If you have been neglecting your loved one because of other concerns, pull out all the stops and treat them to a night to remember.

24. THURSDAY. Frustrating. At some point during the day most normally easygoing Taurus people may wish they had not bothered to get out of bed. Very little is likely to go your way. Practically everywhere you turn you may encounter difficulty and problems. You need every ounce of that capacity to endure for which Taurus people are famous. Although the outlook may appear bleak, indications are that it will be very short-lived. You can put it down to being just one of those days. Avoid confrontation of any kind, even at home; you are unlikely to gain anything by it. Later, treat yourself to a long hot bath and an early night to dispel the gloomy mood.

25. FRIDAY. Satisfactory. Now that yesterday's difficult conditions have passed, you can more than make up for the lack of progress. Communicating with your opposite number, especially business partners, is starred as a means of resolving outstanding problems. Keeping an open mind is likely to ensure a satisfactory outcome. Consider looking up an old associate. What they have to say could help you in your present situation. There is a chance you will be asked to make a trip at short notice; an overnight stay should not be necessary. Indications are that you will deal with the matter quickly. This is a good day for taking tests or examinations, especially to get a needed license.

26. SATURDAY. Misleading. This is likely to be a taxing day. You will probably be obliged to put on a confident exterior, even though you might be feeling a little unsure of yourself. Your efforts are apt to pay off; others are unlikely to see through your mask. Your good ideas will be welcome even though you do not seem to believe in them yourself. Recent events in your personal life may have left you and your loved one feeling emotionally drained. A long walk could be a wonderful tonic for you both and would also provide a good opportunity to talk in depth together. Give yourselves a break for the day. If you keep a journal, record your innermost thoughts but be sure it is for your eyes only.

27. SUNDAY. Pleasant. This is a good day for bargain hunting. You can be confident that all offers are genuine. Try to track down a secondhand household item that is in surprisingly good condition. A difference of opinion between two people who are close to you is likely to flare up. You will probably be successful in the role of peacemaker; you can then be instrumental in bringing them back together again. If you are out and about, an unexpected but exciting invitation may make you linger. Keeping those close to you informed of your whereabouts can allay their concerns. If you are a member of a political party, you will probably be asked to dig deep for a contribution. Consider increasing insurance on valuable family possessions, especially heirlooms.

28. MONDAY. Variable. You will probably have to do more than your fair share of household chores. Fortunately you have plenty of energy. Coupling this with a methodical approach will probably get you through in short order. Taurus students may find it especially difficult to concentrate. Take copious notes; in this way you can go over them in your own time and your own pace. A question may be raised over a clause in a legal document. Keeping careful notes of what is said and by whom will probably work to your advantage. Avoid someone who brings out the worst in you. Taurus people are often masters of stonewalling others; this tactic is better than letting yourself become provoked and angry.

29. TUESDAY. Productive. This is a good day for catching up with administrative chores left over from last week. Payment for a holiday might leave a hole in your pocket, but indications are that it is money well spent. This is an especially favored time if you work in the media or in publishing. Imaginative ideas combine well with a capacity for keeping your feet firmly on the ground. If you are involved in any long-term litigation, some good news is likely. If you are job hunting, consider an offer that includes occasional trips abroad. Although Taurus people often prefer to stay close to home, indications are that an overseas experience will be valuable. A visitor due in town today is likely to meet with some delay.

30. WEDNESDAY. Demanding. You are likely to feel the sting of any legal moves made yesterday. It looks as if you have put your opponent on the offensive. Try your best to make this a case of irresistible force meeting immovable object. Taurus people are known for standing firm, no matter what the opposition does or says. Guard against a tendency of becoming oversentimental. If you are attached, your partner is likely to complain of being hemmed in by you. Or you may become outraged at the sight of someone getting the runaround. Avoid overindulging in food or alcohol. There is a risk that what you say or do while under the influence may give you cause for embarrassment, even regret, at a later time.

JULY

1. THURSDAY. Disquieting. The new month could start with a job interview or promotion prospect. This could be quite a challenge, especially if it is for a position which is much better paid than your current one. If you are asked to name the salary you are seeking, do not sell yourself short; it is important to recognize your own worth. If you know that you are underpaid for what you do, now is a good time to push for a pay raise. Do not allow yourself to be put off with lame excuses. If an increase is not forthcoming, it could be time to start looking elsewhere. You may have to cancel out of a social engagement because of financial restrictions.

2. FRIDAY. Difficult. An ongoing conflict with someone at work may be due to a personality clash. Matters could come to a head today when you cross swords with each other once too often. It may be helpful to ask an objective third party to sit in on your discussions; in this way you stand a better chance of reaching a workable compromise. The Taurus nature tends to be extremely forbearing, but this is a time when you should not let others take advantage of you either in your professional or personal life. Make a stand for yourself even if this creates an unpleasant scene. Clearing the air now can save you from problems in the future.

3. SATURDAY. Fair. If you have had a busy week, start the weekend at a lazy pace. Enjoy a quiet morning at home. Catch up with the less strenuous domestic chores. The shopping mall is likely to be busy. You may decide to put off a shopping trip with a friend until another time. Your social life could be costing you a lot of money at the moment. It can be revealing to work out exactly how much you have been spending on going out. Think of some cheaper alternatives for the next few weeks; keep in mind that you do not have to spend a fortune in order to have a good time. It may be hard to break the ice with a certain guest this evening.

4. SUNDAY. Enjoyable. You are almost sure to be in the mood for company. If you have not made any advance plans, you may find that others are willing to join in on a spontaneous get-together. Take the initiative and call your friends. This holiday is good for entertaining at home, whether just family or a larger group. If there has been some friction between you and a loved one recently, there should be the chance to set the record straight today; do not let stubbornness stop you from making the first move. This is a favorable time for heeding advice from someone older; you could benefit from their experience. Put your trust in someone you know well.

5. MONDAY. Slow. You will probably not be in a particularly communicative mood. You can get the best results by working alone. Other people's suggestions can sound like interference; you may have to remind yourself that they are well intentioned. Your usual routine is unlikely to prevail today. It can be hard to accommodate changes when you had the day mapped out in your own way. Try to meet people's needs without letting your own suffer. Single Taurus people should think twice about reviving a romance from the past; circumstances may already have changed in a way that has not occurred to you.

6. TUESDAY. Changeable. You may still feel the need to keep others at arm's length. If you have some leave due you, this is a good time for taking a day off. Just having some time solely to yourself could be all that is needed to restore your good spirits. If you have no choice but to work, hold on to your earthy sense of humor; there could be more than the usual ups and downs. Someone's sharp remarks or hasty words are probably not designed to hurt; they are more likely to be just thoughtless or blurted out in a moment of stress. It is up to you to keep a sense of perspective and not overreact to what is said or not said.

7. WEDNESDAY. Successful. You should start the day in a positive mood. Problems of the past few days can now be shaken off. You could be very much in the limelight at work. You may even look back on this day later and realize that it was a turning point in your career. Let your confidence shine through if you have to deliver a speech or make a presentation of any kind. Business transactions of all kinds can be finalized. There may be cause for celebration when you conclude a lucrative deal. A promotion could be offered to you without your having sought it; give it serious consideration before announcing your intentions.

8. THURSDAY. Tricky. You may have to take on extra responsibilities in the workplace. Do not shy away from them or make half-hearted efforts. This is a day when your attitude is being noted by those who have power and influence. The Taurus staying power can stand you in good stead. You may not be seeing eye-to-eye with another family member at the moment, but guard against picking a fight. There is a risk of causing greater hurt or offense than you really intend. Diplomacy should be the watchword in all of your dealings. Be prepared to meet others halfway and you can count on them doing the same for you.

9. FRIDAY. Mixed. You may have a tendency to be absent-minded. If you are going out, make a conscious effort to keep track of your personal belongings. There is a greater risk of losing something valuable or even being the victim of a pickpocket. Keep your wits about you. In the workplace do not leave any personal possessions unattended; you could be putting temptation in a thief's way. The working week is apt to end on a high note as far as money is concerned. There is a chance of earning a bonus, maybe through profit sharing. If you want to eat out this evening, choose a restaurant with an excellent reputation for both food and service as well as a relaxed atmosphere.

10. SATURDAY. Cautious. If you go out shopping, make an extra effort not to overspend. It could be wise to pay for everything you buy in cash rather than using a credit card or check. In this way you are more likely to be realistic about costs. Avoid taking out credit in stores unless it is interest-free; even then, keep your borrowing to a manageable amount. High repayments could soon become a millstone around your neck. Guard against making too many demands on a new relationship at this time. If you are too quick to seek a commitment you may end up driving someone away from you because they value their independence.

11. SUNDAY. Rewarding. The earlier part of the day is a good time for putting your home in order. Catch up on domestic chores which were pushed aside last week. This is also a favorable time for making a start on decorating or home improvements of all kinds; you could see some quick results. Later in the day favors looking for a secondhand car or other means of transportation. If your own mechanical knowledge is limited, take along someone who knows what to look for. Their advice could save you from making an expensive mistake. Do not forget to make a promised telephone call; someone is relying on you more than you realize during a stressful time for them.

12. MONDAY. Rewarding. This is a productive start to the working week. It can be easier to settle down to written work of all kinds. You may be able to strike a lucrative deal. Be quick to commit new ideas to paper; they could form the basis for your next job. The mail could bring a long-awaited letter. This is a good day for dealing with both personal and professional correspondence. In your business dealings try to tie up loose ends over the telephone rather than arranging a face-to-face meeting, especially if your offices are not close.

13. TUESDAY. Sensitive. Short journeys are unlikely to be trouble-free. Bring along some extra cash in case you need to take a taxi when public transportation or your car lets you down. In the workplace you may be snowed under with administrative tasks. Easy solutions to problems appear to be in short supply, making decisions impossible in certain cases; you need more information first. Waiting for someone to get back to you can be frustrating; you may need to pester them. In your personal life, tread carefully. Arguments can easily flare up with very little provocation. Think before you speak and avoid making demands of any kind.

14. WEDNESDAY. Confusing. This is likely to be a tiring day. You may feel as if you have too much on your agenda and not enough assistance. In the workplace make sure that you are not covering for a lazy colleague; they may have to be reminded about pulling their own weight. Do not let a superior delegate more work to you if you are already battling what you have. Point out that there are only so many hours in the working day. Be sure to read the small print of any offical paperwork; it may not be as straightforward as it at first seems. A loved one may be acting out of character, but it is probably best to leave them to their own devices for now.

15. THURSDAY. Easygoing. In the workplace you may be under far less pressure than usual. As a Taurus you normally prefer to work at your own pace rather than being rushed along by others; this is a day when you should be able to do exactly that. The day favors creative work of all kinds. The more you are able to use your artistic skills, the greater your chance of job satisfaction. Working with children could also have some especially rewarding moments. Take a leaf out of a child's book by adopting a more simplistic approach to life. You may realize that you have been taking something or someone too seriously for your own good.

16. FRIDAY. Fair. You can probably achieve the most by sticking to straightforward tasks. Anything which demands too much creative input or originality can be hard to crack; you could end up wasting too much time on it. If you are out shopping, this can be a good time for buying clothes or personal accessories. Taurus parents may come across some bargains in children's clothing or shoes. You may be tempted to back out of a night on the town if you are feeling tired, but it could be worth making the effort; you should get your second wind. Taurus singles may make some progress with a new love interest by playing hard to get.

17. SATURDAY. Enjoyable. This is a pleasant start to the weekend. Sports matches of all kinds are favored, whether you are participating or just going along as a spectator. If you have children, try to plan activities which include them; they could make the occasion more fun. If a youngster close to you has been having difficulties, this is a day when they could be back to their old selves. Be extra lavish with praise and affection. You may be feeling cautious if you are embarking upon a new romance, but there is every chance that you are on safer ground than you think; relax and enjoy yourself without being self-conscious.

18. SUNDAY. Unpredictable. The day might not go strictly according to plan. Someone may spring a surprise on you or ask you to change your arrangements at short notice. Try to be as flexible as possible. Allow yourself to be talked into something out of the ordinary. If you have a spare room at home, this is a good time for renting it out. Someone may ask about it rather than your having to advertise. The extra cash can make all the difference in struggling to make ends meet each month. It is best to set a time limit rather than making the arrangement open-ended. In this way you have an end in sight if the situation does not work out well.

19. MONDAY. Buoyant. This is an excellent start to the week for Taurus employees. Changes which are instigated in the workplace now are likely to work very much to your advantage. Even though the Taurus nature is often suspicious of innovations, this is a time when it is important not to resist change. In your business dealings do not stick to tried-and-trusted methods just because they seem safe; you can afford to be more adventurous. Your innate common sense will always back up your good Taurus intuition. This can be a lucky day for Taurus people who are house hunting; an offer is likely to be accepted quickly.

20. TUESDAY. Disturbing. Do not expect an easy day on the whole. For married Taurus men and women there is a greater risk of an argument before you or your spouse leaves for work. This can weigh heavily on you during the day, making it difficult to devote yourself fully to work matters. It can be helpful to figure out exactly what issues are involved before you attempt to make up. There may be points which have to be made once and for all. In the workplace there is a greater risk of a clash with someone in authority. You have to be assertive when it comes to discussing a matter which is important to you; do not let it be dismissed as a whim of the moment.

21. WEDNESDAY. Difficult. Your Taurus powers of patience and diplomacy are likely to be put fully to the test. It may seem as if you are unable to get a straight answer to a straight question. Your best policy is to rely on others as little as possible. Keep in mind the saying that if you want something done well, do it yourself. A superior could be on the warpath at work. Stay out of the line as fire as much as possible or you could find yourself in a no-win situation. A misunderstanding with your partner could lead to a full-scale argument later in the day. You may both need time to cool off before you attempt to make up.

22. THURSDAY. Quiet. For Taurus people embarking upon a new romance this can be a four-star day. You may sense that the relationship is starting slowly, but this is a good sign. The chance to build a sure, steady relationship should be welcome. If you are unattached at the moment, an admirer may become known to you; you may wonder how you have managed to miss the signs. In the workplace this is a good day for meetings with partners or other key associates. Face-to-face dealings of all kinds are likely to be useful. For Taurus business people, conditions favor entertaining an important client at lunch or after work.

23. FRIDAY. Variable. There may be good news on the financial front. If you are married this may come through your spouse getting a pay raise or receiving a large bonus. If money has recently been left to you, the details could now be finalized. This is a good time for chasing up an insurance claim or any other money owed to you. Review your long-term financial situation. If your employer does not provide a pension, you may want to start one of your own. An endowment policy can also be an effective way of providing for the future. Shop around for the best deal; quotations could vary considerably. Do not loan or borrow money.

24. SATURDAY. Useful. If you have been worrying over an emotional problem you may not feel that you can discuss it with anyone close to you. Consider seeing a counselor; some objective, professional input could be the key. Or reading a book related to the issue could also set you on the right track. This can be an excellent time for all endeavors aimed at self-improvement. You need to understand how your own mind works before you can figure out what makes someone else tick. Later in the day you can put a new or existing romance on a more intimate footing. Be prepared to let down your barriers and reveal your true emotional self.

25. SUNDAY. Pleasant. You need to spend at least part of the day by yourself, but avoid being a complete hermit. Think twice about turning down a social invitation; it could be just the thing to bring you out of yourself. Your nearest and dearest are likely to be sensitive to your moods. Feeling close to someone and realizing how deeply they understand you can do wonders for your relationship. A past grievance can now be forgiven and forgotten. You are likely to be on the receiving end of other people's generosity. Allow someone to treat you if the offer is clearly sincere; you can always return the gesture on another occasion.

26. MONDAY. Tricky. For Taurus business people this is a time when negotiations with contacts at a distance can be tricky. You might have no choice but to arrange a trip to meet with them in person. Relying on correspondence may prove insufficient in the long run. A relationship with someone from another country or culture can be interesting but demanding. Trying to understand the differences between you might not be as easy as you assume; you both have to make allowances. Communication is the key to successful relationships of all kinds. In your personal life do not expect others to be mind readers; clearly state what you want as well as how you feel.

27. TUESDAY. Deceptive. Make every attempt to sidestep efforts to involve you in politics of any kind. There is a greater risk of innocent words being repeated out of context at a later date. It can be wise to leave other people to resolve their own disputes, no matter how much you would like to offer an opinion or advice. You could end up being accused of taking sides; stay as neutral as possible. Do not believe gossip or rumors; they are unlikely to be based on fact. Guard against making any decisions on the strength of secondhand information, especially concerning your overall personal relationships or your love life.

28. WEDNESDAY. Disquieting. Career issues are in the limelight. Some Taurus business people may have the chance to assume a position of greater power, including the chance to earn more money. If you are competing for a promotion with an associate you need to keep a sense of perspective; guard against being governed purely by your professional ambitions. It can be important to maintain a healthy working relationship regardless of who wins the promotion. Try to avoid putting in overtime this evening. Your absence from home may not go over well with a loved one who already feels unvalued or underappreciated by you.

29. THURSDAY. Unsettling. In the workplace someone new in a position of authority may be instigating changes. This could be a case of a new broom sweeping clean. It may take a while to get used to their way of doing things, especially if it is difficult to understand the advantages of their methods. However, this is a time when it is important to be open to change. Tried-and-trusted methods have their place, but take on new challenges as well if you want to move onward and upward. Consider signing up for a training course or a review class. A job interview may not go as well as you hope; be prepared to chalk it up to experience.

30. FRIDAY. Tedious. This is a slow end to the working week. Be willing to pitch in on teamwork of all kinds. You should be able to improve a working relationship with a colleague even if you have not seen eye-to-eye in the past. For Taurus people who want wider social horizons, this is a favorable time for joining a club or association. Outside interests can put you in touch with new people. Tread carefully if you have your eye on someone special; you need to find out more about them before you make your interest obvious. Steer well clear of someone who is just ending a long-term romance.

31. SATURDAY. Happy. This promises to be an enjoyable start to the weekend. You are apt to be socially in demand. Friends who have not been around for a while may make a point of getting in touch. Set aside work matters wherever possible and concentrate on having some fun. Join forces with a friend who is always a tonic and who shares your earthy sense of humor. Try to find time for a sport or a hobby; some real relaxation is just what you need. For Taurus people who are unattached, this could be an important day. You may realize that what started as a friendship is now developing into a romantic attraction on both sides.

AUGUST

1. SUNDAY. Rewarding. For Taurus people who are politically minded, this can be a good day for taking part in a peaceful demonstration. Be willing to lend your voice to a cause which you feel strongly about. Volunteer work of all kinds can be satisfying; you may also make new friends in the process. This is a favorable time for meeting up with old friends or with relatives you have not seen in a while. Recalling the good old days can be fun. At the same time you may also learn more about your childhood or your ancestors from someone whose memory goes back considerably further than yours. A romance which has been casual or on-and-off can now be put on a firmer footing.

2. MONDAY. Favorable. The working week gets off to a productive start for Taurus people. The day favors confidential meetings of all kinds. Problems can be sorted out privately without the need for any type of mediation. For Taurus people who are self-employed, this is a favorable time for long-term planning. A budget for the next six months could be adjusted to make it more effective. If you are hatching a new scheme, keep it under wraps for the time being, especially if you are trying to stay one step ahead of a competitor. Devote this evening to relaxation, either by yourself or with someone who is easy company.

3. TUESDAY. Confusing. Tread carefully if you have to raise a sensitive issue with someone. You could easily rub them the wrong way if they sense that they are being criticized. Having to sort out other people's errors can be time-consuming as well as annoying. Allow extra time for filling in forms and for written work of all kinds; it could take much longer than you anticipate. Friction on the home front can be difficult to handle. You may not be able to work out just why someone is behaving as they are; ask them to be more direct. Try to avoid making any firm commitments; you may find that you are unable to keep a promise.

4. WEDNESDAY. Disquieting. You may be under pressure to fall in with someone else's plans. Do not go along with these unwillingly; you will only end up nursing resentment. It is up to you not to let others impose upon you. Demonstrate that you have a mind of your own. At work you can afford to have more confidence in your own abilities; you probably know more than you realize. A superior may have more faith in you than you have in yourself. Although someone may approach you with a business proposition, this is unlikely to be a favorable time for instant decisions. Be noncommittal. Give yourself at least the rest of the week to check out the finer details.

5. THURSDAY. Enjoyable. This is a good day to shop for personal items. If you want to update your wardrobe, take along a friend whose taste you admire who can help you make the right choices. Be on the lookout for bargains in jewelry or other accessories. You may stumble across the perfect gift for a friend's birthday or other special occasion. At work the morning is the best part of the day for meetings. You should be able to race through agenda items. If you decide to put something to a vote, you may find that you have almost unanimous support. This evening favors eating out at a restaurant that is cheap and cheerful and serves home-cooked meals.

6. FRIDAY. Variable. Make a point of bringing all your household bills up to date. Consider paying regular expenses with direct withdrawal from your bank; this can save you time and trouble. If you realize that you have overdrawn your account, ask a friend for a temporary loan in order to keep bank charges to a minimum. If you are claiming unemployment or other government benefits there is a greater risk of payment being delayed. It is best not to totally trust the system; make a telephone call to find out what the problem may be. In the supermarket plan your meals around items which are either reduced or on special sale.

7. SATURDAY. Unsettling. Your general expenses are likely to be high at the moment. Avoid spending on the strength of a check which is supposedly in the mail; it may not materialize. If you receive a bonus or a tax rebate, salt away some of it in a savings account to provide yourself with a financial safety net. Some Taurus people may find that a relationship has finally reached a make-or-break stage, forcing a decision between renewed commitments or going for a clean break. Avoid drifting along in the hope that things will sort themselves out; you could only be prolonging the inevitable confrontation. Go out with a group of friends tonight rather than as a twosome.

8. SUNDAY. Pleasant. Even if you normally sleep late on weekends, you may decide to get up earlier today. Treat your partner to breakfast in bed to put them in a good mood for the rest of the day. Make a point of reading the newspaper to catch up with current affairs. A walk or a swim can boost both your mental and physical energy. This is a favorable day for spending some time with a brother, sister, or other relative. Their intimate knowledge of your past can be invaluable when it comes to discussing a personal issue or making an important decision. Enjoy a relaxing pastime later in the day, such as reading or just watching television.

9. MONDAY. Frustrating. If you live with one or more roommates you may be craving greater privacy or order in your life at the moment. Living with other people can have its drawbacks in this respect. If your lifestyle is not really compatible with these people, start looking for a place of your own. If you have just moved into a home with your partner you can expect some initial problems while you adjust to each other's ways. This is apt to be a time of trial and error. However, if something specific annoys you, find a pleasant way of saying so. This evening favors writing letters, making telephone calls, or e-mailing to friends.

10. TUESDAY. Mixed. In the workplace the morning is best for making presentations or sales pitches. Winning the attention of your audience should be easier than you expect. In your business dealings this is a good time for visiting new clients. You are apt to strike up mutual rapport from the word go. Do not worry about being too formal. Others are likely to respond to a more relaxed or even chatty approach; a hard sell could put them off. Pressure is likely to build as the day wears on. Meeting a deadline could be touch-and-go. This evening it is important to put a loved one at the top of your list of priorities, giving your full time and attention.

11. WEDNESDAY. Difficult. Upheavals in your personal life could be affecting you more than you realize at the moment. You may find it harder to concentrate on work matters. Try to take the pressure off yourself. Stick to tasks which will produce quick results. Try to postpone any occasion which would require you to be at your sharpest. A certain individual may seem determined to pick a quarrel with you. If you are on the receiving end of someone's spite, it is wisest not to enter into any conversation at all. Protect your own authority and reputation. An ongoing dispute in a personal relationship needs to be confronted and resolved once and for all.

12. THURSDAY. Fair. Children are likely to cause extra expense. You might have to go without something yourself in order to meet their needs. Try to make the sacrifice willingly. Keep a close watch on youngsters if you are visiting someone's house or are shopping; they are more likely to break or damage an item which you will feel honor bound to pay for. Creative work of all kinds can be satisfying since your imaginative powers are working well. However, you could come up against some stumbling blocks if you are restricted by a tight budget. Make sure that your ideas are practical and not overly expensive.

13. FRIDAY. Easygoing. This promises to be an easy end to the working week. You may be able to successfully conclude some project. Some single Taurus people may be developing a crush on someone at work or in the neighborhood. This can be exciting, but guard against idealizing the person. Keep in mind that if you put someone on a pedestal they are sure to fall off at some point. When you are fun to be with, other people will naturally be drawn to you. You will almost certainly be in the mood for a night out. Round up your friends, or go out with your workmates. Try out a new venue rather than sticking to the same old haunt.

14. SATURDAY. Deceptive. Taurus people who work full time may have had very little personal time recently. A large part of today could easily be taken up with housework and other domestic chores which have piled up during the week. Consider the possibility of employing someone to help out at home. For some Taurus people, this could be a necessity rather than a luxury. Someone who is out of sorts could bring you down with them rather than letting you cheer them up. There may be more to their bad mood than meets the eye, but they may be unwilling to take you into their confidence at this time. Your best policy is to maintain a healthy distance.

15. SUNDAY. Good. Keep household chores to a minimum. This is a day when it is important to make time for your loved ones, especially if you are all very busy during the workweek. If you live with your family, organize an outing which would suit everyone. Someone may be waiting to have an important conversation with you. Trust your good Taurus instincts if asked for advice; you are almost sure to be on the right track. This is a time when you can also benefit from other people's experience if you need guidance. Strive to establish greater intimacy this evening with the most important person in your life.

16. MONDAY. Satisfactory. This is a busy start to the working week. You may be offered the chance to get involved in the start-up of a new project which appeals to you. A colleague who is more experienced than you may be willing to let you pick their brain; you could learn a lot if you are prepared to listen. Be careful, however, not to neglect more routine tasks; putting them off could cause you more work and trouble in the long run. Working from home could be difficult today because it can be harder to find the self-discipline to keep going. Minimize distractions by turning on your answering machine and working in the quietest room with the door shut.

17. TUESDAY. Stressful. You need to be extra tactful when dealing with colleagues or business associates. If there is a matter to be resolved, do not let it seem that you are trying to apportion blame; someone could easily become defensive. Concentrate on how to put the matter right rather than complaining about it going wrong in the first place. If you are positive, others are likely to follow suit. If an error comes to light which is clearly your fault, be quick to assume responsibility. A genuine apology can win you renewed respect. Avoid raising a sensitive issue with your partner unless you have their undivided attention.

18. WEDNESDAY. Disquieting. It can be difficult to get in gear this morning. In your working life you may have to take on more responsibility than usual. Covering for an absent colleague could double your workload. Try to be extra well organized, but at the same time do not push yourself too hard. Consider whether you are doing too much for other people. People may be quick to call on you rather than relying on themselves. A romance may be causing you more trouble than it is worth. If you are feeling weary of constant battling, this could be a good time for taking a break from one another. In this way you will see if your life is better apart or together.

19. THURSDAY. Manageable. If you work on behalf of a charity, this is a propitious time for fund-raising activities. You may find that the general public is more generous than usual. It can also be easier to enlist volunteer help for a special occasion. In the workplace expect others to be especially helpful. Someone who has been extremely busy now has time for you. Taurus singles are more likely to meet new people through work. Someone who asks you out may not appear to be your type, but you have nothing to lose by agreeing to a date; you are apt to be pleasantly surprised. This evening favors a dinner party at home or at a restaurant.

20. FRIDAY. Pleasant. The end of the working week is an excellent time for financial transactions of all kinds. In your business dealings this is a day when someone may finally put their money where their mouth is. A company merger is also favored. If you are in the process of setting up a business of your own, now is the time to finalize your financial backing. Shop around for the best interest rates if you have to take out a loan. If you are house hunting, this is a starred time for arranging a mortgage. This evening favors a small gathering or going out as a twosome. If you are entertaining someone special at home, create an intimate atmosphere with candlelight and soft music.

21. SATURDAY. Fortunate. This weekend is an excellent time for making a fresh start in a relationship. As a Taurus you are known for your stubbornness and a tendency to bear a grudge for too long. However, if you recently quarreled or turned down a reasonable request, now is the time for forgiveness and affirmation. Remind yourself of each person's virtues and strengths rather than dwelling on their shortcomings. If you are out shopping, keep a lookout for bargains in home furnishings. Anything which lends beauty and grace to your home should be worth buying if on sale. Send flowers or champagne as a special thank you for recent hospitality.

22. SUNDAY. Happy. The positive mood of yesterday continues into today. Avoid sitting around indoors. The best fun is to be found in the open air. Head for the beach, the golf course, or the countryside. A change of environment can be therapeutic, especially if you are stuck in the city during the week. This is an excellent day for long-distance traveling by car or by plane. A vacation started today should live up to all your expectations, particularly if you are going abroad. If you have not already taken your summer vacation, scan the advertisements in the travel section of the newspaper; there may be a last-minute bargain.

23. MONDAY. Tricky. This is unlikely to be an easy start to the workweek. If someone is passing the buck in regard to a problem at work, there is a greater risk of it landing on your desk. It is up to you to set the record straight rather than taking blame which is unwarranted. In your business dealings you may come up against someone whose tactics are suspect. It is important not to lower your own ethical standards. Someone who tries to damage your reputation will probably only succeed in hurting their own. If you are involved in a new romance you might have your first argument. Working through the problem can bring you closer together in the long run.

24. TUESDAY. Demanding. If you are unemployed at the moment, intensify your job-hunting efforts today. Read advertisements carefully; there is no point applying for jobs for which you are underqualified or too experienced. Sign up with as many employment agencies as possible; in this way you avoid putting all your eggs in one basket. Someone may delegate work to you without clear instructions. Wait until you are sure of what is required before pushing ahead; you could waste valuable time if you guess wrong. A friend who is not their usual cheerful self may deny having a problem; read between the lines to figure out how you can help.

25. WEDNESDAY. Productive. This should be a successful day in the business world. A deal which is signed and sealed promises to be lucrative both now and for the future. Give yourself a well-deserved pat on the back for personal triumphs which have taken a long time to achieve; you deserve your moment of glory. If you are applying for a promotion or for a higher paid position, give careful thought to your references; they could swing the decision in your favor if the competition is tough. You may be finding it harder than usual to divide your time fairly between work and home. Do not allow yourself to be pulled in all directions; be clear about where your priorities lie.

26. THURSDAY. Stressful. Conditions today are confused. This is likely to be a day when demands put you at full stretch. Queries or problems relating to your work should be handled through proper channels. If you belong to a union, your representative could sort out a matter for you in a short time. Removing obstacles can give you the chance to plan ahead with more energy and optimism. You need to keep your wits about you in business negotiations of all kinds. A certain individual is just waiting for the chance to put one over on you. A friendship could come under strain if you are too demanding; consider whether you are expecting too much.

27. FRIDAY. Fair. This is a straightforward end to the working week, although a tendency to daydream can make it hard to concentrate in a meeting. You may forget to ask crucial questions unless you write them down in advance. A difficult working relationship may be causing you some anxiety, but it can be hard to put your finger on exactly what is wrong. It may just be a personality clash which you cannot do much about. Do not allow yourself to be talked into a night out if you sense that you need some restful time at home. Recharging your batteries in readiness for the weekend could be your wisest choice for this evening.

28. SATURDAY. Enjoyable. This is likely to be a sociable start to the weekend. Turn a shopping trip into a day out by inviting along a friend. If you are looking for a special purchase, two heads can be better than one. If your social life has been somewhat slow lately, now is the time for planning ahead. Having a special occasion to look forward to can make all the difference to your mood. You may want to purchase tickets for a concert or a comedy show. Accept a party invitation for this evening. There is a greater chance that you will find yourself among like-minded people. Romance could be in the cards for single Taurus people who are ready to settle down.

29. SUNDAY. Challenging. You need to spend some time by yourself. Others may accuse you of being too introspective, but it is the only way that you can resolve an intensely personal issue or dilemma. Seeking the counsel of someone who has known you for a long time could be helpful later. Do not allow yourself to be talked into a social event which does not really appeal to you; you may just end up wishing you had stayed home. Avoid taking on anything demanding; just resting and relaxing at home can be therapeutic. If you anticipate an important day at work tomorrow, some advance preparation could give you a definite edge.

30. MONDAY. Confusing. Take the day off if you are in need of a long weekend and have leave due you. However, do not be tempted to skip work at the last minute if you know that others will have to cover for you. There is a greater risk of creating bad feeling if you are irresponsible. If you have recently broken off a relationship, you might be wondering about the wisdom of your action. Before renewing contact, ask yourself if your differences can be reconciled. If you know in your heart that you are essentially incompatible, it can be wiser to allow yourself some recovery time and then find someone new to fill the void that now exists in your life.

31. TUESDAY. Useful. Most working Taurus men and women are likely to be in a buoyant mood this morning as you start the day with renewed enthusiasm. Job satisfaction plays a large part in determining the quality of life. Make sure that you do not take on more than you can comfortably handle; you may later regret putting yourself under too much pressure. Examination results received today are likely to be better than expected. If the idea of returning to full-time education appeals to you, now is a good time to find out about the coming academic year. Put the past far behind you and look ahead with confidence.

SEPTEMBER

1. WEDNESDAY. Unsettling. Guard against letting others undermine your self-confidence. You may be the object of someone's jealousy; their criticisms are therefore likely to be unnecessarily harsh. Keep in mind your strengths rather than concentrating on your weaknesses. In this way you can take someone on from a position of equality or even superiority. Making an enemy at work is not likely to be as disastrous as you imagine; it can be a much better option than allowing yourself to be intimidated. Someone may secretly admire you for sticking to your principles despite strong opposition. A dispute with your partner will require extra patience and empathy.

2. THURSDAY. Disquieting. Personal upsets are likely to be more intense than usual. You may be finding solace in food or drink. Although this can be a temporary comfort, guard against letting it get out of hand. If you want to lose weight there is no point starting a diet in a half-hearted fashion. Joining a weight-loss group could reduce your stress as well as your pounds, giving you help in working out your goal and how to achieve it. Think carefully before accepting a social invitation which you know will prove expensive. You may only be able to afford it if you sacrifice other pleasures; it may not be worth it.

3. FRIDAY. Exciting. This is a dynamic end to the working week for Taurus professionals. Your earnings from a business deal could surpass your expectations; there may be good cause for a celebration. This can also be a lucrative day if you work on commission. If extra money comes your way, earmark at least part of it for something special. Do not let it get eaten up by bills or just day-to-day living. This is a promising day for Taurus people who work in the entertainment field. You should find that you are in your element at an interview or audition. Conditions also favor signing a work contract of any kind.

4. SATURDAY. Variable. If you are usually too busy to spend time shopping, this is a good time for ordering from a catalog. You may also be able to spread the cost of your purchases. Make sure that there is the option to return goods which are not satisfactory for any reason. If you are taking a test today you may be more nervous than you had expected. A quick review or a practice session beforehand can help calm you down; you then have every chance of sailing through. If you have never learned to drive or to swim, this is a good time for booking some lessons. A social event this evening may be slow getting off the ground; try to put other guests at their ease.

5. SUNDAY. Happy. You may not be in the mood just to laze around the house. This is a good time for a short journey to visit friends or relatives who live some distance from you. A brother or sister could be especially glad to have your company. Make a conscious effort to get in touch with people you have not seen in a while. You may be able to rescue a friendship which has been slipping away from you. If you are involved in a casual romance at the moment there could be some changes in the near future. At least one of you should now be ready and eager to talk about a more stable and committed long-term relationship.

6. MONDAY. Mixed. A social get-together may not go according to plan. Friction between certain individuals is almost certain to surface at some point in the day. If the dispute does not involve you directly, stay well out of the line of fire. It is probably pointless trying to play umpire; let others fight their own battles. If you recently split up from a partner you could find yourself at loose ends tonight. Look up old friends; picking up the pieces of your social life has to start somewhere. Also keep in mind that it is better to be single than in the wrong relationship. Be as honest as possible with yourself.

7. TUESDAY. Satisfactory. You may have assumed that you did not make the best impression at a recent job interview, but there could be a call out of the blue to say that you are a finalist or even to offer you the position. If you are at home this is a good time for tackling the housework. Clean out cupboards or drawers which have become hoarding places; you could come across an item you thought was lost. The time may have come to part with memorabilia from a past relationship, particularly if many of the memories are sad or painful. Freeing yourself of excess emotional baggage can be liberating and far less stressful than you expect it to be.

8. WEDNESDAY. Sensitive. If you are involved in a permanent romantic relationship you might be tempted to stray. However, keep in mind that any indiscretion is likely to catch up with you at some point. You may regret giving someone cause for jealousy. The underlying issue may revolve around personal freedom or satisfaction. Rash behavior could result in hurting the most important person in your life as well as confusing you. Try to figure out what is wrong with your current relationship before chasing after someone new. A child needs to be treated with extra patience. Take their problems seriously so that they know they can confide in you.

9. THURSDAY. Useful. Creative work of all kinds is likely to be easier than usual. Discussing your ideas with a colleague can be productive; their input could spark off a new train of thought. Make sure that you are not disturbed while writing or thinking; interruptions could ruin the flow. There may be a chance to combine a business trip with pleasure, especially if you have to travel a long distance. This is a favorable time for entertaining clients, perhaps at a sporting event as a spectator or participant. A new contact could prove invaluable. If you need legal advice of any kind, seek it today to put your mind at ease and expand your options.

10. FRIDAY. Changeable. Make allowances for a friend who is caught up in a new romance. It may be some time before they pass the starry-eyed stage; in the meantime you may not see very much of them. Look up other friends so that you have a choice of company for a night out. If you rely on just one person you are more likely to be let down. Meetings of all kinds can be constructive and are likely to run on schedule. Make sure that you have your say in any group discussion, especially about issues which affect you directly. Later in the day get some physical exercise on your own or with a group. You may also decide to treat yourself to a sauna or massage for relaxation.

11. SATURDAY. Fortunate. A health problem may show signs of clearing up spontaneously. However, if you are at all worried about the condition, do not stick your head in the sand. If something is wrong you can only make it worse by ignoring it. This is a good time for tackling practical jobs around the home, such as decorating or repairs. A hobby of a practical nature can also be satisfying. If you are looking for a new place to live you may be put in touch with someone in search of a housemate; follow up the lead without delay. This evening can be a good time for hosting a party. Steer the conversation to spiritual beliefs.

12. SUNDAY. Buoyant. This promises to be a pleasant day on the whole. You might decide to abandon routine tasks when visitors turn up unexpectedly. If you are normally the chef on weekends, someone may insist on giving you a break today. Or you may want to suggest going out for brunch or dinner for a change. Meeting someone from your past, maybe an old flame, should live up to all your expectations. Visiting old haunts can bring back a lot of happy memories. Taurus people who are unattached could meet someone new just when least expecting it. There is a greater chance of instant attraction on both sides; enjoy being swept off your feet.

13. MONDAY. Demanding. You may not relish the prospect of work. However, if you cannot take the day off, your best policy is just to put your nose to the grindstone and make the best of it. If work is delegated to you make sure that it comes with clear instructions, even if you have to ask more than once. You may not be able to muster much enthusiasm for other people later in the day; conversation can be tiring or plain boring. Someone with a stack of problems should be kept at arm's length until you feel more energetic. Try not to cancel out of a social arrangement at the last minute; someone could be counting on your presence more than you realize.

14. TUESDAY. Frustrating. You may find time slipping through your fingers if you are not careful. In work matters try to be more methodical; make a list of the jobs to be tackled, then put them in order of priority. You will then be able to see if you are making any significant headway. Business dealings can be frustrating. A certain meeting may result in a stalemate. Consider whether you should give the matter any more of your valuable time; you could be going up a blind alley. If you have your eye on someone new in a romantic sense, bide your time but do not play too hard to get. If you are too cool you could miss an opportunity for long-term happiness.

15. WEDNESDAY. Rewarding. For Taurus people who are self-employed it can be a smart move to start the day with advice from an accountant. Tax-saving ideas could be welcome at the moment; your business may not be as financially healthy as you think. Send out reminders for unpaid invoices if you need to improve your cash-flow situation. This is a good time for chasing up a tax rebate or an insurance claim; find out when you can expect a check. You cannot afford to be flippant in a romantic relationship. Even if you have not yet thought about the future, your partner could have some definite ideas. Be prepared to lay your cards on the table and say exactly what you are thinking.

16. THURSDAY. Changeable. You are apt to spend most of the day in an introspective mood. A personal matter that is on your mind does not have an immediately obvious solution. Your sense that you need time to think things over is probably correct. The same applies to a business problem. Do not allow yourself to be pushed into making instant decisions, especially concerning matters which involve a significant amount of money. Judgments of all kinds need to based on fact as well as on your instincts. If you are under too much pressure at work, ask for help. A superior may be willing to lighten your load or find you a temporary assistant. Get to bed early tonight.

17. FRIDAY. Stressful. Any hopes of a quiet end to the working week are likely to be squashed early on. It could pay to get to work earlier than usual; crises can spring up from out of the blue. The blame is likely to fall on you even if an error was not originally your fault. A promotion or a new job can be exciting at first. However, there is a greater risk that you will inherit old problems or a chaotic filing system. With some projects you might have to start all over again from scratch. If you are single and someone is giving you extra attention at the moment, do not be too quick to jump to romantic conclusions; wait and see where their interest may lead.

18. SATURDAY. Mixed. If you are going away for the weekend, try to make a really early start. Traffic is likely to be heavier than usual. If you have a plane to catch, allow yourself extra time. Double-check the times and places for all arrangements; there is a greater risk that you have outdated or just plain wrong information. If you have a sensitive issue to discuss with a loved one you should be able to pick the right moment when they are more responsive than you had dared hope. Your communication skills are particularly good. Spend this evening in the company of like-minded people with whom conversation flows smoothly.

19. SUNDAY. Happy. This is the perfect day for celebrating a special occasion of any kinds. If you are hosting a get-together at home, make sure that you have plenty of food and extra drinks; you could have more guests than you anticipate. Bringing together members of your family should be successful. Generations can mix easily; there should be no difficulty in including children in your plans. You may find that you have played matchmaker between two of your friends you recently introduced to one another. If you have a new partner you are almost sure to fit into their social circle as their friends go to great lengths to make you feel welcome.

20. MONDAY. Uncertain. The morning is the more productive part of the day. Taurus people who work in the field of education should feel more than satisfied with today's progress. Working with children can be especially rewarding. If you are single, romance with someone from a different country or culture could be in the cards. Later in the day can be difficult at work. You may find it impossible to come to grips with a certain project. Do not struggle on for too long. It may be best to wait until you can get some additional guidance. Do not hesitate to apply for a promotion, but be prepared for some stiff competition. Any promise made to you should be put in writing.

21. TUESDAY. Good. This is a promising day for Taurus professionals. A board meeting or a discussion with those in positions of power can be especially productive. It may become obvious that you have more backing than you realized. If you work in direct sales it should be easier to secure appointments with the real decision-makers. Negotiations of all kinds should be straightforward; you should have the right information or arguments all thought out. In your personal relationships it can pay to be more assertive; asking for exactly what you want rather than being passive can work wonders. Avoid being overly dramatic, however.

22. WEDNESDAY. Disquieting. Career issues are still in the forefront. If you feel that you have outgrown your current job, it may be time to move on and seek new challenges. However, do not discuss your job hunting too openly in your workplace; wait until you have something definitely lined up before making your intentions known. You may have to consider taking a salary drop in the short term if you want to retrain. Being short of money for a while can be bearable if you know that you are moving toward your true vocation. This evening is a good time for visiting older relatives or an elderly neighbor.

23. THURSDAY. Rewarding. Work matters are apt to be more varied than usual. Having to cover for an absent colleague can give you the chance to glimpse a different side of the job. You can learn a lot from other people if you ask the right questions. If you are going on a job interview, have your own questions to ask at the end. Demonstrate that you have done research on the company; you can make a good impression by showing that you are well informed. A friend may announce plans which take you completely by surprise. Give them support even if you sense an element of recklessness in their decision-making process.

24. FRIDAY. Exciting. This is a challenging end to the working week. Taurus people usually like to stick to doing what comes naturally and easily. But today you could be offered a professional opportunity which would be foolish to turn down. You have nothing to lose by giving it a fair chance. If you have been unemployed for a while there could be a job offer today in a field you had not previously considered. Again, give it a go; you could be in for a pleasant surprise. In your social life do not be a stick-in-the-mud. By going along with spontaneous suggestions you could be letting yourself in for a memorable time with friends or co-workers.

25. SATURDAY. Disconcerting. In many ways this can be a testing time for the special relationship in your life. You may suddenly realize that you are at a crossroads. If you can freely and sincerely make a commitment at this time, there is every indication that your relationship will last. You may need to discuss an intensely personal problem or dilemma that has its roots in your past. Be wary of talking with anyone who cannot be relied upon for true sympathy and understanding. The last thing you need at the moment is someone dismissing a problem that is of major importance to you. Accept a social invitation this evening; it could be a real treat.

26. SUNDAY. Fair. If you are guilty of having behaved badly, your conscience will probably not let you ignore the matter for long. Think of a way of making it up. An apology can be a good start; a gesture such as flowers or an invitation to dinner would also help smooth it over. This is a time when actions speak louder than words. You are likely to brood over small things. You probably have given someone too much power over you if the slightest negative thing they say or do can wound you deeply. A relationship which is not working out as you hoped needs to be taken less seriously for the sake of your own peace of mind.

27. MONDAY. Mixed. This is a busy start to the new workweek whether you are at home or on the job. Fortunately you are in the mood for challenges. Bring new energy to bear on a difficult project. Problem solving of all kinds can be easier because you are now willing to look at the matter from a fresh angle. Heed any hunches; your Taurus intuition is likely to be in top gear. Your own life is very much in your own hands. Try not to rely too much on other people for help or encouragement; self-motivation can be your best guiding force. Avoid surrounding yourself with people who only say what you want to hear.

28. TUESDAY. Frustrating. Do not try to take the law into your own hands on any occasion. A clash with authority is almost certain to leave you in a difficult position. At work someone may pull rank on you because they are intent on getting their own way. The temptation to give up a job on the spur of the moment can be strong despite the Taurus trait of steadiness. However, do not give your notice unless you are already guaranteed another position elsewhere. Being without a regular income could soon get you down. You may need to burn off excess nervous energy later in the day. Engage in some sport or go out to a nightclub; letting your hair down can do you a world of good.

29. WEDNESDAY. Satisfactory. You may want to make some changes in your personal appearance. Do not be tempted to skimp on cost. If you want your hair restyled, make an appointment with a top salon; you could live to regret going somewhere inexpensive. Do not buy clothes without trying them on first so that you can really tell what they do for you. Keep your receipts in case you want to return a purchase. If you seem to never get around to certain jobs, try scheduling some definite time on your calendar to tackle the work. When you make a point of planning to do something you are more likely to actually achieve it.

30. THURSDAY. Changeable. Too much routine is likely to get on your nerves. In the workplace it may help to ask for a different project to do or learn; a superior may otherwise assume that you are happy with what you have. This is a good time for reviewing your personal finances, especially if you are paid at the end of the month. A lot of your salary may be already pegged, but some careful budgeting could save you from an overdraft or from having to dip into savings. If you have a yen to travel, plan a short break such as a weekend away. Allow extra time for journeys of all kinds. Stay close to the phone tonight.

OCTOBER

1. FRIDAY. Fortunate. This promises to be a satisfying end to the working week. Communication and cooperation with colleagues are essential, especially if you have a deadline to meet. Strive to establish a good working relationship with a certain individual, whose skills complement your own. The new month should start off with welcome news on the financial front; money due you could now be repaid in full. Treat yourself to an item you have wanted for a long time. The start of the new month is also an excellent time for new resolutions concerning your health and general well-being. Remedies based on a holistic approach can be especially effective.

2. SATURDAY. Easygoing. You should start the day in particularly good spirits. Write down a dream which you feel is significant even if you do not understand it at first; its meaning is apt to become apparent later on. Use the earlier part of the day for writing letters or making telephone calls; someone will appreciate your efforts to stay in touch. If you brought work home with you this weekend, try to get it out of the way as early as possible. A loved one may feel far down on your list of priorities if you do not make time for them today. Try to go along with their wishes rather than imposing your own. Making someone feel special can make you feel the same.

3. SUNDAY. Variable. This is a good time for embarking on house decorating or improvements of all kinds. However, do not take on a project which really requires the services of a professional or you could do one job and make another. Spend some time in the garden, raking up fallen leaves and other debris. Also consider planting winter vegetables if you have the space in your garden or even in a window box. Entertaining at home will probably be more fun than going out. Family and friends should mix easily. Conversation may go on late into the night; it could be a time for sharing confidences.

4. MONDAY. Challenging. If you are starting a new job or project, be prepared to be thrown in at the deep end. This can be exciting if you approach the challenge in the right spirit. Enjoy the learning process rather than letting it panic you; keep in mind that nobody expects you to know everything right away. In your business dealings you need to have a clearer head than usual. Trust your Taurus reactions; they will let you know if something is wrong or if someone is not to be trusted. In your personal life remember that you do not have to explain your decisions or justify your actions unless you choose to do so. Make up your own mind, then stick to it.

5. TUESDAY. Satisfactory. The extra pressure you have been under at work lately should ease off today. Someone may offer to take a difficult task off your hands, which can do a lot to relieve your burden. A business appointment you are nervous about is likely to go much better than you expect; you may realize that your fears were groundless. This can be a good time for getting in touch with family members, especially if they live at some distance from you. Even if you do not have any special news to share, just touching base can be a comfort to a relative. The ideal plan for this evening is a cozy evening at home.

6. WEDNESDAY. Mixed. Taurus parents may have cause for concern about a child. A day off school can mean that you must rearrange your own schedule on short notice. Difficulties at school may be the root cause of uncharacteristic behavior. If you are worried make an appointment to see the teacher; there should be ways in which you can help. In your love life this is a time for caution. A new relationship should be allowed to grow at its own pace; exercise Taurus patience. You may alienate someone if you push for a commitment too soon. If you are married allow your spouse more space for their work or for their own friends.

7. THURSDAY. Cautious. If you are embarking upon a new romance you may feel as if you are walking an emotional minefield. Someone who has been badly hurt in the past will need to learn to trust you; this may take longer than you realize. At the same time, you must guard against becoming a doormat. The key lies in being accommodating without compromising your own needs. As a Taurus you often attract those who need security; think about what you are getting into before you rush to their rescue. Financially you may have to do some juggling in order to meet all of your current expenses. Luxuries may have to be sacrificed for a while longer.

8. FRIDAY. Manageable. If you have an ongoing health problem, this is an auspicious time for starting new treatment. If conventional medicine has proved ineffective, consider alternative remedies such as acupuncture or homeopathy. You may not get instant results but should feel that you are on the right track. Advice from others should not be dismissed out of hand. If you take the time to stop and consider their words, you may have to admit that they have judged the problem correctly. This is not a time for keeping any worry to yourself. Just being able to discuss it can lead to finding the right solution.

9. SATURDAY. Happy. This is a cheerful start to the weekend. Those around you should be in an optimistic mood, which can quickly rub off on you. This is a lucky day for Taurus people who are thinking of moving. There is a greater chance of finding the right place at the right price. Ask your friends and colleagues rather than relying on agencies or newspaper advertisements. Your best chance of success is probably through word of mouth. Get some physical exercise, which will boost your energy rather than depleting it. This evening favors a night out on the town with friends or workmates who are always good company.

10. SUNDAY. Calm. Try to get all household chores out of the way by lunchtime so that you have the rest of the day for pursuing your own interests or just for putting your feet up. If you are entertaining at home, do as much preparation in advance as possible; you can then be free to enjoy the company of your guests rather than being stuck in the kitchen. If a friend or relative wants to cancel an arrangement with you, be willing to let them off the hook; there is nothing to be gained by making them feel guilty. Try to take disappointment of any kind in stride; welcome alternatives may soon come along to delight you.

11. MONDAY. Misleading. In a personal relationship that has been going through an up-and-down period, it can be hard to gauge the mood from one moment to the next. Listening attentively could help. This is a time when you need to just listen rather than talk or offer advice. However, if someone is being downright difficult, leave them alone. It may prove impossible to resolve certain issues without a confrontation. If you cannot win someone over to your way of thinking, at least try to reach a compromise. If a work worry is weighing on your mind, talk it through with someone whose judgment you respect.

12. TUESDAY. Quiet. This is a good day for work which requires close collaboration with colleagues. Meetings of all kinds can be wrapped up quickly as long as everyone sticks to the items on the agenda. Issues which arise unexpectedly should be dealt with at another time. If you have set your sights on a new job or a promotion, guard against becoming complacent. You may have to prove yourself more than you realize. Make sure that your professionalism and general conduct are beyond reproach. A new relationship could benefit greatly from some time alone this evening. Choose a relaxing restaurant where you can talk for hours, or have dinner together at home.

13. WEDNESDAY. Profitable. In your business dealings this is a good day for sorting out financial matters of all kinds. Taurus entrepreneurs may come across a new venture which would be worth backing. Investments made at this time are likely to prove lucrative as long as you are cautious and unemotional. In your personal life this is an important day. You may gain deeper insights into the psyche of someone who is increasingly special to you. A casual relationship can now become more serious because you have now won each other's trust and respect. Discussing your feelings and exchanging confidences can lead to greater intimacy.

14. THURSDAY. Changeable. At work you are likely to be involved with matters which require total concentration and dedication. This can cause other matters to just go out of your head. Make a point of checking your calender for any appointments or tasks which may otherwise slip your mind, then reschedule them for a time when you are under less pressure. If you can afford to lend some money you may want to bail a friend out of a financial crisis. Make sure, however, that the terms of the loan are clear from the very beginning. If you need to secure a loan for yourself, shop around for the best interest rates if you cannot borrow from a friend or relative.

15. FRIDAY. Disconcerting. Problems which arise at work are likely to be due to other people's errors or slapdash methods. Although it can be hard not to get angry with a colleague who has let you down, they may not have realized how much you were counting on them. If you work as part of a team, it is important for everyone to pull their weight. Avoid doing more than your fair share of work; voice your objections, strongly if necessary, if you are overburdened. Written work can take a lot of time, especially if you are working toward a degree. More background reading may be necessary for better understanding.

16. SATURDAY. Slow. This can be a difficult time if you are trying to learn a new skill or study an academic subject. Do not be tempted to give up in a moment of frustration; your enthusiasm should return if you just stick at it. Try to devote at least part of the day to a hobby or other outside interest. It can be easy to let your leisure time get swallowed up by domestic tasks. Try to organize your time rather than letting it slip through your fingers. Although you may be attempting to get a new relationship up and running, this is a time when you probably cannot force the pace. It may take longer to get to know someone than you expect, maybe because of shyness or uncertainty on both sides.

17. SUNDAY. Sensitive. This is likely to be a quiet day on the whole. You need some time to yourself; keep your social plans to a minimum. For example, you may want to skip an afternoon get-together but talk on the phone later on today. Turn your thoughts toward your long-term future. Think about what you want to be doing or where you would like to be at this time next year. Only you know whether or not you are already on the right track. Setting smaller goals on the way to your main aims in life can be helpful. A major career change should be discussed with your family or with one or two trusted colleagues.

18. MONDAY. Useful. If you have no pressing work matters to attend to, this is a good time for taking a day off so that you can have a long weekend. Working from home can be more productive than going into your place of business. You should find it easier to settle down to the day's tasks if you minimize the chance of interruptions. If you work in a managerial capacity, this is a good time for spending time with staff members on a one-to-one basis. You may be able to talk someone out of resigning if you give them extra practical support and encouragement. A family dinner this evening is a good setting if there are important household matters to discuss.

19. TUESDAY. Disquieting. A working relationship which has taken a long time to develop may still be far from ideal. Remind yourself that you cannot like everyone; nor can you expect everyone to like you. Keep your relationship purely professional. Do not take any critical comments or differences of opinion personally. If you are going on a job interview or attending a special function, take extra trouble with your personal appearance. First impressions could prove very important. Your partner may need some sympathy this evening, either about work or family matters. Give your whole attention rather than listening with only one ear.

20. WEDNESDAY. Challenging. The spotlight is on your work this morning. This is an excellent time for making a career decision with regard to a new position or advanced training. If you sense that you have not found your true vocation in life, this is an excellent time for taking advantage of some professional career counseling and guidance. You may be presented with possibilities which had not occurred to you before. For some Taurus people there is a chance to turn a hobby into a money-making venture. This could eventually mean the ideal situation of getting paid for doing work that you love.

21. THURSDAY. Variable. Friends who are better off than you may assume that you will join in on certain social arrangements. If these are clearly beyond your means, say so. Do not let someone pay your way if you suspect that there may be strings attached. Someone who is being unusually friendly or cooperative may have an ulterior motive. It is up to you to determine if you are being manipulated in any way; this means not taking anything at face value. A little skepticism could stand you in good stead. If you are single, guard against being swept off your feet; someone's charm may be only superficial.

22. FRIDAY. Useful. This is a time when the wisest counsel can be your own. Your powers of intuition are at their strongest; be guided by what feels right. In your business dealings keep your latest plans to yourself until you are ready to go full steam ahead. In this way nobody can push you into premature or hasty decisions. An ace up your sleeve can be your best weapon when it comes to taking on your rivals. Single Taurus people should not make an interest in someone too obvious. Subtle signals are likely to be the most effective way of stirring interest; you can then become the pursued rather than the pursuer. A newcomer may make a surprising request; help if you can.

23. SATURDAY. Tricky. The early part of the day may bring news of someone you lost contact with a while ago. Think twice about reviving the relationship if you are doing so only from a sense of duty. This is a good time for clearing out the deadwood in your life; save your time and energy for those people who really matter to you. An older relative's advice or comments concerning your personal life can be irksome. You may need to be more assertive, pointing out that there are areas in your life which are strictly private. A social occasion this evening may not live up to your expectations. Have an alternative in mind if you are eager for a night out.

24. SUNDAY. Excellent. This is one of those perfect Sundays when you can relax and feel at ease with the world. Loved ones are willing to let you do as you choose; someone may even go out of their way to spoil you or spring a surprise treat on you. Even if you are feeling physically lazy, you probably still want some intellectual stimulation. Seek out the company of people who share your interests. Someone who can always contribute to a conversation no matter what the subject may be especially fascinating. Taurus singles are likely to be attracted to someone challenging who makes the ordinary seem extra special.

25. MONDAY. Changeable. The day gets off to an easy start, but do not be lulled into a false sense of security. In the workplace pressure is likely to increase as the day wears on. You may be called upon to make snap decisions in the absence of a superior. In your business dealings you could come up against someone who has more power than you; they will probably not hesitate to wield it. Your best policy is not to show that you feel intimidated. Keep your cool; then you should be able to think on your feet. A date this evening may get off to a rather nervous start. Admitting your shyness could be the best way of breaking the ice.

26. TUESDAY. Mixed. The morning is the more demanding part of the day. A quarrel with a household member can make you late as well as putting you in an irritable mood. Words which are flung at you in the heat of the moment should not be ignored. They may indicate that there is a matter which requires deeper discussion when you have both cooled down. In your working life a meeting could take longer than expected. Try to keep the day's timetable flexible so that you do not have to leave halfway through an important debate. This evening is a good time for going out to dinner with someone special at a favorite restaurant.

27. WEDNESDAY. Stressful. Today's mail is likely to include one or more household bills. If you receive a final payment notice, try to settle it right away. If a bill is much larger than expected, you may be able to extend the payment deadline. Try not to let money worries depress you; anxiety will only make you feel bad without solving anything. Think practically. Prioritize your expenses. Many of the day's tasks may be unchallenging or dull. You can achieve the best results by putting your nose to the grindstone. Whatever gets ignored today still must be tackled at some point; you might as well clear the decks now.

28. THURSDAY. Unsettling. If you recently borrowed money from a friend, try to settle with them today. They may need the cash but feel too awkward to remind you. Think twice before arranging a new loan or extending your credit. Some careful economizing could see you through without having to incur extra long-term debt. Imagination can make a little money go a long way in the supermarket. Keep alert for special offers and for produce which is in season. Plan your meals ahead, especially if you have a large family to feed. Make a point of visiting someone who is hospitalized or is recovering at home from an illness or accident.

29. FRIDAY. Fair. If you want to go on a winter vacation, perhaps for the Christmas period, this is a good time for checking with a travel agent. Find out about special offers for advance bookings. Be realistic when it comes to assessing the cost of a trip; there are always hidden extras to be taken into account. Someone close to you may be about to embark on a course of action which you consider unwise. Couch your opinion in diplomatic terms if you are asked for it. Keep in mind that everyone has to learn from their own experience. This evening is a good time for going to the theater or to the movies with a date or your mate.

30. SATURDAY. Sensitive. If you have a busy working life, try to devote today to your family. A loved one may be waiting for a chance to discuss an important matter with you. If you are always preoccupied you may come across as unapproachable. Make a point of encouraging intimate conversation with your family members. Self-employed Taurus may have reached the stage where work has to be turned down because it encroaches too much on personal needs. Keep in mind that money is not everything. Accept a party invitation for this evening; there is every chance of meeting interesting new people and starting a new friendship.

31. SUNDAY. Disquieting. Do not wander too far from home. If the weather is bad, the prospect of staying warm and dry can be far more tempting than any social invitation. Do not allow yourself to be dragged away from your easychair unless it is an offer you really cannot refuse. This is not an auspicious time for a family gathering. There is a greater danger of getting caught up in other people's squabbles when all you want is peace and quiet. If you live with a roommate, house rules may need to be discussed. It is important to reach democratic decisions on issues such as TV program selection or housework.

NOVEMBER

1. MONDAY. Calm. The new month gets off to a pleasant start. If you have some leave coming to you, this is a good time for taking a day off so that you can run some errands. If you have the option to work from home, you may decide to do so today. This can be a particularly productive day for Taurus people who are house hunting. Drive around the area of your choice to get a clearer picture of what is currently on the market and at what prices. If you are trying to sell property there is a greater chance of finding a buyer today. Enjoy a quiet evening at home. Get to bed earlier than usual.

2. TUESDAY. Variable. Work which requires creative skill can be especially challenging today. Bounce your ideas off other people, but guard against collecting too many opinions; you run the risk of making a project more complicated by listening to anyone and everyone. If you are working with children, vary the activities more than usual. Put aside any activity which is clearly failing to capture their interest or imagination; you can always rework it into a better format for another time. Resist the temptation to tell a little white lie no matter what the motivation; there is a greater risk of being embarrassed by the truth.

3. WEDNESDAY. Productive. Work is more likely to be a pleasure than a duty. You may be entrusted with more interesting tasks than usual. Make time for a colleague who is new to the job; they could benefit from your patient guidance. You could rediscover your artistic or creative talents. If you have any musical ability, this is a good time to learn to play an instrument. Writing poetry or prose can also be satisfying. Taurus parents may want to encourage children to take up hobbies of an artistic nature. A new romance started today is likely to bring you a great deal of long-term happiness. A sporting event can be great fun tonight.

4. THURSDAY. Excellent. The morning is the best time of day for work which requires originality. Run-of-the-mill tasks are apt to take up a lot of your time later in the day. If close concentration is not required, it can be pleasant to listen to some music or to a radio program as you work. In your business dealings try to tie up loose ends; you should be able to bring at least one project to a successful conclusion. Long-distance travel is favored, either for leisure or business purposes. Do not hesitate to strike up a conversation with a fellow passenger; you could have some entertaining company or even begin a new friendship.

5. FRIDAY. Confusing. Take extra care with work matters, especially if you have to make a presentation to a client or to a superior. Cutting corners may seem like a good idea at the time, but you may later wish that you had taken the trouble to be more thorough. In your business dealings someone is set on tripping you up. You need to have all the answers at your fingertips in order to come out on top. Try to reschedule a business engagement if you feel that you are not sufficiently prepared. Any health problem is likely to be a result of overdoing. Try to reduce your workload if you have taken on too much; delegate or reschedule.

6. SATURDAY. Difficult. It can be quite an effort to switch off from work matters, especially if you had to leave an important project up in the air over the weekend. You may feel that you have not used your working hours as effectively as usual this week, but do not be too hard on yourself. Try to learn from your mistakes. When you figure out how or why something has gone wrong you are less likely to repeat the error in the future. Although a personal relationship could be going through a difficult patch at the moment, it is important not to resort to drastic measures. Stay calm; do not be rushed into any final decision. Avoid issuing an ultimatum unless you really mean it.

7. SUNDAY. Uncertain. You may feel at odds with the world and all those around you. Even someone who is normally easy to talk to may not take your side in regard to personal issues. A partner may pull out of a social arrangement without giving you a good reason, leaving you feeling angry or neglected. You could easily talk yourself into arguments, especially if you go on the attack. Guard against blaming others for things which are not really their fault. Do not be too quick to side with someone in a family dispute. There is a risk that you have heard only half the story. A good book is your best companion tonight.

8. MONDAY. Sensitive. If the weekend has not been particularly satisfying you will probably be glad to get back to work. The last thing you need at the moment is time to brood over an argument or misunderstanding. The other person involved has probably already forgotten about it; you should try to do the same. A positive attitude can rub off on those around you. You may have been taking a certain individual far too seriously. A lighter touch can improve both your professional and personal relationships. Rely on your good Taurus sense of humor when a situation threatens to blow out of proportion; laughter can win others over to your side.

9. TUESDAY. Unsettling. Joint finances may require some discussion. If one of you earns considerably more than the other, you need to guard against a power imbalance. Your sense of togetherness can be affected if your income is not fairly divided. Money can be an issue in more ways than one at the moment. Single Taurus people should guard against getting involved with someone who has already displayed a lack of generosity. Meanness with money can indicate meanness with other things, such as affection. Someone who does not pay their way on social occasions needs to be pulled into line. This evening is a perfect time for a heart-to-heart conversation with a loved one.

10. WEDNESDAY. Rewarding. If you have money to invest, shop around for the best deal. A professional could give you sound advice. This is not a time for wild speculation, but some calculated risks could pay off. Consider increasing your life insurance coverage or making a will, especially if you are the main breadwinner in your family. If life seems humdrum at the moment, it is up to you to make some changes. Plan a special night out, either for a group or with your mate or partner. If you are married, find ways of breathing new romance into your relationship. Give a little more than you expect to get.

11. THURSDAY. Useful. This is an especially productive day for Taurus people involved in research. The right information can be easier to unearth than expected. You may be able to beat a deadline. For self employed Taurus people, this is a favorable time for financial planning. If you are looking for an accountant, check out someone recommended by a friend or a colleague. An anxiety about a personal relationship could be all too familiar. If you suspect that you are repeating old patterns, consider going for some counseling that could shed light on your own behavior or choices. A self-help book could also be enlightening.

12. FRIDAY. Variable. Although this week has had more than its fair share of ups and downs, the dust should settle today. Pressure at work is likely to be greatly reduced as some of your tasks are taken off your hands. Someone who has been breathing down your neck should now be happy to leave you alone. There may be time for a long lunch with a friend or colleague. If you are going away for the weekend, aim for an early departure in order to miss the rush hour. This evening favors cultural pursuits of all kinds, especially going to the theater or the ballet. Live music or comedy can also be entertaining. If you drink, do not drive; call a cab or take the bus.

13. SATURDAY. Mixed. If you are unemployed you may get a lucky break today. There is a greater chance of picking up some temporary work, perhaps of a seasonal nature. Do not turn down any opportunity; once you get your foot in the door, another offer may follow naturally. If you have been through a tense time with an older relative, this is a favorable day for a fresh start. Many of your differences may be due to the generation gap. If you show tolerance you are more likely to get the same in return. Agree to differ wherever possible. This evening favors attending a formal occasion or hosting a sit-down dinner at home.

14. SUNDAY. Unsettling. The morning is likely to be the more pleasant part of the day; you should be able to suit yourself. Family duties must not be shirked later on, even if you are not in the right frame of mind. You may have to visit your partner's relatives. You can boost your popularity by being extra charming and entertaining. If someone seeks your advice, make a point of speaking the unvarnished truth even at the risk of causing some temporary pain. This is not a time for saying just what you think someone wants to hear. Your own experiences can benefit a younger relative, especially in the world of work.

15. MONDAY. Fair. This is likely a busy start to the workweek. If you are at home, be prepared for a constant stream of drop-in visitors or telephone calls. You may run into friends if you go out shopping; stop for coffee and catch up on the local gossip. At work this is a good time for getting on top of administrative tasks, such as filing and report writing. Taurus business people are apt to be more effective in the office rather than on the road. You can tie up a lot of loose ends over the telephone rather than arranging face-to-face appointments. A drink after work may turn into a late night out on the town.

16. TUESDAY. Manageable. In the workplace do not allow your time to be taken up with pointless discussions. You may feel that someone is splitting hairs or continually going off on tangents. If you are chairing a meeting of any kind, make sure that it runs on schedule. In this way you are showing respect for other people's time as well as your own. Business dealings with overseas contacts can be especially productive. If you are currently looking for work you may be asked to consider a position overseas, possibly in the field of education. This is a propitious time for dealing with legal matters of all kinds. A court decision is likely to go in your favor, although an appeal is possible.

17. WEDNESDAY. Slow. You are especially sensitive to other people's criticisms. Listen carefully to what they have to say. There is a greater risk of jumping to the wrong conclusions if you react too quickly. If you work for a charity you may be entering your busiest time of year. If fund-raising has been slow, come up with a contigency plan now. A celebrity sponsor or some media publicity could jump-start your campaign. You cannot afford to be complacent. Other people may bring their problems to you. Be willing to help, although giving too much of yourself can be wearing. Guard against obsessive behavior in a new relationship.

18. THURSDAY. Enjoyable. This is likely to be a fun day on the whole. In the workplace you may get a chance to shine or to take the limelight in some way. Praise and recognition from a superior for recent efforts can give your ego a well-deserved boost; make the most of your moment of glory. For Taurus professionals this is a propitious time for wining and dining current or potential clients. You may pick up some useful information which would not be divulged under ordinary circumstances. Your social life is taking an upwards swing. You are apt to be in demand; enjoy your popularity. This evening favors celebrating a special occasion of your own.

19. FRIDAY. Good. This should be a productive end to the working week. You are unlikely to be hampered by distractions or interruptions, making it easier to give your full concentration to the matters at hand. Taurus professionals may be approached on the quiet by another company. Although it can be flattering to be head-hunted, make sure that your final decision is based on all aspects of the position being offered rather than by the financial benefits alone. Put job satisfaction on the top of your list of priorities. This evening favors a small dinner party. Gather your favorite people around you for good conversation and some fun.

20. SATURDAY. Stressful. There is a possibility of a family dispute. You may feel you are banging your head against a brick wall when it comes to asking someone to understand you. Now could be the time to stop trying to live up to other people's expectations; in your heart of hearts you probably already know that their demands are unachievable. If your patience is exhausted, stop trying to put on a brave face. It may do someone good to be told that they have hurt you. If you are under pressure to join in with certain Christmas plans which do not really appeal to you, stand your ground and make your own choices. You may be left waiting by the phone for a promised call tonight.

21. SUNDAY. Satisfactory. The work that you have been putting into a special relationship may now start paying off. You deserve to feel a sense of triumph at having gotten through a rocky patch. You can now enjoy a sense of true togetherness. Give special thought to your closest friends; try to come up with some original ideas. Browsing around a market can be fun; you could pick up all sorts of useful bargains for yourself or for gifts. Cancel out of a social occasion tonight if you have a big day tomorrow. A good night's sleep can be the best preparation for the important work awaiting you. Plan your wardrobe for the entire week.

22. MONDAY. Demanding. On this demanding start to the working week you may feel overwhelmed by the amount of work you are faced with. Do not panic. Make sure that you are being methodical; have a plan and the work should soon get back to manageable proportions. A superior may be in a difficult mood, changing their mind over a matter which you thought was resolved. It may not do any harm to point out the inconvenience or disruption that this causes you as well as your colleagues. In your business dealings, double-check the accuracy of all paperwork, especially mathematical computations. There is a greater risk of discovering an error when it is too late to correct it.

23. TUESDAY. Changeable. The morning is the most productive part of the day; you should be able to race through work or chores. This is a good time for reworking your budget. Figure out how much you can afford to spend on nonessentials. Remember hidden extras, such as cab fares on occasions when you cannot use public transportation or do not want to drive. If you will be hosting a party or get-together, plan the menu now. Taurus men and women who are unattached may be starry-eyed about someone new on the scene, but do not come on too strong. The best policy is to first build a strong friendship, then see what develops.

24. WEDNESDAY. Fortunate. If your work involves serving the general public, expect to be constantly on the go. Chances to earn extra cash are plentiful, although you may not see the benefits for a while. You may be in the mood for liberal spending rather than saving; money can go out just as fast as it is coming in. You may be spending more on your social life than usual; enjoy the extravagance rather than feeling guilty about it. This can be a good time for a reunion. Getting together with old school friends or former workmates can be fun. If you are traveling, expect delays and plan accordingly.

25. THURSDAY. Tranquil. Thanksgiving Day promises to be enjoyable in all ways. You are apt to be on the receiving end of other people's goodwill and generosity. A selfless gesture from someone can restore your faith in human nature. If you have been waiting for special news of any kind, your patience is likely to be rewarded. Single Taurus people may wonder why someone recently met has not called as they promised. They could contact you today with a full explanation. This is an excellent day for getting to know someone in your personal or working life on a deeper level. Be willing to reveal your true feelings.

26. FRIDAY. Mixed. This is a busy end to the working week. Administrative tasks of all kinds can be time consuming, but do not be tempted to dash off a report or an important letter. It is vital to pay extra attention to detail. If you are going on a job interview be prepared for some searching questions; the interviewer may be testing your ability to think on your feet. If you have an important document or artwork to mail off, send it certified or registered so that you can be sure that it will arrive on time. A night out at a local haunt can be fun, especially if you meet up with friends.

27. SATURDAY. Variable. If you work on weekends, be prepared for another busy day. Retail stores are likely to do a roaring business. Self-employed Taurus people should be encouraged by today's turnover. At home most of the day can be taken up with housework and other domestic chores. Make sure, however, that you put aside some time for yourself as well. This evening is not a good time for entertaining at home. You could feel that all you have done is let yourself in for a lot of hard work. Eating out can be far more relaxing and does not have to cost a lot. Avoid talking shop if you are socializing with your workmates and also with other friends.

28. SUNDAY. Disquieting. There could be a lot of friction at home. If you sense that someone is nursing a grievance, it may be best to confront them head-on. Once you know what the problem is you should be able to do something about it. Do not allow yourself to be a victim of the silent treatment or of a guessing game; this is both unnecessary and emotionally wearing. It usually takes a lot to rouse Taurus people to anger. However, this is a day when it may do no harm to blow off some steam; someone may then realize that they have pushed you too far. Avoid an occasion where you are likely to run into someone from the past who you would prefer not to see.

29. MONDAY. Confusing. The morning is the easier part of the day. In the workplace you should be able to get the week off to an encouraging start, but do not be lulled into a false sense of security; your good mood may not last throughout the whole day. Someone who is negative or pessimistic could easily bring you down if you let them. A work matter which lands on your desk later in the day could be disconcerting as you realize that it will take a long time and a lot of effort. Be sure to ask for some assistance, even if you have to use up a favor. Major decisions of all kinds almost certainly need to be slept on so that you can consider all possibilities.

30. TUESDAY. Fair. For Taurus parents, child-care arrangements could fall through. If someone frequently lets you down, this is a time for locating someone more reliable. If your children are approaching school age, find out about the public and private schools in your area; one could have a definite advantage over the others. A new romance may end as quickly as it began. Try not to brood over what might have been; you may eventually feel that you had a lucky escape. Chalk up the episode to life experience. Later in the day is a good time for sports if you play for the fun of it rather than just to win.

DECEMBER

1. WEDNESDAY. Frustrating. The new month gets off to a slow start. A certain work matter could grind to a halt if you are relying on someone else's input or waiting for information from an outside source. Associates may need to be spurred into action, especially if you have a deadline to meet. You could be entrusted with confidential information. Prove that you can keep a secret by making sure that it goes no further. Do not confide any personal or professional matters of your own to anyone who has not already demonstrated that they are trustworthy. If a brilliant idea for a Christmas present for a loved one dawns on you, keep it under wraps despite your excitement.

2. THURSDAY. Difficult. Dealing with a health problem can be especially wearing. If you have a medical appointment, ask someone to go with you for moral support as well as company; there could be a lot of waiting around. Exercise your right to a second opinion if you do not have full confidence in what you are being told so far. A recurrent health problem could have its roots in an emotional difficulty; it may be worth obtaining some counseling. Although you may feel that you need extra love and attention, if you are single guard against thinking of a friend as a lover; you probably already have the best relationship.

3. FRIDAY. Changeable. Taurus workers are apt to be even happier than usual to reach the end of the workweek. You may feel that life is too much work and not enough play at the moment. If you have not made some social plans for the weekend, now is the time to do so. Having something to look forward to can raise your spirits. If you are unemployed, this is a favorable time for finding a temporary or part-time job of a seasonal nature. This could keep you afloat financially while you look for something more permanent. A meeting with an old friend or business associate may fall flat when you discover that you no longer have much in common.

4. SATURDAY. Disconcerting. If you have been working hard you may realize that you have been neglecting the most important people in your life. It is up to you to spot their signs of dissatisfaction or repressed anger; do not just sit and wait for it to explode around you. You can do a lot to put things right if you take the initiative. This is a good time for finding out more about your partner's line of work; in this way you can be more understanding when they need to talk about a work-related problem. If you have just started a new relationship you may already have some doubts about your compatibility; if you ignore these you could soon be sorry.

5. SUNDAY. Demanding. Issues in regard to your personal independence or freedom within a relationship could arise. If you know that you are guilty of being too possessive with your partner, this is a time to try to be more easygoing. There is no need to feel left out or unvalued if they wish to do something alone. Keep in mind that living in each other's pockets can be unhealthy in the long run. If someone is cramping your style, take a firm line in claiming some personal space. Do not allow yourself to be pushed into any arrangement which does not suit you; you will only end up feeling resentful. Get some extra sleep tonight.

6. MONDAY. Buoyant. If life has been generally difficult lately, welcome today's decided change for the better. The morning is the best time for all matters which require good communication skills, such as teaching or interviewing. Taurus employers may decide to hire someone on the strength of their enthusiasm rather than solely on their qualifications. Your workload could be lightened when someone goes the extra mile to help you; be sure to show your appreciation. A business matter which you expect to be troublesome could turn out to be plain sailing after all. A spontaneous night out with that special person in your life could be memorable.

7. TUESDAY. Manageable. Try not to worry too much about a personal matter. Keep in mind that quite often the best solution can be the most obvious one; ask yourself if you are making a problem more complicated than necessary. In your business dealings this is a propitious day for financial transactions of all kinds. Be tough if you are involved in negotiations for your professional services; someone will probably pay you at least the going rate once you win their confidence. For Taurus singles, a love interest from the past could come back on the scene. It may prove to be a case of being lucky in love the second time around.

8. WEDNESDAY. Confusing. This is not an especially productive day in the workplace. You may find it difficult to concentrate on a matter which needs your total attention. If it is not urgent, put it aside for a day; you should be able to approach it with a clearer head tomorrow. If your analytical skills are not at their sharpest today, stick to routine tasks; in this way you will not feel that you have wasted the entire day. You may have to break some bad news to someone. Think carefully about how to phrase it, but do not fall into the trap of beating around the bush. Be gentle but crystal clear. Trust your good Taurus judgment.

9. THURSDAY. Rewarding. This should be a particularly rewarding day for Taurus students. Even though you may already be winding down for the holiday break, you can do some of your best work today because the pressure is off. Do not be tempted to skip a seminar or lecture; you could come away with some valuable insights and information. This is a lucky day for Taurus people who are seeking work. There is a greater chance of finding just the job you have in mind. If you have not yet made any definite plans for the end of the year, there may be invitations to join others for a vacation trip. This may not be traditional but is still worth serious consideration.

10. FRIDAY. Mixed. Your mail is likely to include a stack of Christmas cards. Greetings from someone with whom you do not want to reestablish contact can be irksome. Keep in mind that there is no need to return a card just out of politeness. If you stay silent they should get the message. In the business world this is a good day for sending cards or token gifts to valued customers. Include the people whose business you would like to cultivate. Placing orders now for any special food for the holidays could save you a lot of time and effort. This is also a favorable time for buying tickets in advance for a Christmas show or New Year's eve party in a hotel.

11. SATURDAY. Stressful. If you are looking for Christmas cards, you might decide to buy them from your favorite charity as a way of making a donation. If you have cards or parcels to send, make a point of getting them mailed today in order to guarantee that they arrive in time. As the next to the last shopping weekend before Christmas, you may be out shopping but not able to find all the gifts you have in mind. If something proves too expensive, come up with a different gift idea. An event this evening may not be quite what you expect; maintain your sense of humor if you find yourself in a bizarre situation.

12. SUNDAY. Variable. Be careful not to overdo things. Keep in mind the importance of having some quality leisure time, especially if you had a hectic workweek. You will probably prefer just to sit around and chat with friends or loved ones. Chores can always wait for another time, so let yourself off the hook. Conversation at dinner is likely to center around spiritual or ethical values. As a Taurus you are often unmovable in your beliefs, but today you could now find yourself rethinking or even adjusting a long-held view. Someone with well-thought-out controversial opinions can give you food for thought.

13. MONDAY. Good. This is a positive but busy start to the workweek. Take a little time to plan ahead. You have to organize your day more carefully than usual if you are going to honor all of your personal and professional commitments over the next few weeks. The festive spirit is probably very much in evidence. This is a good time for putting up decorations at work or for going out for a Christmas lunch with colleagues or business associates. Make sure, however, that you get all essential work done beforehand; there is very little chance of your getting back to it later in the day. Socializing can be very good for business.

14. TUESDAY. Tricky. A squabble may break out between you and those you live with, possibly about noise levels. This is a good time for establishing house rules if you can get everyone together; discussion can work far better than a shouting match. Work is unlikely to go according to plan. You need to allow for the unexpected; try to stay flexible. Also make a point of exerting the Taurus easygoing nature even when everyone around you is beginning to panic. Later in the day try to finish writing your Christmas cards and get them ready to mail. Some may require a letter as well in order to bring a friend up to date on all your recent activities.

15. WEDNESDAY. Disquieting. The day is unlikely to start off the way you would like. Even if you did not have a late night, you could still be feeling tired or under the weather this morning. Only take the day off from work if you know that colleagues can easily cover for you. Someone will not thank you for putting them under extra pressure at the moment. You may not feel equal to creative or intellectually demanding work. Try to stick to routine tasks which do not require much effort. A personal relationship which has been going through a difficult time may be reaching a stalemate. You will need a lot of empathy in order to get it back on the right track.

16. THURSDAY. Mixed. You may find yourself under a lot of pressure at work this morning. If someone clearly has unrealistic expectations now is the time to say so rather than laboring on in silence. Also stop to think if you are creating more work for yourself than necessary; a sense of urgency may be misplaced. This is unlikely to be a favorable day for finalizing business transactions of any kind. A certain individual may deliberately be painting you a false picture. Do not rely on secondhand information; check it out for yourself. This evening is likely to be the most pleasant part of the day. Some time alone can be very restful and rejuvenating.

17. FRIDAY. Successful. You may get the chance to earn some extra cash. Although this will probably disrupt some of your personal plans, the financial rewards could make the temporary inconvenience worthwhile. If you go Christmas shopping it could be helpful to patronize smaller stores. Even a thrift shop may prove to be good hunting grounds for original gifts. Taurus business people should have more than a few invitations to join clients or associates for lunch or after work. An office party can be a lively affair, but keep your behavior on the sedate side while superiors are around.

18. SATURDAY. Misleading. The early part of the day can be the best time for Christmas shopping. Try to get as early a start as possible so that you miss the worst of the crowds. Although you might be set on buying generous gifts for certain loved ones, there is a greater risk of overspending. Try to be strict about sticking to your budget. You do not have to spend a lot in order to demonstrate your affection; the thought that goes into the gift is what truly counts. Do not rely on someone to pass on an important message for you; it could easily be forgotten in the rush of the day.

19. SUNDAY. Difficult. You may wonder what has happened to the festive spirit. Others appear too busy or too preoccupied to make any effort at goodwill. Tension in a personal relationship may reach the boiling point. You may have been spending too much time together; a break from each other's company could help. Avoid making a final decision about a romance, even if you feel that you want to call it off. Instead, see how you feel once the festive season has come and gone. Family plans for Christmas may not be easy to resolve in a way that makes everyone happy; compromise is necessary from everyone.

20. MONDAY. Enjoyable. Today's mail may bring a card from someone you missed on your own list. Fortunately there is still time to send a card back right away. Taurus people who do not have family ties may still be debating which invitation to accept for Christmas; decide today or you could end up being at loose ends. Try to finish your Christmas shopping; inspiration is likely to strike as you look around the shops. As a safety net, gift certificates can be a sound option for children or teenagers on your list. Do not pass up a social invitation for this evening; it could be much more fun than you imagine.

21. TUESDAY. Disquieting. This is a demanding day at work. A business decision which involves considerable expense may need more thought before you go ahead. A friend who has been going through a hard time may need extra moral support at this time of year. Do not let them sink into depression. An invitation to join you in celebrating will probably be accepted gratefully. You could be asked to donate money to a charity even though you are already feeling the pinch financially. Try to give a little rather than nothing at all. If you have any spare time over the next few days, you could find volunteer work helping those less fortunate than you very rewarding.

22. WEDNESDAY. Variable. Any hopes of an easy day at work are likely to be squashed early on. Covering for colleagues who have already started their Christmas vacation could be the reason for extra pressures. Make a point of questioning additional responsibilities which are being foisted upon you by a superior. There is no reason why you should suffer from their lack of advance planning or poor organization. Putting in overtime now will not go over well with your loved ones. The children in your life should be given priority over the next few days. Allow extra time for traveling. Be extra vigilant on the highway if you have to drive any distance.

23. THURSDAY. Happy. If you have been too busy to feel the festive spirit you may easily get into the Christmas mood today. Other people's high spirits can soon rub off on you. Work matters are likely to calm down. There is probably very little that you can do to advance certain projects until the New Year, so concentrate on having some fun and enjoying yourself. Taurus business men and women may opt for a long lunch with a key client or associate. If you are at home, making final preparations can be fun. Spending time with people who are special in your life should take precedence. Keep children's presents carefully hidden away.

24. FRIDAY. Stressful. If you are spending the Christmas vacation away from home you need to be well organized today. In the rush to get away on time you could be absentminded. Double-check your packing list, at least for the essentials. This can be a notoriously bad time of year for break-ins. Make sure that your home is secure if you are going to be away. Family get-togethers or reunions of any kind may take a while to get into full swing. If you are acting as host, make sure that one particular guest is not feeling left out in the cold. Any family feud or friction which threatens to cast a cloud over the proceedings should be smoothed over as quickly as possible.

25. SATURDAY. Merry Christmas! The best celebration this year may be in the comfort of your own home. An early start to the day is likely, especially if you have children. However, the day might take a while to get in top gear if you are suffering from the effects of a late night. As tempting as it can be to overdo the food and drink, you will probably enjoy the day much more if you exercise some moderation. At least try to pace yourself. It will probably be easier not to even attempt to stick to a strict time-table. Meals should be leisurely; clearing the table and washing the dishes can always wait until later. Express thanks for all of your gifts, even one that is not your size or style.

26. SUNDAY. Enjoyable. This is a good day for getting out, especially if you spent the whole of yesterday indoors. A walk in the park can blow away the cobwebs. This is also a favorable day for visiting relatives who did not spend yesterday with you. If you are at home, visitors are likely to drop in. Make them welcome by having plenty of food and drink on hand which is quick to prepare. If a loved one is away you might feel their absence more acutely today. Bridge the distance by treating yourself to a long and leisurely telephone call. Accept a party invitation for this evening, or throw an impromptu party of your own.

27. MONDAY. Manageable. If you have young children, anticipate boredom setting in rather than waiting for it to happen. Arrange to visit friends, or take them to a movie. At home, games which can be enjoyed by all age groups can be great fun. This is a good day for sporting events, whether you are participating or just going along as a spectator. Be willing to join in on any outing of a spontaneous or unusual nature. If you are single, be brave enough to take the initiative with someone who has captured your romantic interest. Capitalize on the spirit of the season and invite them to a special party or other gathering.

28. TUESDAY. Successful. This is a good day for checking out the sales. If you received money as a gift at Christmas, treat yourself to some new clothes; you could find some genuine bargains. If you have been playing host, an invitation to a friend's house for later in the day will probably appeal to you. Enjoy being on the receiving end of someone else's hospitality. A pleasant encounter with someone from your past is a possibility. There is a greater chance that a broken romance can be patched up if you are both willing to work at it. If you recently argued with a friend, be the first to make a peace overture.

29. WEDNESDAY. Fair. If you have to go to work it may not be as arduous as you expect. You can probably get away with attending only to the essentials. It could be wise to spot-check your financial situation. You may find that you have overspent even more than you realized. However, keep in mind that you can always make a fresh start at economizing in the New Year. Someone close to you who has not had a good Christmas may need your company. Be liberal with your sympathy without letting them feel too sorry for themselves. However, someone who is overdemanding should be kept at arm's length until you are willing to help them.

30. THURSDAY. Fortunate. You should be feeling in top form and still have plenty of energy for socializing. Invitations are likely to be plentiful; see how many you can fit in. If this is a working day, you can still expect to have a lot of fun. Getting together with colleagues and exchanging news as you work can provide you with plenty of entertainment. If you are looking for work there could be an offer of a job to start in the New Year. The day favors group events of all kinds, with the emphasis on informality. Family gatherings are also likely to be successful. It can be especially heartwarming to spend time with an older relative.

31. FRIDAY. Happy. This is likely to be a happy end to the year on the whole. Romantic prospects for single Taurus people look especially promising. Someone who has captured your interest may want to see in the New Year with you. At some point in the day try to find a few moments to reflect on the year's achievements before you set yourself new goals and make new resolutions. Try to value the lows of the year as well as the highs; you probably have learned a lot from them. There may be a choice of parties for this evening. Select the one where you can guarantee to be with those who are special to you when the clock announces that you are now in the year 2000.

TAURUS
NOVEMBER–DECEMBER 1998

November 1998

1. SUNDAY. Mixed. On this sociable day even if you live alone people are likely to drop by or call to suggest going out together. Someone may go to great lengths to persuade you to join them, in part because they need some moral support. Overcome your initial impulse to stay home. The more adventurous you are, the more fun you will have. There is a risk of running into someone you would prefer to avoid, but you should be able to sidestep getting trapped into a one-on-one conversation. A family get-together can be a lively affair. Minor friction or squabbles should not be taken too seriously. Have a camera on hand so that you can update the family photograph album.

2. MONDAY. Quiet. If you are owed some time off, this is the perfect time for taking a day to yourself, especially if those you live with are out for the day. You are sure to benefit from time alone; your need for company or conversation is minimal. Solitude gives you the space you need to think through any personal issues. The time is not right for gathering other people's opinions; decisions need to be made independently and irrespective of what others might think. In your business dealings this is a day for playing a lone hand. Draw upon your past experience. Keep more ambitious plans a secret for a little while longer.

3. TUESDAY. Uncertain. A health problem may require consulting a doctor. If you have an appointment with a specialist, be sure to get answers to all your questions. Writing them down in advance can be helpful. If a friend or colleague is hospitalized, try to find time to visit, or at least send some flowers if time is at a premium. You may not feel very energetic. It can be difficult to arouse enthusiasm for routine tasks. However, force yourself to deal with at least the most pressing matters. In your working life guard against using up too many favors. Spontaneous offers of help could have strings attached; it may be better to struggle through as best you can on your own.

4. WEDNESDAY. Good. Taurus people are recognized for a high degree of ambition. This is a favorable time for pushing yourself forward in the workplace. Do not be afraid to draw attention to your recent achievements if you sense that they have been overlooked by those in power; sometimes you need to blow your own horn. Taking on more responsibility without being asked, or putting in some overtime, should impress the right people. This is a good time for shopping for clothes. Try out new colors or styles. Seek advice from someone whose taste you admire. Feeling good about the way you look can boost your self-confidence. For Taurus singles, this evening is a propitious time for a first date.

5. THURSDAY. Disquieting. Take a close look at your financial position. If you have just been paid, now is the time to work out a budget for the rest of the month; do this with your partner if you have a joint account. There is a chance that you may not be as well off as you think. Your current expenses may be greater than your income, but efforts to economize in little things could soon even the balance. For instance, in the supermarket be alert for special sales and resist imported delicacies. Also give some thought to your long-term finances. If your employer does not provide you with a pension, now is a good time to start one of your own.

6. FRIDAY. Frustrating. Creative work of all kinds can be frustrating. What at first seemed to be a good idea may now prove impractical or too expensive to pursue. In any of your dealings, a problem is unlikely to be resolved just by throwing more money at it. It may be best to just cut your losses now. Someone close to you could break a promise; find out their reasons before going on the attack. They are probably facing problems and deadlines of their own. A new love interest might not live up to your expectations. If someone is not as free and unattached as they had led you to believe, now is the time to bow out with your dignity intact.

7. SATURDAY. Difficult. You may feel very much on your own at the moment, especially if you have just ended a relationship. Guard against patching up a friendship or romance in the belief that someone is better than no one at all. It should be more productive to concentrate on the advantages of being free to come and go as you please. This is a time for some self-questioning. You can learn a lot about yourself if you put your own behavior under the microscope. Acknowledge your faults while at the same time reminding yourself of your many strengths. Looking at childhood experiences can give you clues to your current behavior patterns. A brother or sister may be able to shed more light on certain events that are only hazy memories to you.

8. SUNDAY. Excellent. Recent efforts in a personal relationship should start to pay off. Your own soul-searching may have provided you with a new insight and a fresh approach. A deeper understanding of a significant person in your life can bring you a great deal of contentment and reassurance. This is a starred day for celebrations of all kinds, including a wedding or engagement. Different friends and all generations should mix easily. This is also a good time for introducing a new partner to your family or social circle. Forging closer bonds with a child can be rewarding. Be lavish with love and praise when they seek your approval.

9. MONDAY. Lucky. This is a busy start to the workweek. Plan your time carefully so that you can get through all that awaits you. If you are starting a new job or taking on new responsibility, you may wonder what you have let yourself in for at first. Enthusiasm and a willingness to learn can carry you through. By the end of the day you should feel that you have made an impressive start. If you are house hunting at the moment there is a greater chance of finding the place of your dreams. An owner who is in a hurry to sell may accept an offer much lower than the asking price. A gamble could pay off, but do not risk more than you can afford to lose.

10. TUESDAY. Rewarding. If you are at home, race through the usual domestic chores so that you have some time for yourself. If you have children make sure that they are pulling their weight at home according to their age and ability. Encouraging more self-reliance can be healthy for both them and you. On the job this is a good day for teamwork of all kinds. Be willing to lend your time and expertise to those who are less experienced than you. A certain working relationship is going from strength to strength. If you are looking for work at the moment, do not hesitate to get in touch with someone who could pull some strings on your behalf.

11. WEDNESDAY. Successful. For Taurus professionals this is a good day for being office-based. You should be able to tie loose ends and clear out your in basket. If you have to arrange meetings, ask others to come to you rather than the other way around. This is a favorable time for off-the-record discussions. If you have a grievance at work, you may be able to resolve it yourself without involving a superior or going through official channels. If a loved one is more withdrawn than usual, take the trouble to find out what is wrong. Offering sympathy or true interest could be all that is needed to lift their spirits and clear the air.

12. THURSDAY. Stressful. At work you are apt to be under more pressure than usual. If you are racing against the clock in order to reach a deadline, you may have to skip a lunch break or reschedule less urgent matters. Stress can show up as physical symptoms, such as a nagging headache or an aching back. Consider whether you are taking on too much all at once or are making unnecessary work for yourself. If it is a case of being overburdened, ask a superior to lighten your load. In a personal relationship be quick to spot undercurrents of discontent. People are unlikely to volunteer information; you will have to come right out and ask them what is wrong.

13. FRIDAY. Fair. Working with children should be especially rewarding today, although you may have to tap into extra reserves of patience from time to time. Keep in mind that you may have to exert your own authority. In work matters guard against a tendency to rush headlong into a new project without sufficient advance preparation. Do not brush off advice from a colleague; it could get you over a hump. Enthusiasm alone is not sufficient when it comes to selling others on a new idea. They expect you to back up your claims with facts and figures. Socializing after work could develop into a late night out. Dancing or playing a team match can be excellent for working off stress.

14. SATURDAY. Satisfactory. Even if you do not normally work on the weekends you might choose to put in some extra hours today at home or in the office. A particular project that has fired up your imagination can make you impatient to push ahead with it. If your working life has become boring, now is a favorable time to begin planning a change. Look at the help-wanted section in quality newspapers. Send off application for jobs that appeal to you. Later in the day the emphasis is on having fun. Opt for the company of those people who are positive and exciting companions. This evening favors seeking the unusual rather than the commonplace.

15. SUNDAY. Good. This is an active day. Do not waste too much time sleeping in or lazing around the house. The morning is the best time for physical exercise of all kinds, with the emphasis on fitness rather than competition. If you are playing in a team match, have fun as well as just trying to win. This is a good time for eating out rather than cooking at home. Choose a favorite restaurant, or accept an invitation to a friend's house. Social gatherings of all kinds are likely to be successful. You may get the chance to play matchmaker between two of your friends or even neighbors.

16. MONDAY. Deceptive. Do not push yourself too hard, especially if you start the day feeling physically under par. Taking a day off could actually nip an illness in the bud. Do not fall into the trap of believing that things will not get done without you; someone else is capable of taking over in your absence. This is a good time for making changes in your diet, whether you want to lose weight or just eat more health-consciously. Boost your system with extra vitamins and more sleep. Traveling could take longer than expected. Keep your timetable flexible so that being delayed does not create a crisis or throw you into a tailspin.

17. TUESDAY. Variable. There may be surprise news from a colleague perhaps announcing a promotion, transfer, or acceptance of a new job. Although you may be sad to see them go, this could be a cloud with a silver lining for you. Changes can create opportunities for you much sooner than expected. A superior is apt to be in a difficult mood. It is probably safer to ignore their irritable outbursts or excess criticism; they may be under more pressure than they are willing to reveal. A personal relationship should bring you a great deal of contentment at the moment. A new romance is likely to progress swiftly, especially if you share a number of outside interests.

18. WEDNESDAY. Fortunate. There is very little to hold you back. It should be easier to tackle difficulties with a positive and determined attitude. Your cheerfulness is bound to rub off on those around you, making work more of a pleasure than a duty. New friendships made at this time are apt to be lasting ones. If a certain relationship has been causing you anxiety lately, this is the perfect time for a fresh start. Try to wipe the slate clean of old grievances and problems. Make some plans for the future together rather than dwelling in the past. Happy news for someone close to you is likely, perhaps inspiring you to plan a surprise party for them.

19. THURSDAY. Fair. If it is difficult to make financial ends meet at the moment, there may be a chance to earn some extra money. Drive a hard bargain if you are selling your services; you cannot afford to take on work for anything less than the recognized fee. Do not offer discounts to anyone unless there is a case of genuine hardship. Keep in mind the importance of putting a proper value on what you do. Taurus employees who are expected to put in overtime should insist on extra pay or compensatory time off. Keep a personal issue to yourself for now. You need to analyze your own feelings before seeking out other opinions.

20. FRIDAY. Unsettling. Administrative work of all kinds can be troublesome. You may be tempted to put off writing letters or returning telephone calls, but at least try to clear away the more urgent ones. If you have forms to fill out, be sure to include all relevant information. Otherwise you could hold up the proceedings. Ask for clarification if there are questions which you do not fully understand; guesswork is likely to be wrong. Business proposals or decisions should be put in writing in order to avoid a possible misunderstanding. Confirm any social arrangement for this evening, especially if it was made some time ago.

21. SATURDAY. Variable. Children can be especially demanding. If you do not feel able to keep up with them, get some extra help. Try to arrange for another parent to swap child care sessions with you. In this way you can be sure of time for yourself. If you are going shopping, head for a mall which provides a good mix of stores. Someone close to you may make you angry. If you keep your negative feelings bottled up you will succeed only in creating an even more tense atmosphere. No matter how painful a subject may be, this is a time when open, frank discussion could be profitable. Just be sure you are talking together, not lecturing or preaching at someone.

22. SUNDAY. Buoyant. This is the perfect time for a day away from home, especially if the weather is unusually good. Make an early start. Drive or take the train to revisit a place which has special memories for you. Traveling is likely to be not only trouble-free but enjoyable. Cultural activities of all kinds are also favored, such as visiting a museum or art gallery. An exhibition related to a special interest should be well worth a visit. If a loved one now lives abroad or will be away for some time, treat yourself to a long-distance telephone call. Talking together can lift your spirits and make them seem closer. Give free rein to your Taurus creativity this evening.

23. MONDAY. Disquieting. This is unlikely to be an easy start to the workweek. Legal matters of all kinds need to be handled with extreme caution. An adversary could have several surprises in store for you. If you are embarking upon litigation of any kind, be prepared for a long battle. Ask yourself if the issue at stake is worth long-term stress. It may be better to cut your losses. Seek professional advice. If you are taking an examination today or interviewing for a job you may feel that you have not done yourself justice. Others, however, are likely to have the same feelings. Avoid carrying a large amount of cash; there is a danger of losing it or of spending too freely.

24. TUESDAY. Fair. The morning is the easier part of the day. If you have written work of any kind to do, aim to complete it by lunchtime. You should also find studying easier in the morning, when there are likely to be fewer distractions. Get some extra help with a subject that is a struggle for you. Later in the day there can be some unforeseen problems in the workplace. You may have to think fast on your feet, but try to avoid making a major decision without first consulting those who will be affected most. Joint finances may require some discussion this evening. Be honest with your partner if you know that you have been over-spending recently.

25. WEDNESDAY. Good. It is a fortunate day for an interview. Although some questions may come as a surprise to you, it should be easy to talk with a potential employer. Competition is unlikely to be as intense as you fear. You may be offered a position on the spot. Meetings of all kinds should be successful, and they should run on time as well. In the workplace this is a favorable day for dealing with financial matters such as departmental budgets or filling out expense forms. If you are self-employed, find time to confer with your accountant. Some ingenuity by a financial professional can mean a lower tax bill for you at the end of the year.

26. THURSDAY. Mixed. An upset among family members may not be as serious as you at first believe. An older relative may go to great lengths to ensure that you are not blamed for events which are out of your control. Let this person know how much you appreciate their support. If you are unemployed do not hesitate to use contacts you already have, perhaps from a former job. A certain individual is willing to put in a good word for you if you ask. Later in the day you need to handle a proposition with great care, especially if a large sum of money is at stake. Do not give financial backing to any venture which appears risky.

27. FRIDAY. Disconcerting. In your working life you may sense that there is a great deal going on behind closed doors at the moment. It is probably best to ignore any rumors which are flying around; they are unlikely to be based on fact. Make a point of distinguishing between hearsay and actual evidence. In this way anyone who is bent on making trouble will soon have the wind knocked out of their sails. If someone close to you is acting out of character, do not question them too closely. Trust that they will confide in you when the time is right. Single Taurus people could strike up an immediate bond with a stranger this evening.

28. SATURDAY. Fair. With the holiday season less than a month away, it is not too soon to make a start on your Christmas shopping. Careful budgeting could pay off. Work out what you can afford to spend on gifts, especially if you are buying for a lot of people. It may be helpful to agree to a price limit with family members if money is tight. If your plans involve a break with tradition, do not postpone letting your family know. It can be hurtful to spring sudden changes on them at the last minute. If you need to discuss a sensitive subject with a loved one, pick a good moment today. Tact and delicacy are essential to reaching a compromise solution.

29. SUNDAY. Exciting. Your plans for a quiet day are unlikely to come to anything. This is a time when you may be asked out unexpectedly. Someone may refuse to take no for an answer, so you might as well go along with their plans right from the start. You will be glad that you did. Meeting an old flame, or friends from your past, can lead to a fun occasion. In romance this is a time for following your heart rather than your head. Too much analyzing could lead you in the wrong direction. You can afford to follow your good Taurus instincts, even if others accuse you of being headstrong. If you are married, treat your partner to a special day out; they are sure to welcome some loving spoiling.

30. MONDAY. Difficult. Taurus people who work full time are likely to suffer from Monday morning blahs today. An attack of the blues can be difficult to shake off. You need to exert greater self-discipline to get through the day's tasks. A personal problem could be weighing on your mind, making it almost impossible to concentrate fully on other matters. Try to take the pressure off yourself wherever possible. Someone could be playing mind games with you. It may be time to get angry rather than depressed, forcing them to acknowledge that they have pushed you too far. When others see that you are not going to back down you are apt to get your way.

December 1998

1. TUESDAY. Productive. This is a busy day and not the time for sitting on the fence. The more enterprising you can be, the more likely you are to succeed. Test out unusual or unconventional ideas and approaches; they could serve you better than traditional methods. Proving that you can lead as well as follow is the way to impress a superior. Do not take for granted a possible promotion at work. You need to stand out from the crowd. An older relative, perhaps a parent, may surprise you by sharing exciting plans of their own. Be sure to give them your enthusiastic support. Do not put off purchasing airline tickets or making other travel arrangements.

2. WEDNESDAY. Uncertain. If you are starting your holiday shopping, guard against a tendency toward extravagance. Do not spend as if money grows on trees. You are apt to regret your impulsiveness when it comes to balancing your checkbook later. Try to pay in cash rather than using a credit card. Avoid taking on new credit unless it is interest-free and with affordable repayments. If you are looking for a place to hold an office party, be prepared to shop around; prices could vary considerably. Socially you are apt to be in demand. However, guard against booking up too many evenings and leaving no free time for yourself.

3. THURSDAY. Variable. If you are unemployed or struggling to make ends meet, be sure that you are claiming all the benefits to which you are entitled. There may be extra help available for fuel bills during the winter months, or a group ready and willing to provide extra food. Taurus business people approaching the busiest time of year may decide to boost advertising or launch special offers. The extra sales that publicity produces could soon cover the initial layout. For Taurus men and women who are weight conscious, now is a good time to start a diet. Although you may not be able to shed surplus pounds during the festive season, at least you can avoid putting on more weight.

4. FRIDAY. Easygoing. This quiet end to the week should come as a relief if you have been especially busy. Deal with a backlog of smaller tasks which were put aside during busier times; in this way you can start next week with an uncluttered desk. If you need more insurance coverage, be sure to shop around for the best deal. This is not a lucky time for buying a secondhand car; mechanical problems may only come to light after you have bought it. Pinning someone down to a definite arrangement for this evening or the weekend could be difficult. Have other options up your sleeve so that you are not left high and dry.

5. SATURDAY. Mixed. Make a list of people to whom you want to send Christmas cards. If you are buying your cards today, consider buying from a charity as a way of making a donation. Taurus people who are artistically inclined may decide to make cards or gifts. This is also a good way of keeping children occupied. Household chores are likely to take up more time than usual. Pace yourself when it comes to work which is physically demanding; there is a greater risk of overdoing. Opt for a quiet evening at home rather than a night out on the town. You need extra sleep before holiday parties fill your weekends.

6. SUNDAY. Disquieting. This day may not go according to plan. There is a greater possibility of arrangements being canceled on short notice. Someone's excuse for letting you down could sound somewhat lame. Taurus people who are unattached should not invest too much hope in a new romance. There are reasons a new relationship will not get past the starting gate. Do not sit at home and wait for a telephone call. Either make the call yourself to find out what is going on, or keep busy with your own interests. This is a favorable time for broadening your social horizons in order to create more romantic opportunities for yourself.

7. MONDAY. Fair. If you are in the process of buying or selling property, this is a good time for putting pressure on the right people. Try to complete a contract before Christmas. Your concerns can get ignored if you do not make enough of a fuss. Shop around for the best mortgage. The atmosphere at work is apt to be tense at times. Make allowances for a colleague who is clearly under a lot of pressure; offer a helping hand if your own workload is lighter than theirs. Guard against being too possessive with your partner or another close family member. They may need some extra time to themselves.

8. TUESDAY. Satisfactory. This is an especially productive day for Taurus people who work from home. You should find it easier to settle down to tasks which require close concentration. If you can take some time off, this can be the perfect day to catch up with domestic chores or just laze around in the comfort of your own home. Meeting a friend for lunch can be fun. This is a propitious time to apply for a loan if you want to make home improvements of any kind. If you are going shopping, be alert for unadvertised bargains. Treat yourself to flowers or a flowering plant for your home or place of work. You may also want to send flowers to a friend.

9. WEDNESDAY. Rewarding. Your worries about someone close to you may be unnecessary. If you step back you should see that they are far more capable than you are giving them credit for. There is probably no need for you to run to their assistance unless you are specifically asked for help. If you are looking for Christmas presents for children, you may be dismayed by the prices. Remind yourself that a little imagination can go a long way; be prepared to shop around as well. The chance to earn some extra money may come along. Married Taurus people may benefit financially from the good fortune of a close family member or in-law.

10. THURSDAY. Disquieting. You may have cause for concern about a child, especially a teenager. You need to find a way of drawing them out if they are being uncommunicative. Do not make light of a problem they disclose to you. It may seem trivial to you but could be very serious to them. A short-term romance may not be working out as you had hoped. It may be best to tactfully stop seeing each other if you know in your heart that you are simply not compatible. Do not fall into the trap of finding the hat and then making it fit; you deserve better. Do not dwell on disappointments of any kind; chalk them up to experience and move on with your life.

11. FRIDAY. Misleading. Do not attach too much importance to other people's promises. Although they may be sincere at the time, they could soon be sidetracked by other matters. If you need to guarantee that something will be done or delivered on time, take personal responsibility for it. Nor should you entrust an important message to a third party. Think twice before lending money to a friend or colleague; it may be some time before you are repaid. The same warning applies to your possessions; there is a greater risk that they will not be returned in good condition. In any business dealings all agreements should be confirmed in writing.

12. SATURDAY. Successful. If you have not already started your Christmas shopping, this is a good day for doing so. If you know what you are looking for before you set out, you should be able to get a lot done in a short time. Ideas can come to you as you browse around. Place orders now for flowers or other fragile gifts. You should have lots of energy today. Physical exercise, such as a workout or a swim, may appeal. This evening is favorable for a formal occasion. It should be easier to break the conversational ice with people you meet for the first time. Look your best; first impressions are likely to be lasting.

13. SUNDAY. Mixed. In contrast to yesterday, take life at a slower pace today. Tiredness can creep up on you; sleep late this morning if you get the chance. Later in the day seek out the company of people who always accept you just as you are. Avoid a social occasion where you have to put on a bright face or make superficial conversation; you could end up feeling drained. If you are entertaining at home, try to do most of the preparation before guests arrive. In a new relationship this is a day when you can establish deeper intimacy. Spend time together away from friends or family members. A candlelight dinner can set the stage for asking that all-important question.

14. MONDAY. Changeable. If you have cards or packages to send, do not delay mailing them off. In this way you can be sure that they will arrive in plenty of time. A card from someone in your past may be delivered to you. Taurus business people should make a point of sending a card or gift to valued customers. This is also a favorable time for arranging a festive get-together with colleagues or associates. If your work involves serving the general public, this is sure to be a busy day. You need extra patience when it comes to dealing with a difficult customer; do not risk your good business reputation.

15. TUESDAY. Exciting. Career issues need some attention. Think more about long-term opportunities. This is a good time to sign up for a course which will start next year; learning a new skill could improve your job prospects as well as being fun. This is an excellent day for an office party or a Christmas lunch with others in your line of work. Make sure, however, that important tasks are finished in the morning; you may not get back to your place of work until late in the day, if at all. You are probably in the mood for a night out and should not be short of offers. Friends make the best social companions, allowing you to relax and be yourself.

16. WEDNESDAY. Rewarding. This is one of those days when people are apt to bring their problems to you. Even if an answer is not required, your sympathetic ear is sure to be appreciated. If someone asks for advice, your best policy is to be bold; do not say just what you think they want to hear. In your business dealings this is a favorable time for off-the-record discussions. You can learn far more about someone if you make a meeting unofficial or talk over the lunch table. If you have been somewhat guarded in a new relationship, now is the time to let down your barriers. Exchanging stories from your past or talking about your emotional needs can bring you closer together.

17. THURSDAY. Fair. If you have not yet decided on Christmas plans you could be tempted to take a trip. Even if your financial position is not as good as you would like, a special offer may be difficult to refuse. Do not forget to budget for hidden extras when away from home. If you are unemployed at the moment there is a chance of picking up some last-minute seasonal work. Many charities are busy at this time of year and may be looking for volunteers. Doing some unpaid work for them for a while could lead to paid job opportunities. If you have money in the bank, make a point of donating a sum to your favorite charity.

18. FRIDAY. Sensitive. If you are finding it hard to meet the expenses of Christmas you may receive an offer of financial assistance, perhaps from a friend or relative who is better off than you are. The offer is likely to be sincere, so there is no reason not to accept it. If you are paid today you could find more than you expect in your pay, such as a generous Christmas bonus. If you are buying presents for children, think up an ingenious hiding place so that they are not discovered in advance. Do not allow yourself to be pushed into partying tonight if you are not in the mood. A cozy evening at home could be more to your liking.

19. SATURDAY. Manageable. You probably cannot escape the crowds on this last shopping weekend before Christmas. Go to a mall close to home. Finding the right gift for someone who is usually difficult to buy for can be easier than you expect. A gift certificate for tapes or tickets to a concert can be a good idea for teenagers, especially if you are not sure of their tastes. If you are going out of town for the Christmas break, this is the perfect time to depart. Long-distance traveling should be problem-free. Later in the day pay special attention to children. Make reservations now for an event coming up next week. A small gathering at home is favored this evening.

20. SUNDAY. Variable. Tread carefully if you become involved in a discussion about religion. Someone who holds views that are very different from yours could take exception to an opinion you express. Make it clear that you respect their beliefs even if you do not agree with them. If you intend to host holiday festivities at home this year, do some forward planning now. Decide on menus which cater for everyone's tastes or special needs, especially for a guest who is a vegetarian or on a low-fat diet. Stock up on snacks and drinks. A friend or neighbor who is at loose ends would probably welcome an invitation.

21. MONDAY. Confusing. If you are at work this week you may have to cover for colleagues who have already started their holiday vacation. Parts of their job could be a mystery to you, but if you keep good records of what you have done or decided you will not go wrong. Someone in authority may ask you to take on extra work or responsibilities. Guard against accepting too much at this late date. Family commitments have to come first, especially for Taurus parents of young children. Do not risk drinking and driving under any circumstances this evening. Arrange to use public transportation or to travel with a designated driver who will not drink.

22. TUESDAY. Difficult. It is pointless to try to maintain your usual routine. Work matters are apt to be chaotic; it may be impossible to get in touch with the right people. Some matters have to be put on the back burner until after the Christmas break. At home there may still be a lot to be done. The more organized you are, the more efficient you will be. Make a list of tasks or shopping; delegate as much as possible. Pick up extra wrapping paper and decorations to be on the safe side. Last-minute travel plans can be time consuming. Purchase tickets in advance rather than trusting luck to get you aboard on a standby basis.

23. WEDNESDAY. Good. Even if this is not your favorite time of year, you should feel the festive spirit rubbing off on you. At work the pace is likely to slow down. Colleagues can be in high spirits and very much in a holiday mood. You should be able to take a long lunch break or finish early. If you are at home, try to finish all of your preparations so that you avoid a last-minute panic tomorrow. Neighbors or friends are likely to drop by unannounced; have food and drink in plentiful supply. This evening is a good time for hosting a party. A card in today's mail may remind you to send return greetings right away.

24. THURSDAY. Fair. You are unlikely to be short of social invitations, but lack of money could be a drawback. Although you expect to overspend at this time of year, a check on your finances could tell you that the situation is getting out of control. You might need to avoid an occasion which you know will prove expensive. If you are at work, try to clear your desk by lunchtime, especially if you are leaving early to go out of town. Checkout lines in the stores or bank could be long; allow plenty of time. Plan an informal supper at home if you have guests arriving sometime this evening. An early night may be welcomed by everyone.

25. FRIDAY. Merry Christmas! If you have young children you can expect an early start to the day. Their delight should soon rub off on you. Festive cheer and goodwill should be in abundance. Let the day's events flow at their own pace rather than sticking to a timetable. Even though this is traditionally a family day, the more people you include in your celebrations the more fun you are likely to have. Invite a neighbor who may be alone to come for dinner or dessert. Other people's generosity can be overwhelming. The special person in your life may have gone to great lengths to spoil you. Your own gifts should also be well received.

26. SATURDAY. Easygoing. This is likely to be a slow day. If you have guests, allow everyone to sleep late and then serve brunch. You and your family may want to relax in front of the television this afternoon. A gift related to a hobby or a new book can be absorbing. Also be willing to play with children who are impatient to try out new toys or games. You may not be in the mood for strenuous exercise; but a gentle walk can blow away the cobwebs and work off a few calories. You are apt to feel the absence of a loved one acutely. Do not shrink duty calls to relatives who live at a distance.

27. SUNDAY. Mixed. A desire to withdraw for a while may have to be put on hold while you visit in-laws or other relatives today. Try to be gracious even if it is a visit you would prefer to avoid. A family get-together may not go as smoothly as you hope. Remind yourself that it is not always possible to get through a holiday period without some people arguing or bickering. Avoid taking sides in any dispute which does not directly concern you; in this way you can stay out of the line of fire. Playing host can start to wear thin. Find some time for yourself this afternoon and let others entertain themselves.

28. MONDAY. Demanding. You may experience a letdown now that Christmas is over, but there is still New Year's Eve to come. Make definite plans for this occasion if they have not yet been finalized. It can be hard to muster enthusiasm if you are back at work. Do not expect too much of yourself; it will take a while to get back into the swing of things. Someone who is already trying to pile on the pressure should be kept at arm's length if possible. If you are at home tackle clearing up and putting your domestic affairs in order. Find time to write thank-you letters for gifts or hospitality that you received.

29. TUESDAY. Pleasant. If you were given money or a gift certificate it could be burning a hole in your pocket. This is a good day for a shopping trip, especially to stores that have already started their sales. Good bargains can be found if you are looking for clothes; treat yourself to a new outfit for a forthcoming party or other special event. In the workplace this should be an easy day; you only need to keep things moving along at a steady pace. Exchanging news or late gifts with colleagues can be fun. A friend who has been away is eager to get together with you soon. Lend your support to a charity that is holding a fund-raising event or soliciting donations.

30. WEDNESDAY. Sensitive. Try to avoid arguments over money. If you have a joint account with your partner, point out that you can always start economizing again in the New Year. If your love of good food means that you have piled on the pounds, this is a good time for planning a diet, although it may be easier to start in the New Year rather than now; in this way you are more likely to stick to it. Someone close to you may not have had an enjoyable Christmas. Be alert to the signs even if they are not saying much; a shoulder to cry on may be just what they need. Be willing to go along with the wishes of a loved one this evening; they may be relying on your cooperation.

31. THURSDAY. Challenging. Take time to reflect on your achievements over the past year. Consider whether you have accomplished all or most of what you wanted, both in your personal affairs and in your professional life. You may realize that some of your goals were overly ambitious. However, aiming too high is better than aiming low. If you are hosting a party tonight make preparations well in advance. If you have a choice of events for this evening, opt for the one where you will know the most people; do not risk feeling out of place and uncomfortable. Be with your partner or special someone when the clock strikes midnight.

Having A Good Psychic Is like Having A Guardian Angel!

Love, Romance, Money & Success
May Be In Your Stars....

Get a **FREE** Sample
Psychic Reading Today!!!

1-800-799-6582

FREE
Love
Advice

Does he really love me?

Will I ever get married?

Is he being faithful?

Call To Find Out How To Get Your

FREE Sample
Psychic Reading!

1-800-869-2879